BEGINNING YOUR
JOURNEY

NASPA.
Student Affairs Administrators
in Higher Education

MARILYN J. AMEY
& LORI M. REESOR

EDITORS

REVISED AND EXPANDED | FOURTH EDITION

BEGINNING YOUR

JOURNEY

A Guide for New Professionals
in Student Affairs

NASPA™
Student Affairs Administrators
in Higher Education

Beginning Your Journey: A Guide for New Professionals in Student Affairs

Published by

NASPA–Student Affairs Administrators in Higher Education
111 K Street, NE
10th Floor
Washington, DC 20002
www.naspa.org

Additional copies may be purchased by contacting the NASPA publications department at 202-265-7500 or visiting http://bookstore.naspa.org.

Library of Congress Cataloging-in-Publication Data
Amey, Marilyn J.
Beginning your journey : a guide for new professionals in student affairs / Marilyn J. Amey and Lori M. Reesor, editors. — Fourth edition.
    pages cm
Includes bibliographical references and index.
ISBN 978-0-931654-79-4
1. Student affairs services—United States. 2. Student affairs administrators—In-service training—United States. 3. Student affairs administrators—Professional relationships—United States. 4. Student counselors—Vocational guidance—United States. I. Reesor, Lori M. II. Title.
    LB2342.92.A64 2015
    378.1'97—dc23

2014046886

ISBN: 978-0-931654-79-4 (Print)
ISBN: 978-0-931654-80-0 (e-Book)
ISBN: 978-0-931654-73-2 (e-Book)

Printed and bound in the United States of America

FOURTH EDITION

Contents

ACKNOWLEDGMENTS

The editors of this book are grateful to the contributing authors who shared their wisdom and experiences with the readers. These are leaders in our profession of student affairs, and we are appreciative of their participation in this book.

The contributing authors of this book wish to thank the many new professionals who added their stories to this text. Their willingness to share experiences and insights made this a rich experience for us all.

We also thank those authors who participated in writing earlier editions of *Beginning Your Journey*. Although they chose not to be involved this time, they allowed new contributing authors to continue with and build on work included previously. We appreciate Randi Schneider, Michael Dannells, Melissa Hazley, Florence Hamrick, Brian Hemphill, and the late J. Douglas Toma who lent their expertise and colleagueship to earlier editions of this work.

Finally, the editors want to extend a special thanks to Rachel Osowski, administrative assistant in the Office of the Vice President for Student Affairs at the University of North Dakota. She was central to coordinating our efforts, distributing and receiving drafts from contributing authors, and being the center of our collaboration throughout.

Writing this edition of the book continues to invigorate the editors and contributing authors, and gives us confidence in the future of our profession as we guide future leaders. We are grateful for this opportunity to contribute in this way.

INTRODUCTION

Marilyn J. Amey and Lori M. Reesor

"New professionals are the future of our profession." This is a common phrase heard when a seasoned staff member addresses a group of newcomers to the profession. Our graduate degree programs concentrate on providing students with the theoretical and practical experiences that will help them succeed in the student affairs profession. As we know, however, these programs are diverse in their teachings and emphases. It is crucial that NASPA be an active voice in the development of new professionals; this book is one way of demonstrating that commitment.

The purpose of this book is to help ease the transition from graduate student to full-time professional and to increase the retention of new professionals in the field. It is not intended as an administrative cookbook but rather as an examination of key issues facing new professionals and ways of thinking about the challenges and opportunities in careers in student affairs. The issues facing those entering the profession have a certain degree of comparability, whether one assumes a first professional position or moves into student affairs from a career in another field; and whether one is employed at a community college, a liberal arts college, or a research university. Understanding organizational culture and its impact on work, thinking through career configurations, reflecting on the aspects of collegiate life that affect the way work unfolds, exploring the values and belief systems of the field—all these issues confront new professionals. For more experienced professionals who are moving into the student affairs arena, past experience, knowledge, and expectations affect perspective and create a different set of needs and concerns. Because of the space limitations of the book, we assume a primary readership of entering professionals and try to capture experiences that those new to the field have in common. We use the term *new professional* throughout the text. We also assume that supervisors, graduate preparation faculty, and other supporters of new professionals constitute a secondary audience for the book, and that they will find the discussion of current issues as seen by new professionals useful.

To identify the most relevant issues, we begin with a brief discussion of the arena in which student affairs professionals work in the 21st century. We work in organizations that are both political and diverse. If new professionals are unaware of the nature of colleges and universities, or do not understand the competing priorities that cause institutional members to negotiate for resources, they can be adversely affected by organizational politics. In addition to its inherent political culture, the higher education system is struggling to achieve a truly multicultural orientation. Numerous authors believe that the future of colleges and universities lies in creating a multicultural environment (Chang, Denson, Saenz, & Misa, 2006; Dancy, 2010; El-Khawas, 2003; Hurtado, Milem, Clayton-Pedersen, & Allen, 1998; Park, 2013; Pope, Reynolds, & Mueller, 2004; Shaw, Valadez, & Rhoads, 1999). They call for changes in institutional climate and culture to accommodate an increasingly diverse student population; for increasing the cultural diversity of faculty and staff; for changing institutional directives, statutes, and policies to reflect the realities of a changing clientele; for increased technological expertise and instruction that accommodate a wider range of learning styles; and for leadership that can facilitate the transformation of the academy into a multicultural environment for the 21st century.

We also recognize the extent to which postsecondary institutions are struggling to redefine themselves in the midst of a technological and global revolution that is changing every aspect of academe—what it means to be an educator, to be a learner, to provide services for students, and even to be a college campus. Although we cannot foresee all the ways in which increased uses of technology will transform the practice of student affairs, it is clear that things are changing. New professionals face the press of politics, fundamental philosophic changes, seemingly unlimited innovation, and boundary redefinition. We have written this book with those environmental constructs in mind.

We believe, also, in the value of hearing from professionals themselves. Therefore, personal vignettes and the "talk" of new professionals are woven throughout the book to give voice to their concerns, strategies, and beliefs. Sometimes, these voices are those of individual professionals, included to illustrate a specific point; at other times, the voices represent amalgams of viewpoints expressed by many. Pseudonyms are used in all cases to protect confidentiality.

Kari Ellingson and Barbara Snyder start off by reflecting on the issues from the perspective of new professionals and senior-level student affairs officers. In dialogic fashion, Ellingson, Snyder, and several colleagues add their voices to the words of others included throughout the volume, speaking directly about the challenges facing new professionals and those who attempt to provide support and guidance. Marilyn Amey, Eric Jessup-Anger, and Connie Tingson-Gatuz discuss the organizational and political realities likely to confront new professionals as they take on full-time responsibilities in student affairs. They present a conceptual model of organizational culture as a framework for thinking through these critical issues. Anna Ortiz, Jonathan O'Brien, and Carla Martinez consider the implicit values that give form and nuance to administrative practice. They define professional and personal ethics, emphasizing the importance of ethics in all aspects of student affairs work. They describe the importance of having an ethical stance to deal with traditional issues such as excessive workloads and student conduct, as well as new issues such as those associated with social networking sites and social justice. Kevin Bailey and Jenny Hamilton examine the complexities of supervision and the role of the supervisor. Using organizational and leadership theories as guideposts, Bailey and Hamilton describe how this relationship is manifested and offer insights for dealing with potential (often inevitable) dissonance.

Camille Consolvo and William Arnold help us think through the issues of collaboration between student affairs professionals and faculty. They highlight some of the challenges and opportunities, and provide useful strategies for cultivating the relationships that support student learning. Matthew Wawrzynski, Ashleigh Brock, and Austin Sweeney focus our attention on the importance of and challenges associated with assessment, which is now so much a factor in student affairs work. They provide guiding questions to help new professionals understand the task of assessing learning outcomes and the important relationships between the work that goes on inside and outside of the classroom. Eugene Zdziarski and Dawn Watkins look at the issue of campus crisis management, which has come to the forefront in recent years. Their matrix shows how a campus can prepare for and implement crisis management processes, and suggests a way of thinking about the small and large issues facing student affairs professionals that is planful rather than reactionary. Grace Bagunu and Danielle Quiñones-Ortega consider the ways in which technology and social media are both part of the fabric of collegiate life and how they affect the work of new student affairs professionals. Effectively using technology and social media can enhance communication, programming, and networking between and among new professionals, their colleagues, and their students. But as the authors point out, it is also important for new professionals to thoughtfully consider their virtual presence and identities in the context of their careers. Lori Reesor, Grace Bagunu, and Luke Gregory discuss various approaches to professional involvement and networking, inter- and intra-institutionally. They describe avenues for participation and issues associated with cross-gender and cross-cultural support systems.

Joy Blanchard and Charlie Andrews tackle a key component of a successful career in student affairs work: finding work and life balance. New professionals need to find a healthy equilibrium as they strive to excel in their personal and professional lives. Blanchard and Andrews offer insights and frameworks for thinking through these key decisions and choices. Jody Donovan and Maria Marinucci take professional development and career planning in a different direction as they explore career paths and advancement opportunities. They discuss various scenarios, including the role of doctoral study, and present ways of envisioning one's future in the profession. Brent Paterson and Christa Coffey lay out strategies for the all-important first job search. Whether you are moving into student affairs from a graduate preparation program or making a mid-career switch, Paterson and Coffey will help you think through your personal strengths, goals, preferred work environments, and so on. They offer helpful tools in an age of numerous application portfolios and careers that span multiple jobs.

Finally, Shannon Ellis brings together the reflections of leaders in the profession. We honor the words of new professionals themselves throughout the book. In the same spirit, we find great value and wisdom in listening to the voices of the leaders who have come before, who helped shape the profession as we know it today, and whose commitment to student affairs remains as deep and unwavering as it was when they, too, were new professionals.

We are reminded of the words of one of these leaders. Although she wrote them more than two decades ago, Margaret Barr's (1993) advice about enjoying work and being an effective administrator is equally relevant today and serves as the foundation for this book. She said, "Enjoy the students"; "Become involved in the institution"; "Maintain perspective"; and "Take time to smell the roses" (pp. 525–526).

References

Barr, M. J. (1993). Becoming successful student affairs administrators. In M. J. Barr (Ed.), *The handbook of student affairs administration* (pp. 522–529). San Francisco, CA: Jossey-Bass.

Chang, M. J., Denson, N., Saenz, V., & Misa, K. (2006). The educational benefits of sustaining cross-racial interaction among undergraduates. *Journal of Higher Education, 77*(3), 430–455.

Dancy II, T. E. (Ed.), (2010). Managing diversity: (Re)visioning equity on college campuses. New York, NY: Peter Lang.

El-Khawas, E. (2003). The many dimensions of student diversity. In S. R. Komives & D. B. Woodard, Jr. (Eds.), *Student services: A handbook for the profession* (4th ed., pp. 45–62). San Francisco, CA: Jossey-Bass.

Hurtado, S., Milem, J. F., Clayton-Pedersen, A. R., & Allen, W. R. (1998). Enhancing campus climates for racial/ethnic diversity: Educational policy and practice. *Review of Higher Education, 21*(3), 279–302.

Park, J. J. (2013). *When diversity drops: Race, religion, and affirmative action in higher education*. New Brunswick, NJ: Princeton University Press.

Pope, R. L., Reynolds, A. L., & Mueller, J. A. (2004). *Multicultural competence in student affairs.* San Francisco, CA: Jossey-Bass.

Shaw, K. M., Valadez, J., and Rhoads, R. (Eds.). (1999). *Community colleges as cultural texts: Qualitative explorations of organizational and student culture.* Albany, NY: SUNY Press.

VOICES OF EXPERIENCE

CHAPTER ONE

Kari Ellingson and Barbara Snyder

A ny new professional faces choices, rewards, and often unexpected challenges as they move from the student role to this new identity. Student affairs professionals are no exception. To learn more about the transitional issues facing new professionals, Barbara Snyder, vice president for student affairs, and Kari Ellingson, associate vice president for student development, both at the University of Utah, met with a group of nine colleagues who were all working at the University of Utah and who had been in the field from 8 months to 5 years.

In this chapter, you will learn about the experiences of: Jeremy, a residential education coordinator; Pablo, an admissions counselor; Erica, a financial aid counselor; Kelly, a career counselor; Katie, an associate dean of students; Belinda, director of the Office of Inclusive Excellence; Garrett, an associate director of orientation and leadership development; Maggie, a residential education coordinator; and Chris, an academic advisor. These

1

new professionals represent different ethnicities, sexual orientations, educational backgrounds, and life circumstances. Although different paths led them to the student affairs profession, a common commitment to students was at the core of their career choice.

Choosing a Career in Student Affairs

No single path leads to a career in student affairs. The entry point is as varied as the individuals who occupy the roles; for example, some are tapped early by a mentor who recognizes their potential while serving as a resident advisor (RA). New professionals are pleasantly surprised to find that the experiences they loved as undergraduates can be turned into a full-time job.

> *I followed the path of traditional undergraduate to graduate student to full time student affairs professional. I knew by my sophomore year that student affairs was for me. I was one of those involved students. . . . I was an RA, on the orientation team, went to conferences, and all of that. I think I'm in student affairs now because I got to work with so many great people and could see the impact they had on others. I wanted to be able to do the same. I love learning and helping it happen for students outside of the classroom.* —Jeremy, residential education coordinator

A growing group of new professionals were the first in their family to pursue higher education. They found the transition difficult with no one to smooth their path, introduce them to resources, or offer helpful suggestions. A career in student affairs offers them the chance to provide the support they themselves found on campus or, in some cases, struggled to find.

> **New professionals are pleasantly surprised to find that the experiences they loved as undergraduates can be turned into a full-time job.**

As a first-generation undocumented undergraduate student, I struggled through my first few years. Multiple barriers, such as lack of financial aid or access to a network and not knowing the educational system in the United States, affected me academically and socially. I was able to connect with inspiring individuals who helped me become heavily involved in student leadership positions. These opportunities opened my eyes to a whole world of possibilities and empowered me to obtain a master's degree in higher education, giving me the tools to work as a student affairs professional and increase access to students with similar experiences. —Pablo, admissions counselor

As a first-generation student, I didn't know resources for us. I had some depression and someone told me about the Counseling Center and I was shocked we had that resource. Then I wanted to talk to someone about another issue and I learned about the Women's Resource Center. Every time someone said that there was a resource, I thought, "I can't be the only person who didn't know about these resources." Now, I want to help other students to find all of these places. —Erica, financial aid counselor

Jeremy, Pablo, and Erica followed a more traditional path, entering student affairs immediately following completion of their bachelor's degree. They were involved as undergraduates and received guidance that helped them realize the impact they could have on others. They almost immediately started in a master's program in higher education or public administration and used this knowledge to inform their practice. Others followed a different path.

I find it ironic that I'm a career counselor since my career path was the furthest thing from being linear. I was in the teaching field for a while, did medical research for a while, and then went and got my master's in counseling. While working on that, I had an internship working in student activities and decided to change my focus almost immediately. I think there's a magical quality about student affairs that draws people in. —Kelly, career services counselor

Mine was similar. I worked in the accounting field after college and one day I thought, "I hate my life." It was not enjoyable. I talked with mentors in the athletic department, rape education, and judicial, all things I was involved with as an undergraduate. They helped me talk through this career change. —Katie, associate dean of students

Regardless of how anyone enters the profession, whether someone has chosen student affairs directly after completion of the undergraduate degree or after a trial period in other fields, all new professionals bring valuable knowledge and skills that serve to enhance the student experience. As mentioned, new professionals might enter student affairs having planned for this career since their first or second year in college, or they might fall into the field while pursuing another goal. Department managers seek to maximize experiences and build working teams by drawing from the strength that individuals bring. New professionals achieve the greatest success by taking time and care to learn from their colleagues and to use their own skills to complement, rather than compete, with others. They should pay particular attention to the background and educational experiences of those they work with and celebrate those who can help them approach problems or issues in innovative and creative ways. Vice presidents for student affairs appreciate, and enhance the experience of, those who work collaboratively with others. Effective student affairs programs are those that meld the institutional identity of more seasoned professionals with the enthusiasm and innovative ideas of new professionals.

Transitioning to a New Identity

Any transition offers opportunities for growth but also presents challenges. New student affairs professionals will find themselves moving into unknown territory. Often the view from the world of the undergraduate or graduate student perspective contrasts with the reality of the professional.

> *When you're a student, you think you're super powerful, you think you're going to change the world, and in graduate school, you learn about social justice and making a difference. Then you come into the profession and you realize, there's a process, there's funding, there's people. It felt like hitting a hard wall. Things can't happen quickly and reality hits you.* —Pablo, admissions counselor

> *As a student, you have more liberty to exercise your freedom of speech. As a professional, you realize that politics are very real, and you can't necessarily say anything you want. There are standards of account-ability for what you say and you quickly realize that you represent more than yourself—you basically represent the institution you're working for. On the other hand, being in student affairs also provides endless possibilities to make change, but you do have to deal with the reality of politics. The new professionals entering student affairs may be leaving a world where they felt competent, viewing themselves as leaders, only to enter a new world as beginners.* —Belinda, director, Office of Inclusive Excellence

When I was working with political campaigns, I was managing a huge budget and then, all of a sudden, I'm a graduate assistant (GA) whose job is making coffee. It was a problem for me to make that shift and then slowly get back to more autonomy. —Garrett, associate orientation director

Maggie discussed the new identity as coming in two phases, first from undergraduate to graduate and then from graduate student to professional, finding the second transition much more empowering.

As a GA, you're working with other GAs who, as undergraduates, were big fish in a very small pond. You get used to being the bright shining star as an undergraduate RA and then you go to graduate school where you are just one of many stars. Now, as a professional, it feels more collaborative. . . . We are all professionals and we all work together toward a goal. —Maggie, residential education coordinator

Those who make the transition from undergraduate to new professional at the same institution face a special challenge.

As an undergraduate, I worked in the dean of students office, in housing, and with the Latino Outreach Center. Now I work in financial aid. I knew the financial aid staff as a student, and while some see me as I am now, others still see me as a 19-year-old student. Sometimes, so do I. That's hard. —Erica, financial aid counselor

The need to see the "bigger picture" was identified as a very steep learning curve. Jeremy stated that as an undergraduate RA, he only needed to worry about "this floor" which, as a graduate assistant, grew to encompass "this building." A new professional is required to consider how decisions affect an entire department or the university while simultaneously helping mentor and educate those who are now RAs and GAs to consider the big picture. The role of a supervisor during this early transition is critical. Kelly discussed the change from receiving constant feedback as a student to the more autonomous reflection required from any professional. The supervisor serves as the transition guide during this period of settling in. One new professional discussed the sense of floundering when his supervisor left the institution shortly after he arrived. While simultaneously discovering the nuances of a new job in a specific department, they are trying to learn the culture of student affairs and, as Jeremy stated, understand the big picture of how student affairs fits into the institutional mission. Supervisors ideally provide this link to the greater vision and introduce new professionals to colleagues who can help them complete their job successfully while providing additional opportunities to expand their experiences and competencies. It is critical for new staff to let their supervisor know of their needs so that he or she can provide needed support and assistance. Looking for others outside of their department from whom they can learn provides an alternative perspective and additional support.

Experiencing Rewards

Student affairs as a career can bring great interpersonal satisfaction. New professionals come to their first position with expectations formed from their undergraduate and graduate experiences. The opportunity to positively impact the lives of students and provide support and mentorship was universally acknowledged as the primary reward.

> *When I see students graduate who I feel like I was able to help get them there—that's very rewarding. Also, in my personal life, I'm involved with social activism, and it's important to me that I chose a job that lets me continue to have that be important.* —Chris, TRIO-Upward Bound advisor

> *Being in this role is so symbolic for other Pacific Islanders in my community to see what they can be, and even aspire to be, in a higher administrative level is great!* —Belinda, director, Office of Inclusive Excellence

> *As a student I had the opportunity to be mentored by great administrators, and as a student affairs professional, I have the opportunity to do the same, to share my network, and create access to their academic experience. Additionally, as an admissions counselor, it is rewarding to see students be recruited, be successful, and graduate from this university.* —Pablo, admissions counselor

The culture of student affairs was identified as a major benefit by the new professionals. Just as this group identified mentoring and providing growth experiences for students, they identified the value of having these same opportunities provided for them by supervisors and administrators.

> *When I started in accounting, I was on my own, but being a new professional in student affairs, people take an interest in mentoring*

and training new professionals. The care that people have for your development in student affairs is great. —Katie, associate dean of students

For me, one of the rewarding parts of being a new student affairs professional is having the ability to really own my position and style. I feel in student affairs that "being you" is welcomed and supported. I was hired for my experiences and for who I am—I get to really own that and be me. —Jeremy, residential education coordinator

As a new professional in student affairs, I find it has been really easy to get involved in professional associations, when that isn't the case in most professions. I started by simply reviewing programs for the National Association of Student Personnel Administrators as much as I could in my graduate program, and then I signed up to volunteer as an editor for a newsletter produced by one of the knowledge communities (KCs). Next thing I knew, I was asked to become more involved to apply for a chair of a KC for Region V, and that turned into volunteering for the Enough is Enough campaign. To me, what is great as a new professional is that if you want the opportunities, if you want to learn more, if you want to be involved, there are PLENTY of opportunities to do so. All you have to do is ask, and then be ready to work hard! —Kelly, career services counselor

As these new professionals have expressed, the rewards of choosing a career in student affairs are deep and life changing. However, because of these rewards, there is a tendency for new professionals to lose some

> **The rewards of choosing a career in student affairs are deep and life changing.**

balance in their lives specifically because of the pleasure of helping students and growing as a professional. During high-stress times, the new professional should remember the many reasons they chose student affairs as a career.

Meeting Challenges

Each new professional faces a unique set of challenges, depending on his or her background, work setting, and specific job responsibilities. The task of embracing these challenges and using them as opportunities to learn about the profession can be difficult. These challenges often lead to the ever-present task of setting priorities, both professionally and interpersonally. These priorities might include time, image, and agenda management.

Learning to say "no" for me, as a new professional, was my biggest challenge; I said" yes" to anything, and I'd stay until 8 p.m. to get it done. Then people would start asking me to do everything, because they knew I would say yes. It's hard to come back from that. —Kelly, career services counselor

A challenge has been being young and not always being taken seriously. It's like I make a suggestion and then I know they are thinking "Let me check with someone older." —Chris, TRIO-Upward Bound advisor

This happens with working with parents, too. Students feel more comfortable talking to me because I'm younger, but I have to fight to be taken seriously in other settings. When parents request to meet with my staff's supervisor and they see me, they often request someone else or are surprised until we start talking or until they see my diplomas. My education and vocabulary have been carefully crafted to make me seem older. —Maggie, residential education coordinator

One challenge is finding ways of weaving social justice into what I do. I didn't do it in accounting—it just didn't come up. It was one of the things I really like about student affairs but thinking about incorporating it was quite an adjustment. —Katie, associate dean of students

Politics are my steepest learning curve. We talked about politics in my master's program, and you hear about it as a student, but when you walk into your first job you quickly begin to find yourself immersed. You must learn to think critically quickly and always represent one's department strategically to not offend others so you can reach collaborative goals. —Pablo, admissions counselor

Establishing your identity, goals, and priorities are challenges that all professionals face. Even seasoned professionals revisit these issues periodically throughout their career as they move to new settings, advance their career, or incorporate changes in their personal life into their jobs. But these tasks are never as salient as during the first several years after entering the field. Because all supervisors at one time were faced with similar challenges, it is incumbent upon them to help the new professional navigate these transitions. Each institution is unique—being successful is not only about knowing the job but also about understanding the culture of each setting. For example, if social justice is a priority for the institution and a passion for the new professional, the supervisor must facilitate opportunities for growth in this area. However, the new professionals must also be willing to ask for assistance while tackling these challenges or to check their perceptions with their supervisor or other trusted colleagues. They should be willing to admit mistakes and seek help. Taking advantage of opportunities or suggesting innovative ideas require a certain amount of risk taking, which often is uncomfortable for professionals at any level. As long as the supervisor is kept informed and help is requested as needed, the fresh perspectives that the new professional brings to old problems can be among the most valuable contributions they can make.

Attending to Self-care

Much attention has been given to the notion of *balance*. This term can create its own set of pressures as the new professional tries to give equal weight to all aspects of life. In reality, there are times when work requires more investment of time and energy such as move-in days in the residence hall. At other times, personal life might have the upper hand. The trick for the new (and seasoned) professional is knowing when and how to prioritize. New professionals are often building a new life in a new city while starting a new job. They are invested in proving their value, establishing professional connections, and developing new skills. Knowing when to take time for themselves and establishing an awareness of healthy self-care behaviors are essential skills to learn early.

> *As much as possible, I leave the office at 5 p.m., recognizing that when the 2 a.m. duty call comes in, I have to be there—and I will be. While my home IS on campus (and only one floor above my office), I still have a distinct time that I try to leave the office. My mentor told me, "Find your balance early on and get ahold of it quickly." And that's what I've done! In supervising GAs, I want them to see that in me. This is an important role modeling piece for me.* —Jeremy, residential education coordinator

I agree about the 5 p.m. time—I try to leave then. I have to do e-mail at night. . . . I just can't get my work done without it, but I need that 2 to 3 hours away after work, maybe golfing or something. If I feel overwhelmed with work, I'll come in on Saturday or Sunday for an hour or two, usually later in the day after I've had time to have some fun. —Garrett, associate orientation director

I have to work at different hours a lot of the time. I have to work on Saturday and I have to work from home sometimes. In the summer, I'm here 18–20 hours a day during Upward Bound. But then I take 2 straight weeks off and it's great. I like to be involved in community work, that doesn't feel like work to me, and sometimes I get to do that as PART of my work. —Chris, TRIO-Upward Bound advisor

I found it was hard to find time for myself when I first moved here. I didn't know anyone and didn't have friends or family in the state. I joined some athletic teams—softball and field hockey. This forced me to get involved in things I like so I HAVE to leave work. Also, participating in professional development opportunities helps me balance myself out. I can go away for a conference or retreat, and this allows me to come back to the office refreshed. —Kelly, career services counselor

Racquet ball helps. You get to bash the ball and take out your frustration! —Erica, financial aid counselor

Self-care can also take the form of developing trusted colleagues at work who can help you with perspective. Pressures don't always come from time constraints, work demands, or family expectations. You might find that balance is missing because of issues discussed previously, such as campus politics or interpersonal differences.

A great friend of mine once said, "If one can find one or two individuals on campus that you can totally trust and vent to, you are golden." I am lucky to say that I have found mentors and colleagues whom I can trust and share my frustrations with. I try to visit and meet with them as much as possible to keep my sanity. —Pablo, admissions counselor

Student affairs professionals tend to be passionate about their work. Helping students and collaborating on innovative projects makes the work stimulating and rewarding. The new professional might confront the choice between equally attractive opportunities and, in an effort to learn more, agree to all of them. One of the greatest challenges for new professionals is prioritizing. Staff who develop good rapport with students will undoubtedly be asked to give more and more of their time. Those who successfully spearhead one new initiative will find themselves rewarded with two more projects. Finding ways to spend time with friends and family, volunteering in the community, and exercising self-care while simultaneously committing to their work responsibilities and professional growth might sound like an impossible task. Like any habit, this takes practice. It also requires a self-awareness of your own stress signals. Learn to recognize these early and identify your own de-stress strategies. Like Erica recommended, maybe it's bashing a racquetball.

> **One of the greatest challenges for new professionals is prioritizing.**

Working with Supervisors and Administrators

New professionals need help defining their jobs while they look for new responsibilities and broadening expectations. They must feel comfortable making (and admitting to) mistakes and asking questions in order to develop the expertise required to advance in the field. They benefit from supervisors who help them navigate the new world that the institution presents and who explain the culture of the new environment when it seems confusing. Supervisors who are able to be positive while remaining challenging allow for opportunities for the new professional to recognize both their successes and their growth edges. And, as has been discussed, they often need someone to tell them to slow down, take a deep breath, and relax.

> *What I want is to be complimented; what I need is for someone to push me, give me constructive criticism, and provide me with concrete advice on what I need to work on to get to the next level.*
> —Pablo, admissions counselor

> *I need someone who can see my strengths but can also see me trying to hide my struggles. I like in student affairs that we have a much more personal touch—more open relationships. It's easy to see where personal issues interfere with the work space but a good supervisor can call me on it when that happens.* —Maggie, residential education coordinator

I'm my worst critic, so what I want in a supervisor is someone who will challenge me but will also support me and tell me some of the good things I'm doing as well. I'm already being hard on myself. I want someone who can advocate for me. —Kelly, career services counselor

I want someone who shares some philosophies and will make me better. I like the philosophy, "Good is the enemy of great." If something is always good enough, it will never become better or great. I don't want someone who does things because "This is the way it's always been done." I like a supervisor who will not settle. —Chris, TRIO-Upward Bound advisor

I've been thinking about this lately. My need is twofold—I want someone who can keep me in the loop when I'm not part of important decisions to help me get on board with it. If I understand where a decision is coming from, I can buy into it more easily. Second, when the opportunity to give feedback is there and I give my supervisor my thoughts, I want them to advocate for my thoughts when I'm not there. —Jeremy, residential education coordinator

For new professionals, access to student affairs leadership is also an important aspect in understanding their new environment. The diverse perspectives from supervisors, directors, deans, and vice presidents for student affairs are helpful when determining the expectations of the new employee's role in their department and where that department fits into the mission of student affairs and the university.

I like that we can build relationships with administrators. When I was working in politics, you only talk to your supervisor and not the candidates, but student affairs is not as hierarchical. You can talk to different people at levels higher than you and it's okay. —Garrett, associate orientation director

My two supervisors are senior administrators. I count on them to give me warnings about the land mines I may step on and about opportunities for professional development. I love honesty as well. My bosses come from a place of yes and, if it's no, they explain the big pictures of why it's a no. —Belinda, director, Office of Inclusive Excellence

Vice presidents for student affairs bear the responsibility of setting the professional climate of the division and promoting a culture of bringing new professionals along through support and encouragement. Additionally, each supervisor is equally responsible for providing this environment for the staff who report to them. Just as the success of a university is determined by the accomplishments of its graduates, so, too, is the success of student affairs programs and services determined by its staff at all levels and their ability to be effective in their work and their lives. Those just entering the field are often the professionals with the most direct contact with students. It is critical that both administrators and supervisors give them the tools they need to be successful as they learn to take their place at the student affairs table.

New professionals should look for leaders and mentors who are open to answering questions and sharing advice, especially those who have successfully established themselves as respected members of the university community. Mentors can be found anywhere, often in unexpected places, and a mentoring relation-

> **New professionals should look for leaders and mentors who are open to answering questions and sharing advice.**

ship should not be limited to one specific supervisor. People from other institutions can become sounding boards. With professional growth, often mentors and support systems increasingly become peers.

When interviewing for future jobs, learn what supervision in that department is like and how comfortable staff feel with the leadership of student affairs. Most senior administrators take great pleasure in working with new staff and helping them grow as professionals. The wise administrator is always aware that the new professional of today is the senior leader of tomorrow.

Voices of Experience

The new professionals involved in this discussion all shared the belief that they were still finding their way. We asked what one piece of advice they would give to those starting in their first professional position in student affairs.

> *You have to have a passion for students and want to help them succeed. Your job is to be the person who opens doors for them.*
> —Erica, financial aid counselor

You have to take time to understand. Understand your role, the department, and the university. Take time building relationships and first understand others and their roles. Essentially, learn and understand before you jump. —Jeremy, residential education coordinator

I came to student affairs from the academic side and I find it to be surprisingly collaborative. The culture is not about "me, myself, and I" like I feel it is sometimes as an academic. You move into student affairs and you can't do anything without a collaborative effort. It's very communal. And I think new professionals should get as many experiences collaborating with as many different areas as you can. —Belinda, director, Office of Inclusive Excellence

Be willing to take chances. When I finished my internship in student activities, someone told me about this job across the country in career services. I had never been to Utah, and had never thought I would enjoy career services, but I took a leap for career services and I love it. Sometimes the situations that challenge us the most, turn out to be the most rewarding. —Kelly, career services counselor

I heard someone from another part of campus say that going into student affairs was "professional suicide." Eventually, I realized that because I care about the students, it was a good place for me to be. My advice would be to always remind yourself why you are here, and WHO you are here for. —Chris, TRIO-Upward Bound advisor

When I decided to make the switch from accounting to student affairs, I sat down with family and friends and talked about what student affairs is and tried to help them understand why I wanted to do this. That was really important for me. Share why you love your work with those who matter to you. —Katie, associate dean of students

Be open to new opportunities and ideas, especially the scary ones. The scary opportunities are the ones where you learn the most about yourself. They are often the hardest decision but the most worthwhile. —Maggie, residential education coordinator

Find that balance in your life quickly and hold onto it. Do it early because it's harder to find it later. —Erica, financial aid counselor

Be ready to be your office champion, be ready to lead, be ready to be loyal to your division's goals, and always keep in mind that students come first. Don't ever settle, keep pushing yourself against all odds, people notice and next thing you know you are there. —Pablo, admissions counselor

I'm a firm believer in the old adage, "Don't sweat the small stuff." Our jobs can be stressful whether you are a new professional or a senior administrator. With multiple demands coming in from multiple sources, it's easy to be overwhelmed. Learn to recognize what is top priority, what is time sensitive, what can be delegated, and what is inconsequential. Don't be afraid to ask for help when you need it. —Kari, associate vice president for student development

Do all you can to prepare yourself educationally and experientially, and then move forward in your career with confidence. Surround yourself with strong, positive colleagues who help you learn and grow and are your strong champions. And champion those around you in their successes; growing together provides momentum that sustains you in our profession. —Barb, vice president of student affairs

Conclusion

Welcoming new staff into a student affairs division represents a challenge and an opportunity for student affairs administrators and supervisors. It's an exciting time for most new professionals eager to get started on a career with infectious energy. Most administrators and supervisors are ready and willing to share the wisdom gained in a career they love in a field that has been exceptionally rewarding. There is also a keen sense of responsibility to ensure the future of student affairs by developing new professionals. At the same time, these new professionals increasingly come from backgrounds that might differ significantly from those in administrative positions. What remains consistent is a firm commitment to creating a positive educational environment for students. New professionals are well advised to take advantage of opportunities for learning from those with more experience while using their energy, passion, and innovative ideas to enhance current practices. Entering your new role with a positive attitude, seeking out new experiences, making mistakes (and learning from them), and preparing for the future are goals that can be met through mentoring and support from supervisors, mentors, and colleagues. This is the nature of student affairs: to learn and grow in our work so that the students we serve receive the benefit. With this common goal, we are all destined for success.

UNWRITTEN RULES: ORGANIZATIONAL AND POLITICAL REALITIES

CHAPTER TWO

Marilyn J. Amey, Eric R. Jessup-Anger,
and Connie Tingson-Gatuz

Higher education is political. Experienced professionals recognize the truth of this statement, but for new professionals in student affairs administration, the political nature of the world they have entered might feel like a cruel joke. They might have studied college administration and perhaps even administrative theory in their graduate programs, but translating textbook examples and theories to the real world can be challenging. This chapter provides some tools new professionals can use to assess their organizational culture and makes suggestions for managing this culture and the politics inherent in it. For the purposes of this discussion, we have used Kuh and Hall's (1993) definition of *culture*:

[The] collective, mutually shaping patterns of institutional history, mission, physical settings, norms, traditions, values, practices, beliefs and assumptions which guide behavior of individuals and groups . . . and which provide frames of reference for interpreting the meanings of events and actions on and off campus. (p. 2)

After briefly describing the political nature of today's higher education institutions, we present several common dilemmas facing new administrators, situations that might not conform to their expectations. Each dilemma is, in part, a product or function of the work environment and, as a result, can be ameliorated through a better understanding of organizational culture. Because new professionals are more likely to see themselves as counselors, programmers, or hall directors than as administrators, they don't always have a context for understanding and dealing with institutional challenges. Therefore, we present an approach to organizational analysis and relate it generally to student affairs work and specifically to the dilemmas confronting new professionals. This approach to understanding organizational culture is not intended as a panacea. We merely suggest that being an effective organizational analyst—that is, understanding the organizational and political realities of the job—is key to addressing essential professional issues that are generally not taught in graduate school.

The Environment of Student Affairs Work

Compared with the corporate and private sectors, educational organizations are often touted as collegial institutions whose members are drawn together by a common mission to serve students and provide an educated citizenry. Lofty goals, rich traditions, ceremonies full of regalia and pomp and circumstance, and an air of elitism are stereotypical images of colleges and universities, and *family* is a metaphor often used to describe their atmosphere (Bergquist & Pawlak, 2007; Birnbaum, 1988). In most cases, the vernacular definition of *collegial* (friendly) might accurately reflect colleges and universities today, but the organizational definition (small in size, shared goals, face-to-face interaction, consensus decision making, minimized status differentials; Birnbaum, 1988) applies less often. Institutional growth or decline, financial strain, diversification, technological advancement, online instruction, entrepreneurial spirit, cultural diversification, and increasing internationalization are just some of the factors that can affect the collegial atmosphere and change the way the college functions.

All colleges and universities are political organizations; they vary in how susceptible they are to political behavior and, therefore, how much new student affairs professionals might be affected (Hirt, 2006). In an era of declining resources, increasing competition for students, and conflicting demands, even small private liberal arts colleges—long held up as a model of the nonpolitical or at least less political (Birnbaum, 1988)—are becoming arenas for coalition building, win–lose games, ambiguous goals, and uneven power distribution.

> *Before I started my first professional job, I had a preconceived notion that politics only took place in public universities. But I quickly learned that politics can even find its way to the religious college environment. We need to be aware of the role that politics plays in our work and, more important, how we choose to deal with it. We can't let it stifle our ability to put students first.* —First-year experience coordinator at a private college

Although the ideas of politics and political organizations tend to have negative connotations, there is nothing inherently negative about politics or its role in decision making and organizational behavior (Bolman & Deal, 2013). New professionals who are unaware of the nature of organizations or don't understand political functioning can be adversely affected quite easily. Becoming a good organizational analyst—a culturally competent student affairs practitioner, as Kuh, Siegel, and Thomas (2001) said—is key to survival and effective practice in a political organization.

At the same time, new professionals need a clear personal identity to avoid being swept away by institutional gamesmanship that can occur when competition for scarce resources increases positioning and posturing. A strong sense of personal ethics, morality, and integrity is an important foundation for effective practice and is key to organizational leadership (Badaracco & Ellsworth, 1989; Bogue, 1994; Young, 2001; see Chapter Three). However, these factors are not often discussed in graduate degree programs, in new member orientation, or even among colleagues. New practitioners must reconcile their personal expectations with the professional realities of the organization.

> **Becoming a good organizational analyst—a culturally competent student affairs practitioner, as Kuh, Siegel, and Thomas (2001) said—is key to survival and effective practice in a political organization.**

Issues of Dissonance Confronting New professionals

No matter how carefully we prepare for a job interview, how thoroughly we question those employed at the institution, how competently we assume the responsibilities of a new job, inevitably, once the newness begins to wear off (and sometimes even sooner), we realize that our expectations don't match the job's realities. The nature of the administrative position, the college or university where an individual works, and the gap between expectations and realities vary from person to person, but new student affairs professionals consistently face similar challenges. Four broad issues of dissonance frequently appear in the literature: academic or experiential preparation; role conflict or ambiguity; lack of systematic evaluation and feedback; and professional opportunities or lack thereof. These issues can often be addressed or reconciled through a better understanding of organizational culture.

Academic or Experiential Preparation

Student affairs graduate preparation programs provide an orientation to the field and initial employment experiences, often in the form of paid assistantships and for-credit practicums. A review of programs listed in the National Association of Student Personnel Administrators' (2014) Graduate Program Directory makes clear that most entry-level graduate programs provide common course experiences for their students. Experiential components of degree programs vary significantly and are most noticeable with regard to how much classroom learning (including theory) connects to work experience and vice versa. It's not always clear whether the combination of in- and out-of-class experiences adequately prepares new professionals to hit the ground running in their first post-degree position and to succeed in the profession (Ambler, Amey, & Reesor, 1994; Renn & Jessup-Anger, 2008).

> *My classes in the master's program were fine; I learned a lot from my assistantship, too—a ton. But it was like living in two different worlds! The faculty hadn't been in practice for a long time, some of them not at all, and the supervisors, well, they just kept saying, "Don't give me theory. This is real life!" I wish we'd had more of an opportunity to bridge the gap. Sometimes it was hard to know which way to go.* —Recreation services director at a midsize public university

The reality is that my coursework and field experience throughout graduate school prepared me for the profession to a certain extent. On many other dimensions, I had to learn so much on the job. But on the other hand, I value my graduate experience because it has informed my thinking about issues that I encounter every day.
—Service–learning coordinator at a private college

Because there is no specific undergraduate academic preparation (i.e., no undergraduate major in student affairs, although some institutions offer a single introductory class), people enter the field from many different disciplines. This is obviously true for positions requiring only a baccalaureate degree but also for those that require a master's degree. Previous work experience is almost as varied as academic major: An admissions recruiter might come from work in the private sector, and a financial aid counselor might come with a law degree. The mix is rich. The generalist nature of entry-level student affairs professionals helps institutions attract a diverse work force. But for new professionals, the generalist approach often leads to insecurity, difficulty relating to peers, a sense that "others must know more than I do," and feeling overwhelmed with all there is to learn.

New professionals might also feel tension because they are trained at large institutions that award master's and doctoral degrees but often choose different kinds of employment settings. The extent to which their graduate preparation program addresses the needs and issues of student affairs work in smaller liberal arts colleges or community colleges, for example, might vary quite a lot.

It seems that higher education professionals are trained at universities, which is a night-and-day experience compared to the small private colleges where many of us work. In fact, most of my peers don't have training in higher education administration. This is often very frustrating for me, because I often feel that I am one of a select few people on campus who are familiar with student development theory, especially when I'm on institutional standing committees. —Academic advisor at a private college

Community colleges are a completely different story. Although my academic preparation in student affairs from a larger university was very enriching, I had to seriously adjust my understanding of our work in the community college environment. Things are changing so fast, especially as we must help as many students as possible go on to pursue a bachelor's degree. —Academic support coordinator at a community college

Role Conflict or Ambiguity

New student affairs professionals are often torn by conflicting job demands, differences of opinion with supervisors, or duties they don't want to perform or aren't comfortable doing, such as firing an employee. Role conflict can be especially hard for those making the transition directly from senior year in college to the first position in student affairs. Although many entry-level positions today require or prefer a master's degree, many others require only a baccalaureate degree; as a result, in a matter of days, someone can go from being a student (i.e., one of the group) to being in charge (i.e., a leader). The dissonance caused by role conflicts can be especially overwhelming at this stage, when organizational understanding, influence, and power to resolve conflicts are often lacking.

What was most difficult was having to separate from the group of Greek leaders. We thought we had developed such a very strong working relationship with them, and everything was going so well. We really thought this was the best group of leaders yet. But while we were at the conference, they all started drinking right there in front of us. We knew they weren't of legal age, and yet they did it right in front us. I'm not sure if they wanted us to do something or not, but we couldn't stay there with them. It would have been like sanctioning their behavior. I just couldn't believe they would put us in that kind of position. I thought we were friends, but they crossed the line that night, and I don't know how to go back now. —Greek advisor at a public university

As an academic advisor, I was the youngest professional in the entire division. Students often mistook me for a peer, and my colleagues often mistook me for a student. I was stuck in an awkward space of trying to assert my new identity. —Academic advisor at a liberal arts college

Another aspect of dissonance is role ambiguity, which arises when the new professional is unsure of the scope and responsibilities of the job, job objectives, and colleague expectations (Rasch, Hutchison, & Tollefson, 1986). Positions might seem very clearly defined on paper, but so much of every student affairs administrative position falls into the "other" category that the true scope of a job seems ever evolving and, sometimes, never ending. Student, colleague, and supervisor expectations also play a role in defining the scope of a position, depending on the organizational culture. In small colleges, for instance, it might be understood that administrators are expected to attend various institutional events regardless of the relationship of the activities to their specific position. At both large and small institutions, committee work might be an unstated but important job responsibility. As with other elements of culture, these expectations might not be clarified until they have been violated in some way.

And although organizational charts and position descriptions provide an interpretation of the reality of the job, many basic functions cut across organizational lines and formal reporting structures (Sandeen, 1996). In part because of the interrelated way offices work together to serve students and in part because of the inherently political nature of educational organizations, new professionals must understand the culture in their primary work unit and also the cultures of other units with which they work on behalf of students. Dissonance can arise as you straddle cultural boundaries, where norms, values, behaviors, jargon, and rewards differ.

Finally, many new professionals face role conflict between their expectations of being ready to take on the world of student affairs and their supervisor's perspective of what preparation entails. This might be particularly challenging for those coming into work environments where most of their colleagues and supervisors are seasoned professionals. Expectations about the pace of change and a preference for immediate results and feedback are just two examples of issues that can cause frustration for new professionals. "Paying your dues" and "working your way up" are less relevant concepts for new professionals who feel they are more current with the use of technology, more closely connected with students, and more accustomed to assessment and evaluation tools than some of their more senior colleagues.

Lack of Systematic Evaluation and Feedback

Every setting has processes or sets of experiences through which newcomers learn norms, values, and behavioral expectations. During this early period of socialization, issues of role conflict are either lessened or heightened (Louis, 1980), as new professionals test their expectations against the realities of the work environment. If the gap is too great, the resulting dissonance might lead to the person leaving the position. Feedback, both positive and negative, is very important during the first few months for closing the expectation gap and relieving dissonance. Most new professionals rely heavily, although not exclusively, on their immediate supervisor for feedback (Carpenter, 2001; Renn & Jessup-Anger, 2008). However, colleges and universities are notoriously weak in providing systematic, timely, and constructive feedback to employees.

> *As a new professional, I expected to get regular feedback from my supervisor. When that didn't happen, I quickly developed feelings of being unappreciated and undervalued. I had to figure out where my source of motivation would come from, since I was thirsty for recognition. My expectations that I would receive mentoring from my boss went unfilled until I started asking for feedback from my peers and from the students that I worked with. I realized that evaluations and feedback can come from sources other than the top.*
> —Student activities advisor at a large state university

The socialization period might not even include training or sufficient training for new professionals to feel that their questions have been resolved. Newcomers, especially those in their first post-degree professional position, might be unsure about the questions to ask or are afraid of appearing insecure, and so might be particularly reluctant to seek feedback actively and early on, thereby increasing their sense of stress and transition dissonance. This is often the case for people of color (who might be underrepresented) and women in units dominated by White men—these people might feel more at risk.

Professional Opportunities or Lack Thereof

Most people accept a position expecting opportunities for personal and professional growth. Professional growth can come through participation in various committees and initiatives on campus that help expand job skills, build networks, and gain important experiences without actually changing jobs. It can come from being promoted, taking on leadership responsibilities, or participating in professional development opportunities off-campus such as conference workshops or webinars. When such opportunities don't materialize, however, creative strategies are called for.

During the interview, I didn't know enough to ask if there were opportunities for professional development. That was a mistake! I sorely needed to continue the opportunity to explore new knowledge and information that I received in my graduate school experience. Opportunities to attend national conferences weren't a priority. So I had to be creative. —Career services advisor at a faith-based college

There are so many professional development opportunities that don't cost much. More and more webinars are sponsored by our professional associations. Some of them are free, and others are a pretty reasonable, especially if you join with others on campus to share the costs. We don't have funds to travel much these days, but I find drive-in summits within our state are very helpful. There is so much on the Internet now to access. —Counselor at a private university

Horizontal movement is one way of enhancing your job and expanding your skills before moving up in the organization (Young, 1990), which can be a good professional development strategy. At the same time—depending on whether the move occurs within or across divisions, at the same or a different institution—opportunities might vary a lot. Previous comparable experience is not always seen as such, so lateral moves can lead to a "life at entry level" cycle rather than offering an opportunity to gain broader experience.

Promotion is most commonly mentioned when thinking of professional opportunity for growth, whether within the same institution or in a move to a new institution. Promotion usually comes with an increase in decision-making authority, control of resources, and opportunities to affect the organization and effect change. Many associate directors, directors, and deans are actually quite constrained by demands on their time, increased responsibilities, increased administrivia, and the structure, values, and norms of their units (Mills, 1993). The aspects of student affairs work that appeal to many new professionals (i.e., working closely with students, programming) are engaged in less frequently or more narrowly by senior administrators. Finally, opportunity is in large part a result of who is ahead of you on the ladder.

When I found out I was going to shift over full time to the advising center after having worked there part time for a year, I was thrilled. They told me my knowledge and expertise were going to be invaluable to the new team, and I couldn't wait to get started. What they didn't tell me was that, in the new structure, the director calls the shots—all of them. I might have expertise, but I'm not getting to use it. Most of the time, I'm just supposed to sit there and do what's handed to me. Now I'm looking to move out. —Advising center counselor at a public state university

As illustrated in this example, a supervisor who is unwilling to delegate important responsibilities or share plum assignments and committee activities limits the growth, development, and institutional exposure of fellow administrators (Amey, 1991). New professionals must be aware of the hierarchical and personnel structures of their organization as they consider their mobility and opportunities.

Each of these four dilemmas can cause dissonance for new student affairs professionals. At the same time, a person can curb the confusion, close the gap between expectations and reality, and learn to deal with the work environment by learning to understand the organizational culture. The degree of dissonance created by these dilemmas (and many others) is a function of the specific institution and unit, so the analytic tools presented are generic. Each new professional must identify the answers that fit his or her individual circumstances, career, and life goals.

Theory to Practice: A Cultural Framework for Professional Survival

New professionals are not likely to find quick fixes to eliminate the gap between expectation and reality as they go about the business of surviving in their organizations and thriving in student affairs. At the same time, many issues that hit new professionals head on, such as those described earlier, are a function of the organization itself and how it works. One strategy for managing these issues is understanding organizational culture and becoming an effective organizational analyst.

The best course I took in graduate school was [on organizational governance], where we talked about decision making and politics, and why things work the way they do, and how to figure it all out. This is what I really needed to know to survive! —International student advisor at a research university college

In the framework presented in this chapter, we adapted Tierney's (1991) six essential components of organizational culture: environment, mission, socialization, information, strategy, and leadership. Understanding the dynamics of culture by analyzing these six organizational components can help reduce the dissonance that results from a gap between expectations and the organizational and political realities of the job. Familiarity with the values, norms, rituals, symbols, myths, and impact of leadership helps a new professional recognize the behaviors and strategies that are most likely to succeed (or not succeed) in the unit.

> *I quickly learned that there is an "institutional way" of doing things. If I questioned why things were the way they were, colleagues would tell me, "Oh, you'll learn how we do things here." If I had a new idea, they would tell me that it would never work here. It seemed like there were insiders and outsiders. If you didn't participate in the indoctrination process of learning the ins and outs, you would always be an outsider.* —Admissions officer at a private college

Understanding culture not only gives administrators a way to assess their institutions and departments but helps them identify appropriate tasks and roles for themselves, reducing some of the dissonance created by role conflict and ambiguity (Hirt, 2006). As Whitt (1993) suggested, "The potential reward [of discovering the culture of an organization] is greater understanding of both the visible and the tacit elements—the furniture, scripts, and invisible props. . . ." (p. 93). But organizational analysis is not the answer for all the difficulties facing new professionals. Making sense of things; being aware of ideologies, rituals, and symbols that motivate and alienate members; identifying key supporters and networks; and conceptualizing leadership as embodying these ideals are all important components of administrative effectiveness and success.

> **Understanding culture not only gives administrators a way to assess their institutions and departments but helps them identify appropriate tasks and roles for themselves, reducing some of the dissonance created by role conflict and ambiguity (Hirt, 2006).**

Environment

Student affairs divisions are not islands unto themselves; they exist within many internal environments (e.g., departments within divisions, levels of directors within departments) and external environments that have an impact on their effectiveness. Some of the external influences are located outside the specific division but within the institution, such as academic affairs, business affairs, and athletics. Others are external to the college or university altogether, such as national Greek organizations, the community, private sector suppliers, and state and federal laws. Not all internal and external environments have great influence, but in some ways these environments shape the context of work for new professionals, even in daily tasks and assignments. New professionals who believe that they only have to pay attention to their direct supervisor are very shortsighted and narrow in their thinking. Supervisors help define the most immediate environments, which is helpful, but new professionals can become so engrossed in performing the tasks for which they were hired that they fail to grasp the larger context. For example, changes in national accreditation standards in professional degree programs such as business or education might at first seem irrelevant to student affairs work; indeed, many new professionals might even be unaware that accrediting agencies exist. But those involved with recruitment, scholarships, educational support services, and cultural support services might see changes in their work as they help students adjust to new (usually higher) academic standards.

An example much closer to home is the importance of understanding what other units in the college or university think about student affairs, particularly faculty. At some schools, for a variety of reasons, the professional staff and the faculty work closely together, especially in areas that affect students. Collegial relationships abound, faculty involvement in programming is the norm, and cocurricular activities are considered valuable contributions to the overall growth and development of students (Cook & Lewis, 2007; Hirt, 2006; Manning, Kinzie, & Schuh, 2006). At other institutions, academic and nonacademic units are more separate and even perceived as antagonistic (Cook & Lewis, 2007; Komives & Woodard, 1996). Individual interactions might be cooperative, but real collaboration is less likely. The interdependence of units and professionals in serving students is either less valued or less well understood. In these settings, new professionals are often dismayed when budgets are discussed to hear their work described as "taking a load off faculty shoulders," "interfering with students' study time," or "not central to the institutional mission." Becoming an effective environmental scanner, inside and outside your immediate office, helps you understand which influences matter most and how others' values and beliefs affect your daily activities. This is a key to success in an institution.

Mission

At some point, every new professional comes in contact with a student handbook or a piece of recruitment material that contains the institution's mission statement. Usually a lengthy and lofty text, the mission supposedly describes what the institution does, how and for whom, and sometimes even provides a discussion of the social, ethical, and educational beliefs that shape the institutional context (Lyons, 1993). Student affairs divisions often have their own mission statements that reflect the larger institutional mission but also describe more specifically the work of the division related to students. Individual units within a division might have their own versions as well. As guiding texts, these various mission statements provide a loose framework for organizing daily activities; as cultural artifacts, they often don't explain what really happens. This is especially true in colleges and universities, which are known for having multiple and competing missions (e.g., providing access for diverse students and increasing prestige by raising admission standards).

> *Don't be naïve to think that residence life is similar on all college campuses. I thought that my prior experiences working in residence halls on a large university campus prepared me for my current experience of working in a residence hall on a small private campus. I was wrong. The mission of the institution reflects the institution's priorities. Even in the residence hall, the policies are dictated by the values of the institution. As a new professional, I wish I had thought about whether my personal values were aligned with the institutional mission before I took the job. If these are not compatible, you will struggle.* —Residence hall director at a private college

Kuh and Schuh (1991) suggested, "The 'living mission' of a college is how students, faculty, administrators, graduates, and others describe what the college is and is trying to accomplish" (p. 12). These descriptions of purpose help new professionals understand more fully what student affairs means in each institution (Sandeen, 1996). Looking for both agreement and disagreement in how others think about the office's mission gives a clearer sense of what the office is about and for whom and how it will work. New professionals can find descriptions of purpose in the comments of the president in a convocation address, in the words of the vice president for student affairs at the fall semester division gathering, in a director's design for professional training, in the staff evaluation criteria, and in the day-to-day talk around the office. The messages might not be the same. The most agreement might exist at small private liberal arts colleges, where frequent interactions among faculty and staff reinforce a set of beliefs, values, and traditions (reflecting a stronger organizational culture). The greatest disparity might occur at a large research university, where multiple sets of beliefs, values, and traditions likely exist even within a division or department. Institutional and, therefore, student affairs unit missions can also be affected by history and heritage, organizational type and complexity of purpose, and type of student served.

Finding consistent messages is only part of the assessment; recognizing places where mission and belief statements conflict is also critical to success as a new professional. When what is said (i.e., the espoused mission) diverts from what is done (i.e., the mission in use; adapted from Argyris & Schön, 1977), the new professional might find a dissonance about unit goals, little sense of common purpose driving or shaping decisions, weak support for work done within the unit by those external to it, and a clash between his or her own value system and institutional or unit activity, or both. Remembering that missions exist both on paper and in the minds and actions of organization members should lead job candidates to ask more questions during the interview process and have a greater awareness of the culture during the early socialization period, when they might otherwise be preoccupied with learning specific tasks and buoyed by the euphoria of a new job.

Socialization

All organizations have rituals and ceremonies for welcoming new members. These activities might be as limited as having newcomers complete employment forms and purchase parking permits or as extensive as orientation programs and staff retreats. Just as we think of orienting students to campus or initiating inductees into student organizations, student affairs units should bring new members into the fold through intentional on-boarding that creates a sense of shared meaning and understanding about the work, the unit, the members of the unit, and the larger college or university; such socialization efforts help enculturate new members and give them some basic skills for navigating the organization. In addition to providing a sense of who's who and what's what, socialization, as Tierney (1991) described it, is a process of becoming aware of and indoctrinated to the norms, beliefs, and values of the organization. This socialization process is related less to administrative functions than to the development of social consciousness; less concerned with short-term job tasks than with long-term direction and purpose. As the new professional develops an identity as a member of a department and the larger student affairs profession, socialization plays a key role in providing knowledge of what is required to succeed.

One factor of both early and ongoing socialization is the professional anchoring of a person's position in the department and the institution. *Professional anchoring* refers to the primary orientation and interaction patterns of a position. For example, does the position demand that you work most often with employees in the same office or unit (internal) or with those in other offices outside the unit (external)? Student affairs usually includes a very interactive, externally oriented set of positions, because members work with so many other people to get the job done. New professionals in advising or educational support services, for example, quickly realize the importance of building close relationships with faculty departments as well as with admissions and student orientation staffs (Amey, 1991; Cook & Lewis, 2007). This external focus keeps the new professional aware of the college or university, its culture, and how it works, because attention is not primarily focused within the unit.

At the same time, many student affairs positions seem internally focused on a daily basis, either within the office or program itself or on students, rather than on interaction with other employees. Such positions tend to be fairly self-contained and emphasize more depth than breadth in professional growth. Advanced positions in student housing and financial aid, for example, might be very specialized and, therefore, won't encourage increased broad institutional knowledge. Individuals in more internally anchored positions might have to create their own opportunities, apart from job responsibilities, for developing relationships and interacting with the broader college community. The networks and support systems you develop help with this, especially as technology makes inter- and intra-institutional connecting easier. Institutional volunteerism, such as committee work, is another excellent way to stay connected outside the office (see Chapters Nine and Eleven).

Information

Tierney's (1991) fourth essential component of organizational culture is information. In assessing the organizational and political realities, an early task of new professionals is to determine what constitutes information, who has it, and how it's disseminated. Even in a highly structured organization—where memos, written records, handbooks and guidebooks, and standard operating procedures are in great supply—information doesn't flow only hierarchically, from the top down. Certainly, this is the case in an institution characterized as more collegial or political (Birnbaum, 1988; Bolman & Deal, 2013). Listervs, instant messaging, online resources, e-mail, and other social media increase the speed and volume of information flow, often making instantly accessible what traditionally was disseminated by an information gatekeeper. But communication explosion does not always mean information accuracy. New professionals must become skilled at gathering information from multiple sources and in multiple forms. Waiting for "official word" might mean missing an opportunity or not being able to avoid or manage a crisis. You need to learn whom to ask for what and who is a reliable source for the information you need to be most effective and efficient. This is not something to figure out at the moment of crisis. In such situations, the relationships you have developed with key colleagues can be critical to getting the job done. Knowing whom to call for the right answer might have nothing to do with that person's position on the organizational chart.

New professionals quickly become aware of how many different points of view exist in a college or university. Gathering information from multiple sources allows for a kind of triangulation through which you can draw conclusions on the basis of areas of agreement among sources (Patton, 1990). This can be critical in curbing rumors, creating coalitions, and seizing creative opportunities. Informal networks also provide important information, serve as critical sounding boards for ideas, and function as ways of gathering feedback for professional growth and development. Learning whom to work closely with and developing those relationships isn't often a conscious activity but needs to be more intentional (Hirt, 2006; Reesor, Bagunu, & Hazley, 2009).

> *Rich and I have a standing lunch the third Thursday of every month. He's been here two years longer than me and works in [another unit], so I'm always looking to him for advice, to figure out what's really going on. He's been great to talk with and introduces me to lots of folks he knows.* —Residence hall director at an urban university

We all sometimes feel as though we don't have enough information or the right facts on which to base decisions and take action. The better we understand the department and institution in which we work, the more we can see what is enough and not feel as though we're being excluded or left to our own devices. New professionals must realize that in addition to being purposeful in developing good contacts and networks, when they don't receive the kind of information they seek, it's not necessarily because someone is withholding it. Asking questions, listening carefully, seeking perspective outside your office, and building a strong informal network helps you as a new professional learn how to gather and broker information more effectively.

Strategy

Many new professionals believe that most decisions are straightforward, that the designated leader has the final say-so, and that their own authority is very limited. Others seek or are hired into an institution that touts a team or participative approach to management, in which everyone is involved in decisions and discussions of mission, goal setting, and evaluation. Still others believe they're being hired into one kind of environment and discover that the reality is very different. It's important to recognize the difference between talk and action, to distinguish between espoused theory and theory in use related to decision making and inclusiveness (Argyris & Schön, 1977), and to learn as quickly as possible how things actually get done. It's not helpful to bemoan the fact that the organization is not the way you hoped it would be; instead, focus on figuring out how it really operates so you can operate effectively within it. How the institution makes decisions and enacts them is what Tierney (1991) called *organizational strategy*.

Becoming familiar with both the obvious and subtle ways in which decisions are made—who is involved and at what level, what the penalties are for ineffective decisions and the rewards for effective ones—is part of understanding your unit. Unfortunately, these things are often learned by trial and error and by observing rather than questioning others. New professionals can begin understanding the strategies used in their own office early in the socialization period by asking some basic questions. Is this the kind of unit where the director signs off on everything before you are allowed to move ahead? Are symbols and symbolic meaning (including something as simple as event T-shirts) prevalent and effectively used throughout the office? At department meetings, is everything discussed, from what to give the administrative assistant on his birthday to next year's budget proposal? If the supervisor casually mentions an upcoming event, do you really have

> **There are many unwritten rules in institutions, divisions, and departments. Find a trusted supervisor and mentor to help you process and navigate the invisible politics and culture of the institution.**

a choice about attending? Does an invitation to be creative and innovative and to take the lead mean only within limits that are not well known? A clear sense of proper procedures, cliques, active countercultures, and informal networks that are common in every organization helps a new professional work more effectively and efficiently, build supportive connections, capitalize on opportunities, and succeed more consistently on behalf of students. One strategy we endorse is using a cultural guide. Guides can be a supervisor, a peer, or a trusted colleague who provides a perspective gained from years of experience embedded within the campus culture.

> *There are many unwritten rules in institutions, divisions, and departments. Find a trusted supervisor and mentor to help you process and navigate the invisible politics and culture of the institution.* —Residence hall director at a large private university

Leadership

Organizational charts supposedly show who the campus leaders are; what they really show, however, is who is in a position of authority, not who is necessarily a leader. An institution has many leaders, and they are not obvious by title or position; you find out who they are by paying attention to who gets things done. These informal leaders are everywhere and at every level, including new professionals. Often, informal leaders wield a lot of power and influence over daily activities in student affairs. A long-standing mid-level director might not appear as strong as her senior-level supervisor, judged on the basis of title and position, but her institutional knowledge and well-established reputation as a team player might allow her to exercise significant leadership throughout the division. Another person might live or work next door to the college president and often can raise important issues and concerns without an appointment, even though he holds an "assistant to" position, which many might perceive as low status. Good practice, organizational intuition, and a willingness to get involved are key to informal leadership, more so than title and place on the organizational chart.

People who choose careers in student affairs tend to look for ways to develop and exercise their own leadership early on rather than assuming that they have to wait until they're senior leaders before they can make a difference. If a leadership culture exists at the institution, you'll see leaders who are and are not in positions of formal authority. You'll also see staff who are lifelong learners, participating in ongoing professional development and organizational learning (Meyerson, 2002; Senge, 1990). They inspire confidence in others and work collectively to create new answers and identify new issues (Lewis, 1994; Meyerson, 2002). In many ways, this situation is similar to the learning imperative that we talk about when we're working with students. In a culture of leadership and lifelong learning, the job title is less important than choosing to exercise personal leadership. This can be an important lesson for new professionals.

> *I never saw myself as a leader before—that really sounded so "out there" to me. I'm a helper, and I guess being the leader always seemed less important. And then I sat on two committees, and there were things to be done, so of course I just jumped in to help get the work done, and all of a sudden everyone is calling me the leader, looking to me for leadership. It was weird! I guess that's what I was doing, but I also kept saying to myself, "Who am I? I don't have that fancy office or a long title." No one seemed to be worried about that but me.* —Multicultural affairs counselor at a community college

As this practitioner learned, there's a close connection between effective leaders and effective followers. The literature primarily focuses on the leadership side of the equation. The bookshelves of senior administrators are full of works by leadership strategists promoting seven steps or five keys or eight things to remember. Although these books have their place, the work of those who promote effective followers (De Pree, 1993; Kelley, 1993; Lee, 1993), team leadership (Bensimon & Neumann, 1993; Heider, 1989), and servant leaders (Bogue, 1994; Pollard, 1996; Wheatley, 2002) is equally important and perhaps more vital to the diverse higher education institution of the future. In addition, because the face of leadership in student affairs is changing slowly, it's important for new professionals to see themselves in leadership roles where role models might not yet exist. Aguirre and Martinez (2002); Astin and Astin (2000); Curry (2000); Hackney (2003); Ideta (1996); Valverde (2003); and Wolverton, Bower, and Hyle (2009) are only a few of the writers who have presented new lenses for identifying leadership that are different from the traditional images and narrow ranges of acceptable behavior. Whether through readings, conference participation, networking, or insightful supervisors and role models, new professionals should seek opportunities to engage in leadership and followership development, and start seeing themselves as potential leaders in their organizations and in the student affairs profession. We suggest new professionals develop a handful of coaches and mentors early on to ensure they have their own personal board of directors to help them develop as leaders and effective followers. (See Chapter Nine for further discussion.)

Conclusion

Cookbook philosophies or how-to lists don't easily resolve the difficult challenges and dilemmas that new professionals face. Becoming an effective organizational analyst changes the nature of the questions to ask during job interviews, questions that can lead to finding a better initial institutional fit. This kind of analysis also offers a different way of making sense of and interacting with the college or university, the student affairs division, the department, its members, and even the job itself.

During the first few months on the job, new professionals are busy learning specific tasks required of their position, adjusting to the new environment, and going through numerous balancing exercises, many of which are addressed in subsequent chapters of this book. At the same time, they need to quickly become culturally competent educators, managers, and leaders who regularly engage in ongoing discovery and rediscovery of their organizational context, its evolving situations, and their own actions (Hirt, 2006; Kuh et al., 2001). If new professionals take an organizational analysis approach to their professional transition, they'll pay attention to issues such as these: What are the important offices with which I will interact? What are the agreed-upon values and beliefs of my unit, and where is there disagreement? How will I get connected within and apart from my office? How is information communicated? Who are the key people to know, and why? Where will my support systems be? How do decisions get made, and by whom? Who are the informal leaders? Using this approach encourages new professionals to ask questions and be aware of certain aspects of their work environments during the first few months on the job and throughout their career. Realizing the importance of understanding the culture of the work setting will also lessen frustration during the socialization period—when gaps between expectations and job realities are common—and provide some guidance on how the new professional can successfully address these tensions.

References

Aguirre, A., Jr., & Martinez, R. (2002). Leadership practices and diversity in higher education. *Journal of Leadership Studies, 8*(3), 53–62. doi: 10.1177/107179190200800305

Ambler, D. A., Amey, M. J., & Reesor, L. M. (1994, March). *Strategies for improving collaboration between faculty and practitioners*. Paper presented at the NASPA Annual Conference, Dallas, TX.

Amey, M. J. (1991). Bridging the gap between expectations and reality. In K. M. Moore & S. B. Twombly (Eds.), *Administrative careers and the marketplace* (New Directions for Higher Education, No. 72, pp. 78–88). San Francisco, CA: Jossey-Bass.

Argyris, C., & Schön, D. A. (1977). *Organizational learning: A theory of action perspective*. Reading, MA: Addison-Wesley.

Astin, A. W., & Astin, H. S. (Eds.). (2000). *Leadership reconsidered: Engaging higher education in social change*. Battlecreek, MI: W. K. Kellogg Foundation. Retrieved from http://www.naspa.org/images/uploads/kcs/SLPKC_Learning_Reconsidered.pdf

Badaracco, J. L., & Ellsworth, R. R. (1989). *Leadership and the quest for integrity*. Boston, MA: Harvard Business School Press.

Bensimon, E. M., & Neumann, A. (1993). *Redesigning collegiate leadership: Teams and teamwork in higher education*. Baltimore, MD: Johns Hopkins Press.

Bergquist, W. H., & Pawlak, K. (2007). *Engaging the six cultures of the academy: Revised and expanded edition of the four cultures of the academy*. San Francisco, CA: Jossey-Bass.

Birnbaum, R. (1988). *How colleges work*. San Francisco, CA: Jossey-Bass.

Bogue, E. G. (1994). *Leadership by design*. San Francisco, CA: Jossey-Bass.

Bolman, L. G., & Deal, T. E. (2013). *Reframing organizations: Artistry, choice, and leadership* (5th ed.). San Francisco, CA: Jossey-Bass.

Carpenter, D. S. (2001). Staffing student affairs divisions. In R. B. Winston, D. G. Creamer, & T. K. Miller (Eds.), *The professional student affairs administrator: Educator, leader, and manager* (pp. 211–244). Philadelphia, PA: Accelerated Development.

Cook, J. H., & Lewis, C. A. (Eds.). (2007). *Student and academic affairs collaboration: The divine comity.* Washington, DC: National Association of Student Personnel Administrators.

Curry, B. (2000). *Women in power: Pathways to leadership in education.* New York, NY: Teachers College Press.

De Pree, M. (1993). Followership. In W. E. Rosenbach & R. L. Taylor (Eds.), *Contemporary issues in leadership* (3rd ed., pp. 137–140). Boulder, CO: Westview Press.

Hackney, C. E. (2003). Struggling for authentic human synergy and a robust democratic culture: The wellspring community for women in educational leadership. *Advancing Women in Leadership Journal, 13.* Retrieved from http://www.advancingwomen.com/awl/spring2003/HACKNE%7E1.HTML

Heider, R. (1989). The leader who knows how things happen. In W. E. Rosenbach & R. L. Taylor (Eds.), *Contemporary issues in leadership* (2nd ed., pp. 161–167). Boulder, CO: Westview Press.

Hirt, J. B. (2006). *Where you work matters: Student affairs administrators at different types of institutions.* Lanham, MD: University Press of America.

Ideta, L. M. (1996, November). *Asian women leaders of higher education: Inclusionary empowerment in pursuit of excellence.* Paper presented at the meeting of the Association for the Study of Higher Education, Memphis, TN.

Kelley, R. (1993). How followers weave a web of relationships. In W. E. Rosenbach & R. L. Taylor (Eds.), *Contemporary issues in leadership* (3rd ed., pp. 122–133). Boulder, CO: Westview Press.

Komives, S. R., & Woodard, D. B., Jr. (1996). Building on the past, shaping the future. In S. R. Komives & D. B. Woodard Jr. (Eds.), *Student services: A handbook for the profession* (3rd ed., pp. 536–555). San Francisco, CA: Jossey-Bass.

Kuh, G. D., & Hall, J. E. (1993). Clinical perspectives in student affairs. In G. D. Kuh (Ed.), *Cultural perspectives in student affairs work* (pp. 1–20). Lanham, MD: ACPA/University Press of America.

Kuh, G. D., & Schuh, J. (1991). *The role and contribution of student affairs in involving colleges.* Washington, DC: National Association of Student Personnel Administrators.

Kuh, G. D., Siegel, M. J., & Thomas, A. D. (2001). Higher education: Values and cultures. In R. B. Winston Jr., D. G. Creamer, & T. K. Miller (Eds.), *The professional student affairs administrator: Educator, leader, and manager* (pp. 39–64). New York, NY: Brunner-Routledge.

Lee, C. (1993). Followership: The essence of leadership. In W. E. Rosenbach & R. L. Taylor (Eds.), *Contemporary issues in leadership* (3rd ed., pp. 113–121). Boulder, CO: Westview Press.

Lewis, P. H. (1994). Implementing the culture of leadership. In S. A. McDade & P. H. Lewis (Eds.), *Developing administrative excellence: Creating a culture of leadership* (New Directions for Higher Education, No. 87, pp. 93–100). San Francisco, CA: Jossey-Bass.

Louis, M. (1980). Surprise and sense making: What newcomers experience entering unfamiliar organizational settings. *Administrative Science Quarterly, 25,* 226–251.

Lyons, J. W. (1993). The importance of institutional mission. In M. J. Barr (Ed.), *The handbook of student affairs administration* (pp. 3–15). San Francisco, CA: Jossey-Bass.

Manning, K., Kinzie, J., & Schuh, J. (2006). *One size does not fit all: Traditional and innovative models of student affairs practice.* New York, NY: Routledge.

Meyerson, D. (2002). Everyday leaders: The power of difference. *Leader to Leader, 23,* 29–34.

Mills, D. B. (1993). The role of the middle manager. In M. J. Barr (Ed.), *The handbook of student affairs administration* (pp. 121–134). San Francisco, CA: Jossey-Bass.

National Association of Student Personnel Administrators. (2014). Graduate program directory. Retrieved from https://www.naspa.org/careers/graduate/graduate-program-directory

Patton, M. (1990). *Qualitative evaluation and research methods* (2nd ed.). Newbury Park, CA: Sage.

Pollard, C. W. (1996). The leader who serves. In F. Hesselbein, M. Goldsmith, & R. Beckhard (Eds.), *The leaders of the future* (pp. 241–248). San Francisco, CA: Jossey-Bass.

Rasch, C., Hutchison, J., & Tollefson, N. (1986). Sources of stress among administrators at research universities. *Review of Higher Education, 9*(4), 419–434.

Reesor, L. M., Bagunu, G., & Hazley, M. (2009). Making professional connections. In M. J. Amey & L. M. Reesor (Eds.), *Beginning your journey: A guide for new professionals in student affairs* (3rd ed., pp. 109–132). Washington, DC: National Association of Student Personnel Administrators.

Renn, K. A., & Jessup-Anger, E. R. (2008). Preparing new professionals: Lessons for graduate preparation programs from the National Study of New Professionals in Student Affairs. *Journal of College Student Development, 49*(4), 319–335.

Sandeen, A. (1996). Organization, functions, and standards of practice. In S. R. Komives & D. B. Woodard Jr. (Eds.), *Student services: A handbook for the profession* (3rd ed., pp. 435–457). San Francisco, CA: Jossey-Bass.

Senge, P. M. (1990). *The fifth discipline: The art and practice of the learning organization.* New York, NY: Doubleday.

Tierney, W. G. (1991). Organizational culture in higher education: Defining the essentials. In M. Peterson (Ed.), *ASHE reader in organization and governance in higher education* (pp. 126–139). Lexington, MA: Ginn Press.

Valverde, L. A. (2003). *Leaders of color in higher education: Unrecognized triumphs in harsh institutions.* New York, NY: AltaMira Press.

Wheatley, M. (2002). The work of the servant-leader. In L. C. Spears & M. Lawrence (Eds.), *Focus on leadership: Servant-leadership for the twenty-first century* (pp. 349–362). New York, NY: Wiley.

Whitt, E. J. (1993). Making the familiar strange: Discovering culture. In G. D. Kuh (Ed.), *Cultural perspectives in student affairs work* (pp. 81–94). Lanham, MD: University Press of America.

Wolverton, M., Bower, B. A., & Hyle, A. E. (2009). *Women at the top: What women university presidents say about effective leadership.* Sterling, VA: Stylus.

Young, R. B. (Ed.) (1990). *The invisible leaders: Student affairs mid-managers.* Washington, DC: National Association of Student Personnel Administrators.

Young, R. B. (2001). Ethics and professional practice. In R. B. Winston Jr., D. G. Creamer, & T. K. Miller (Eds.), *The professional student affairs administrator: Educator, leader, and manager* (pp. 153–178). New York, NY: Brunner-Routledge.

DEVELOPING A PROFESSIONAL ETHIC

CHAPTER THREE

Anna M. Ortiz, Jonathan O'Brien, and Carla R. Martinez

E arly in their careers, professionals encounter ethical dilemmas on a daily basis, requiring them to balance personal values and beliefs with institutional expectations. These dilemmas range from relatively minor decisions to major crises. The fast pace of daily work and rapidly unfolding crises seldom allow time to consult with supervisors or mentors about ethical professional practices. Developmental issues also compound the challenge of engaging in ethical practice. In the midst of developing a professional identity, many new professionals lack the confidence to conduct themselves authentically.

> *One of my biggest professional fears is being confronted with an ethical dilemma. I'm afraid of not knowing what to do or making the wrong decision. I'm a people-pleaser and I hate making decisions*

where somebody will be let down. I believe that development of this competency is ongoing. I will continue to learn about ethics, even after many years in the field. —Greek life coordinator at a large public university

Indeed, when opportunities for reflection and collective learning through dialogue are absent, new professionals are at times challenged beyond their skill and comfort levels, forcing them into compromises and unethical behavior. But with mentoring, guidance, and dialogue, new professionals can develop an appropriate professional ethic.

There is a significant gap between the codes, principles, and theories in the literature that describe ethical conduct and how professionals actually deal with dilemmas in practice (Janosik, Creamer, & Humphrey, 2004). One way to understand this gap is by viewing ethical practice through the theoretical lens of person–environment fit (Holland, 1985; Lewin, 1938). From this perspective, the *person* is a practitioner with a unique combination of knowledge, skills, values, and motives who engages in moral conduct. The *environment* is the institution and its ethical culture. When a practitioner's conduct is aligned with the ethical culture of the institution, he or she is inclined to behave ethically. Conversely, if unethical behavior goes unchallenged, it quickly becomes normalized (Sternberg, 2002).

In this chapter, we present ethical professional practice as an interaction between the new professional and the institution's ethical culture. We also look at how dilemmas and critical incidents provide opportunities to reflect on practice and engage colleagues and students in such strategies as ethical dialogue. Ultimately, our goal is to assist graduate students and new professionals in developing a plan for ethical practice where they can: (a) know and articulate their professional dispositions; (b) gather data on their institution's culture; (c) examine critical incidents using their professional dispositions; and (d) select strategies true to their dispositions and compatible with the values and practices of their institutions.

Ethical Professional Practice

For many professionals, the only opportunity to learn about and explore ethical issues is during a single course in graduate school—an unfortunate fact, because complex ethical issues surface early in a person's career that require more than theoretical knowledge to address. New practitioners must know how ethical issues affect their roles as advisors, administrators, and leaders. Humphrey, Janosik, and Creamer (2004) emphasized that "ethics is at the core [of student affairs] . . . putting the practitioner center stage to serve as both role model and moral conscience for the campus" (p. 676). Two common sources of ethical guidance for new administrators are supervision and codes of conduct.

Ethical Codes and Principles

Codes of conduct and standards are the formal means for communicating how someone ought to behave in a professional community. According to Kitchener's (1985) foundational writing on ethics in student affairs, these codes are usually the new professional's initial guideposts in developing their professional ethics. Student affairs professionals must know the codes and principles relevant to their work and commit to putting them into practice (Humphrey et al., 2004).

Most student affairs professional associations publish their own ethical standards. The Council for the Advancement of Standards (2006b) synthesized the ethical codes across 40 of its member associations in its *Statement of Shared Ethical Principles*. The document identified seven overarching principles among each of these codes: autonomy, non-malfeasance, beneficence, justice, fidelity, veracity, and affiliation. These principles are also consistent with Kitchener's (1985) six ethical principles for student affairs: do no harm, act to benefit others, show respect, honor autonomy, promote justice, and be faithful. These codes are important in helping new professionals establish their own ethics.

> *It's important for me to make decisions where my morals are congruent with the ethical codes of the profession. I do my best to be proactive in predicting any ethical dilemmas that I might face. I have a conversation with my supervisor near the start of each semester to prepare for major dilemmas I might encounter. I also discuss ethical scenarios with my mentor to learn how seasoned professionals handle such situations.* —Assistant director of campus activities at a community college

This new professional anticipates when her ethical principles might conflict in practice. When professionals try to act according to one principle, they often infringe upon another. For example, academic advisers must balance their support for students struggling in rigorous academic majors (autonomy) with the obligation to help them avoid academic disqualification (beneficence and justice). Likewise, new professionals who are loyal to their supervisors (fidelity) might be compelled to reveal what they know when asked about questionable expenses in department budgets (veracity).

The Role of Supervisors

Although there are many resources and individuals to which new practitioners can turn to learn about moral conduct, there's no prescription that explains how to act ethically in a particular situation. In fact, professionals often receive conflicting information and advice, because "ethical standards lack the specificity to differentiate among competing moral beliefs. Thus ethical standards are guides for decision making, but ultimate responsibility rests with the individual to make a moral judgment" (Blimling, 1998, p. 66).

Supervisors of new professionals are critical members of the professional community for assisting new practitioners in adapting to the norms of the profession and the regulations, policies, and cultures of their institutions (Benshoff, 1990; Talley, 1997). This led Klein, Aldana, and Mattera (2013) to assert that "some of the best support supervisors can provide is to assist new professionals in the construction of an ethical framework to guide them in everyday decision making and growth" (para. 10). Supervisors are primarily responsible for conveying institutional values, along with establishing expectations for quality performance. Synergistic supervision (Saunders, Cooper, Winston, & Chernow, 2000; Winston & Hirt, 2003) is an effective approach, which involves giving supervisees timely and ample feedback on performance and constructive coaching to modify their behavior as necessary (Tull, 2006).

The Ethical Practitioner and Professional Dispositions

Employers in student affairs recognize the importance of dispositions and expect new professionals to display them, along with the knowledge and skills they learned in graduate programs and in prior experience. Dispositions are the underlying patterns of thought and emotion that motivate our behavior, which in this case is ethical professional conduct. One study found employers seeking candidate dispositions such as a commitment to diversity and social justice, creativity, enthusiasm, flexibility, and a positive attitude (Hoffman & Bresciani, 2012).

Thinking of ethical conduct as professional dispositions can help new practitioners to identify areas for personal growth across three interrelated aspects of experience: (a) consciousness, an awareness of self and sensitivity to the ethical dimensions of the situation; (b) competency, the knowledge and skills required to respond to a dilemma professionally; and (c) character, the will to act on personal values in the context of practice.

Consciousness

Before taking action, ethical practitioners must be aware of their own biases and assumptions as well as the consequences of their actions (Sundberg & Fried, 1997). Consciousness combines keen personal insight with a sensitivity to the context in which you operate. Self-awareness is critical for new professionals who must assess whether their actions are a fit with the institution (Dalton, Crosby, Valente, & Eberhardt, 2009). A lack of discernment in this area can lead to unfortunate circumstances in which practitioners believe they are doing the right thing, even though their colleagues and supervisors take a different view. Self-awareness in ethical practice is paramount.

> **Cardinal rule number one: Know thyself first. . . . I'm forced to take a daily assessment of who I am and what I value, not only as a person, but as a professional challenging students to do the same.**

> *Cardinal rule number one: Know thyself first. This environment, more than any other, has me in a constant state of reflection. I'm forced to take a daily assessment of who I am and what I value, not only as a person, but as a professional challenging students to do the same. Self-reflection is the pathway to making a real connection with students. How can I expect students to dig deeper and search for purpose in life if I'm not willing to do the same. Every day is an opportunity. Every day is a journey.* —Student activities professional at a small public institution

Besides self-awareness, consciousness entails being mindful of the experiences and concerns of other constituent groups within the institution. Graduate preparation programs and professional associations devote considerable effort to develop this mindfulness through their curricula, publications, and other educational projects. Ethical professionals must be aware of how events on campus and in the larger culture influence the perceptions and behavior of students and colleagues.

One way to help new professionals identify and articulate ethical professional practice is to create an ethical will (Baines, 2006). In ancient times, ethical wills provided a means of communicating personal beliefs, hopes, and advice to future generations at the time of one's death. Unlike legal wills, which bequeath *valuables,* ethical wills impart *values* for the benefit of future generations. Here, we reframe the ethical will as a way to facilitate self-awareness in new professionals by reflecting on their values, motives, and aspirations for ethical practice. To stimulate reflection we offer a series of prompts that new professionals can use to develop their ethical will (Baines, 2006).

1. What is my process of self-discovery and developing maturity?

2. What is my purpose or calling?

3. What are my values and motivations to serve others?

4. What are my hopes for the future?

5. What is my plan for putting my values in practice?

6. How will I know my plans are accomplished?

Once the ethical will is constructed, you can write dispositional statements, which are brief comments designed to concisely convey your ethical commitment to student learning, development, and success. Here are some examples:

☞ I work to include students who live off-campus in activities that can benefit them.

☞ My commitment to open access education, diversity, and student success aligns with the mission of the institution and guides me as I engage with students and colleagues.

Building on professional virtues identified in the ethical will, you can reflect on these questions to develop your statement:

☞ Am I aware of facts and perceptions that constitute ethical dilemmas? (*consciousness*)

☞ How do I put my values and beliefs into action? (*competency*)

☞ Do I have the will and commitment to take action when necessary? (*character*)

Competency

The knowledge and skills required to be a competent practitioner are also fundamental to being an ethical professional. Sources of information about competencies include the *Characteristics of Individual Excellence for Professional Practice in Higher Education* (Council for the Advancement of Standards, 2006a) and *Professional Competency Areas for Student Affairs Practitioners*, which was published jointly by the American College Personnel Association and the National Association of Student Personnel Administrators (NASPA) (2010). In their joint statement, they considered only *ethical professional practice* as the "integral component of all the competency areas" (p. 12). Thus, theoretical and historical knowledge related to the field and skills learned in graduate preparation programs such as management, programming, and helping practices are always implemented through the lens of professional ethics.

Character

Ethical practitioners must have the will to implement their personal ethical code of conduct. Humphrey et al. (2004) defined *character* as those "behaviors that student affairs professionals admire and demonstrate every day in their work" (p. 678). Without strong character, what new professionals perceive (consciousness) and what they can do (competency) will never be implemented. Sometimes taking action is contrary to what is popular with others or threatens to disrupt the status quo. This is when character moves to the center of ethical practice. As Cuyjet and Duncan (2013) observed, there are times when injustice occurs and "remaining neutral with our values or cultural perspectives is not beneficial to the increasing numbers of diverse students who enter our institutions" (p. 307). Before making a decision with ethical implications, any practitioner should ask themselves, "Can I be proud about this decision?" (Dalton et al., 2009, p. 173).

The Environment: Ethical Culture of the Institution

Ethics are culture based. Different cultures hold unique values and might act in a variety of ways when faced with similar situations (Komives, Lucas, & McMahon, 1998). What is acceptable behavior in one culture might not be so in another; therefore, it is important to be cognizant of cultural dimensions in ethical situations (Benjamin, 2004). According to

Rebore (2001), "How human beings should treat one another is thus predicated on certain notions about humanity. Those notions are significantly influenced by the culture and traditions of each society" (p .6). Within a higher education context, culture also plays a role in the ethical standards we hold as a profession. Fried (2003) stated:

> The ethical beliefs of the student affairs profession are grounded in Anglo-American culture. This culture believes in scientific materialism, individual autonomy, achievement and responsibility, a belief in the necessity of progress, and a strong emphasis on the future, rather than the present or past. (p. 411)

This emphasis on individual autonomy is different from many collectivistic cultures and might contradict familial and cultural values that our students or colleagues hold. This makes ethical dilemmas complex, because no universal principles exist that can guide our behavior in all situations (Benjamin, 2004).

The culture of an institution also has an effect on ethical values and standards. "Culture is a quality inherent within an organization that creates an atmosphere setting it apart from other organizations with similar purposes" (Rebore, 2001, p. 62). Higher education institutions have various cultural norms based on institutional mission, history, student population, geographical location, and so on. These cultural norms can be observed across campus through interactions between faculty, staff, and students or can be evident in campus publications and websites (Hellmich, 2007). According to Vaughan (1992), "Culture consists of those things that make an institution distinct: its history, traditions and values, interaction with the larger environment, ceremonies, renewal process—including recruitment and selection of personnel—and evaluation process, including assessment of its ethical values" (p. 21).

The culture of an institution can be very powerful. When these cultural norms promote ethical behavior, "a functional as well as successful organization emerges—one that not only achieves its mission and approaches its vision, but that is also a rewarding place to be a student, employee, and visitor. . . ." (Hellmich, 2007, p. 23). New professionals can become disillusioned when they discover their personal code of ethics conflicts with the cultural norms of their institution.

> *When I interviewed, I didn't realize the true and practical implications of [ethics] and how different my philosophy would be from my*

department director, who said during our professional staff train-
ing that "the number one goal for the department this year is to
make money." This led to several instances of "keeping the customer
happy" at the expense of student development, and a lot of decisions
that I had trouble accepting and supporting. —Director of social
justice programs at a 4-year religious institution

As student affairs professionals, we have the power to contribute to
the institutional culture and promote ethical behavior that over time can
preserve or promote the institution's commitment to ethical standards
(Hellmich, 2007; Vaughan, 1992).

An environmental scan or cultural audit (Whitt, 1993) can help practitioners discover the explicit and implicit elements of institutional culture.
We recommend new professionals conduct an environmental scan of the
ethical issues on campuses where they seek a fieldwork placement or job.

☞ Before making contact with anyone at the institution,
review documents on official websites and reports. Also,
consult student newspapers and social media, such as
Twitter, Instagram, and YouTube videos.

☞ Generate a list of questions that surface during the review
of materials. Refrain from making quick judgments or
allowing biases to influence interpretations; rather, reflect
on concerns and curiosities.

☞ Based on observations and questions, create some preliminary
conclusions about the institution and its students, faculty, and
top-level administrators as well as the role of student affairs.

☞ During a campus visit or interview with campus representatives,
ask questions to clarify the institutional values and mission.

☞ After the visit or interview, (a) correct misperceptions you
might have gathered from your pre-visit investigation;
(b) outline new discoveries or concerns that arose
during the visit and investigate further for clarification;
(c) determine whether intuitional values, norms, and
customs are congruent with your ethical will and disposition
statements; and (d) make a decision about your next steps.

Ethical Strategies: Responding to Critical Incidents

An ethical dilemma is a situation in which two or more ethical principles conflict; professionals must choose from among them to achieve the greatest good (Fried, 1997). This concise definition belies the confusion many practitioners experience when they view dilemmas as either "choices between right and wrong or choosing between two unsatisfactory alternatives" (Janosik et al., 2004, p. 370). Most ethical situations are difficult to resolve because few, if any, options can avoid causing pain or embarrassment to someone.

Difficult situations with ethical implications can be viewed broadly as *critical incidents*, a term that refers to an event that is bounded by time and an institution's culture and history and also involves people, policies, and practices. Some examples of critical incidents include granting exceptions to policy, reporting data accurately, and giving unquestioned loyalty to a supervisor who engages in dishonest behavior (Janosik et al., 2004). In the context of person–environment fit, critical incidents occur at that moment when a practitioner's dispositions clash with the ethical culture of the institution.

> **Critical incidents occur at that moment when a practitioner's dispositions clash with the ethical culture of the institution.**

At first, critical incidents are difficult to anticipate or detect; however, after some time on the job, new professionals learn to identify them quickly. Detecting and reflecting on critical incidents with supervisors and mentors can help new professionals increase their capacity for "choosing ethically defensible perspectives and actions, as well as understanding and being able to communicate the rationales for choices" (Hamrick & Benjamin, 2009, p. 3).

> *If you end up at a place where you are asked to do things that make you feel funny inside, it's probably not the right place for you.*
> —Career counselor at a public college

Professionals respond to critical incidents with a strategy, which Blimling (1998) described as "informal theories that they have elaborated through experience to guide their decision making" (p. 67). Strategies are also the means by which practitioners put their dispositions in action. Thus, although dispositions endure as the basis of ethical behavior, strategies often change to fit the situation.

Blimling (1998) proposed a typology of three professional strategies in student affairs: (a) peace at all costs; (b) win at all costs; and (c) fight when you can win and retreat when you can't. The first two types, *peace at all costs* and *win at all costs*, are at opposite ends of a spectrum. Blimling argued that professionals who prioritize peace over ethical principles risk being seen by others as passive and unable to make difficult choices. Conversely, when they insist that their decision is the only ethical one, they appear to others as inflexible or reactionary. He concluded that the most effective strategy for ethical practice is a middle ground, where professionals know when to engage others over moral concerns or to withdraw and reevaluate.

Another typology of ethical strategies was advanced by Anderson, Harbour, and Davies (2007). Building on Berry's (2003) theory of acculturation, the model posits ethical identity types, including assimilation, separation, and integration. The first two, *assimilation* and *separation*, are contrary positions. Assimilation occurs when practitioners suppress their dispositions out of obedience to the values of the institution. On the other hand, separation refers to an ethical identity that is distinct from the mainstream values of the institution. Assimilation or separation can be useful strategies. For example, new practitioners must quickly learn about the practices and ethical standards in the field. A strategy of assimilation would involve fully immersing yourself in the culture of student affairs to learn as much as possible about the profession. Likewise, a separation strategy can be a healthy defense for practitioners who outgrow their career goals and need time to reflect on what matters most to them.

Anderson et al. (2007) recommended integration as the preferred ethical identity and leadership strategy. As practitioners encounter critical incidents that challenge their personal values, they can acknowledge how their dispositions interact with the values of the institution and make the choice to act in ways that are congruent with the institution's culture and values. Integration occurs over time, in response to ethical dilemmas, and in consultation with supervisors and mentors.

The strategies described here are used by practitioners in response to critical incidents that surface from their interaction with the ethical culture of their institutions. These strategies also lay the foundation for two important tactics in ethical professional practice: dialogue and decision making. Before engaging in either, new practitioners should first reflect on their own ethical perspectives.

Ethical Foundations of Decision Making and Dialogue

Here we use Kidder's (1995) classification of three ethical perspectives that are common in the literature: ends-based, means-based, and care-based. These varied perspectives illustrate a common phenomenon in ethical practice: Individual professionals who comprise a team deeply committed to the same professional value come to very different conclusions about how to respond to the same critical incident (see Appiah, 2006).

Ends-based approaches prioritize the outcome of a decision above other considerations. Also referred to as *consequentialism*, the ends-based decision maker carefully weighs the likely results of a decision based on its consequences or what would produce the most good for the largest number of people. Kidder and McLeod (2005) advised using the cost–benefit test to determine whether the circumstances warrant this approach. The practitioner weighs the risks and rewards of a potential decision and chooses the option that helps the most people in the best way possible.

Means-based decision making, in contrast, is nonconsequentialist. Doing the right thing involves applying universal ethical principles, regardless of the consequences, to all people in every situation. The Golden Rule is an example of a universal principle. Most practitioners know this approach through the work of Kohlberg (1981). The self-righteousness test prompts decision makers to reflect on the true reason behind their choice (Kidder & McLeod, 2005). Is the decision about consistently upholding principles, or is it really about justifying the personal viewpoints or biases of the decision maker?

Care-based decision makers choose a course of action that prioritizes relationships with others. The work of Gilligan (1982) and Noddings (1984, 1999) are closely associated with this approach. The innocent-parties test (Kidder, 1995) helps decision makers evaluate whether this is the best approach by looking at how a decision will affect the well-being of others and the relationships among them.

Although each of these approaches is valid, many student affairs practitioners are drawn to care-based approaches. Nevertheless, as new professionals assume greater authority as administrators, they can find themselves making tough choices with an array of undesirable outcomes. Sometimes, no matter what they decide, people will be hurt and no one will feel good about the result. It's difficult to make decisions through a lens of caring alone, especially because administrators are often judged by their ability to be fair and consistent. For this reason, it's important to develop a process of decision making that is both sound and authentic.

Ethical Decision Making

Practitioners make ethical decisions every day that have significant impact on people and programs. A review of the literature reveals many models and concepts to aid in the ethical decision making process (Benjamin, 2004; Kitchner, 1985; Komives et al., 1998; Mattchet, 2008). We discuss two models that can be helpful.

Nash (1997) proposed a rigorous 10-step protocol for ethical decision making that considers "the major themes, issues, players, and situational factors in a case-dilemma" (p. 4). Prior to making a decision, practitioners are prompted to analyze the facts of an ethical dilemma by identifying codes and principles relevant to the case, filtering the dilemma through personal experience and moral instincts, and then identifying the anticipated impact of a decision on those involved. Although Nash's model is comprehensive and logical, it is rather extensive. It can be cumbersome to use without guidance.

Humphrey et al. (2004) offered a more concise and accessible model, a four-step process grounded in professional values of "honesty, the rights of others, fairness, and acting responsibly" (p. 677). The steps are "(a) identifying the problem; (b) classifying the type of problem in ethical terms; (c) considering the relevant ethical principles, character traits, and professional values; and (d) making an ethical decision" (pp. 677–678).

> *I still have to navigate the balance between guiding students and outright making decisions for them based on my own opinion. I learned to be careful about using my position to push my own agenda. I'm always mindful that I am helping students to achieve their own goals rather than influencing them based on my own views.* —Director of intercultural affairs at a small private college

Vaccaro, McCoy, Champagne, and Siegel (2013) provided a general decision-making framework that can be used when making decisions that are ethical in nature. Finally, Nash (1997) listed a series of step-by-step questions to analyze ethics-oriented case studies. Ethical decision-making models are tools to guide practice. Although they illustrate trusted methods for analyzing a critical incident, they're not the only (or necessarily best) way to approach a dilemma. Because most critical incidents occur in community, it might be best to address them through dialogue.

Dialogue as An Ethical Decision-making Practice

Dialogue is perhaps the most effective way to create and sustain an ethical campus community; it emphasizes that ethical decision making is not conducted in isolation (Fried, 2003; Pope, Reynolds, & Mueller, 2004; Thomas, 2002). Constructing shared ethical views with colleagues involves "acknowledging, understanding, discussing, and negotiating moral, ideological, and political decisions leading to ethical decision making" (Magolda & Baxter Magolda, 2011, p. 458). This process is never easy; all parties must be willing to learn from each other, accept possible shortcomings in their own positions, and be willing to change their views if necessary (Strike & Moss, 2008).

> **Dialogue is perhaps the most effective way to create and sustain an ethical campus community.**

The NASPA Professional Standards Division (2012) offered an "approach to ethical decision making that is based on context and dialogue rather than discernment of universal principles" (p. 2) with three guiding questions:

1. What would the greater good/benevolence/compassion look like in this situation?

    a. Does my intention match the intended effect on the greater good? What are the effects on different groups within this situation (i.e., individual, leadership board, student organization, all student organizations, department of student activities, division of student affairs, etc.)?

2. What thoughts, ideas, behaviors, and relationships will be expanded from what is created by my decision? What will be reduced? Consider all that will be expanded or reduced from a cultural, religious, socioeconomic, and privileged perspective.

3. Does the decision respect my individual values and the integrity of all people being affected by it? How would I feel about this in front of my loved ones if my decision and its effect was featured on the front page of the newspaper, made a TV headline, or was posted on the Internet?

Common Critical Incidents

Next we review common ethical concerns that professionals face early in their careers. We encourage you to use the three guiding questions in dialogue with your peers, supervisors, and mentors to gain a deeper understanding of how their ethics, dispositions, and the culture of their institutions would respond to such critical incidents.

Use of Social Media

There are many advantages of using social media in your work with students. It's a fast and efficient way to communicate about upcoming events, important college dates, and so on. It can also be a great way to connect with colleagues on campus. However, ethical issues arise when new professionals use social media accounts for both personal and work communications. Some common questions, dilemmas, and issues:

☞ Should I "friend" or follow students or colleagues on Facebook, Instagram, and Twitter?

☞ What should I do if I see policy violations on students' social media?

☞ What if I become concerned about students' mental health based on what I see or read?

☞ How should I manage the anonymous nature of bullying or threats on Yik Yak?

Assisting Students in Difficulty

Students come to college with diverse physical and cognitive abilities and mental health and developmental issues. When you work with students, ethical decision points are widespread. Consider these questions:

☞ Do I have the skills, knowledge, and training to best serve this student?

☞ When should I inform my supervisor of concerns that I have for my students?

☞ In helping a student, is it okay for me to gather information from friends, family, or professors?

Job Searching While Employed

Many student affairs professionals conduct their first job search at the end of their master's degrees when the job search is widely shared with mentors, peers, and potential employers. After that first job, deciding to look for a new job can be fraught with ethical concerns for new professionals. Consider these questions:

- ☞ When should I inform my supervisor that I am looking for a new job?

- ☞ Is it okay to leave a job in the middle of the year if I have given proper notice?

- ☞ I have already accepted a position, but I was just invited to a campus interview for my dream job. What should I do?

Establishing and Maintaining Boundaries with Students

Student affairs professionals work closely with students, are often close in age to students, and frequently share personal experiences and information. Close, personal relationships can likely develop. An ethical dilemma occurs when you face the decision to expand those relationships. Here are some situations you might encounter:

- ☞ My staff member just invited me to her 21st birthday party. Is it okay for me to go?

- ☞ I have become increasingly close to one of my Associated Students' board members, and I'm wondering whether it's okay if we go on a date?

- ☞ I consider one of my staff members a good friend. Is that okay?

Power Dynamics in Ethical Decisions

When new professionals have the opportunity to work with more senior-level staff and faculty, they might find themselves in the difficult and awkward position of witnessing unethical behavior by superiors. They might even be asked by superiors to personally engage in unethical behavior.

- ☞ My supervisor routinely asks me to work on evenings and weekends, but refuses to allow me to make up that time by taking a day off here and there. I think this is unethical. What should I do?

☞ The admissions office called to ask that I extend the deadline for priority room assignments for a special admit they have been working with. I think that's unfair, but my supervisor said I have to do it. Do I have any recourse?

☞ I am the hearing officer for a conduct case involving an athlete. The vice president contacted me and asked that I reconsider my decision to suspend the student from campus for a semester. This seems really wrong to me. How can I express my concern without risking my future at this school?

Overall, new professionals must remember that they can be an agent for change to help move the institution toward more ethical practices.

> *Trust your instincts in ethical situations. It's easy to make excuses for why people violate ethics, but by making excuses you are colluding in unethical practices as well. It can be easy to be idealistic or to want to believe the best in people, but it's important you take a stand when you first notice ethical issues.* —Area coordinator at a large public university

Case Studies

The following two scenarios have multiple dimensions of ethical concern for use in small groups or as part of classroom discussion, using the multiple strategies reviewed in this chapter. We refrain from offering solutions to the dilemmas presented to reinforce the notion that ethics are bound by culture and context, often with more than one solution. Nash (1997) offered 10 essential questions to analyze situations and issues from an ethical frame. They are:

1. What are the major moral themes in the case?

2. What are the conflicts in the case that make it an ethical dilemma?

3. Who are the major stakeholders in the case?

4. What are some foreseeable consequences of the possible choices in the case? What are some foreseeable principles?

5. What are some viable alternatives to the possible courses of action in the case?

6. What are some important background beliefs you ought to consider in the case?

7. What are some of your initial intuitions and feelings regarding the case?

8. What choices would you make if you were to act in character in the case?

9. What does your profession's code of ethics say regarding key moral principles in the case?

10. What is your decision in the case? (pp. 2–6)

Scenario #1

Amy is a new professional who advises student government at a community college. At this commuter campus, students feel at home in the student life office, hanging out between meetings, work, and classes. One student, Brian, finds that involvement in student government gives him a sense of belonging, to the extent that his grades have improved. He is elected vice president and begins his term on a positive note. Students, staff, and faculty regard him as a passionate leader with great potential.

However, as the semester continues, Brian's behavior becomes erratic. He is rude with staff and easily agitated in government meetings and class. He initially resists Amy's attempts to help. Eventually he discloses that he recently lost his home and had to access public assistance; he feels that the stress of this situation is the source of his anger. However, his behavior doesn't change.

Amy sees potential and talent in Brian. His behavior is inappropriate, but she worries that if Brian were removed from student government, he would lose his only support system and wouldn't likely get the help and support he needs. Conversely, Amy wonders whether keeping Brian in student government is fair to the other students who were subjected to his angry outbursts.

Scenario #2

John is an international student advisor. He focuses on helping international students feel welcome, because there are so few of them on campus.

Lorena is a first-year student with an energetic personality; recently, she has been stressed and unusually quiet in group settings. Through their conversation John learns that she misses her family and feels lonely. He refers her to counseling services, but Lorena is reluctant to see a counselor. Disappointed, he urges her to make friends in her classes.

The next time John sees Lorena, he notices that she has lost a significant amount of weight. When he asks about her well-being, Lorena shares that she took his advice and reached out to her classmates. At first Lorena was invited to join others out of class. Soon she realized they were only interested in her car. When she confronted them about her concerns, they started being rude to her in class. John suggests that Lorena speak to her professor immediately. Lorena agrees.

A week later, Lorena returns in tears. She explains that the professor refused to discuss the matter and told her to keep personal business outside class. The other students' rude behavior continues, but it's more covert. Compounding Lorena's situation is her parents' insistence that she come home. Lorena begs John to explain the situation to her professor.

John consults his supervisor. He learns that the professor has a reputation for being critical of international students. His supervisor advises that he not get involved. John is torn about what to do. If he intervenes, he will likely upset the professor, hurt Lorena, and damage his own reputation. He also knows the bullying must stop.

Conclusion

As new professionals build and enact a professional ethic, they will undoubtedly encounter challenges along the way. The congruence we advocate requires a finely tuned balance between self, institution, and profession. Careful reflection and consultation help you through inevitable conflicts. You *will* make mistakes as you make ethical decisions and take action. This is an important acknowledgement. Therefore, you need to be kind to yourself as you recover from mistakes, and your supervisors should show empathy and guidance.

> *I can identify when a student or colleague is violating an ethical standard, but I have not advanced to the stage of being able to advise them how to overcome or prevent it from occurring. As I advance in my career, I plan to acquire new insights about ethical professional practice by interacting with seasoned professionals in the field. These colleagues can share stories with me of situations*

when they faced an ethical dilemma and how they went about finding the solution. —Assistant director of academic retention at a community college

These colleagues, a group of caring institutional outsiders (peers, mentors, trusted colleagues), provided a space for this advisor to deliberate ethical dilemmas and critical incidents without fear of repercussion or consequence. Seasoned professionals who enter into dialogue and provide authentic and critical feedback help new professionals see that managing ethical dilemmas, developing their own ethical will and dispositional statements, and enacting them as leaders in their institutions is entirely possible.

References

American College Personnel Association & National Association of Student Personnel Administrators. (2010). *Professional competency areas for student affairs practitioners*. Washington, DC: Authors.

Anderson, S. K., Harbour, C., & Davies, T. (2007). Professional ethical identity development and community college leadership. In D. M. Hellmich (Ed.), *Ethical leadership in the community college: Bridging theory and daily practice* (pp. 61–76). Bolton, MA: Anker.

Appiah, K. (2006). *Cosmopolitanism: Ethics in a world of strangers.* New York, NY: Norton.

Baines, B. K. (2006). *Ethical wills: Putting your values on paper* (2nd ed.), Cambridge, MA: Da Capo Press.

Benjamin, M. (2004). The role of leadership in addressing issues of race and ethnicity: Cultural competence as a framework and leadership strategy. In R. L. Hampton & P. T. Gullotta (Eds.), *Promoting racial, ethnic, and religious understanding and reconciliation* (pp. 123–136). Washington, DC: CWLA Press.

Benshoff, J. M. (1990, April). *Helping ourselves: Ethical practice through peer supervision.* Paper presented at the annual meeting of the American College Personnel Association, St. Louis, MO.

Berry, J. W. (2003). Conceptual approaches to acculturation. In K. M. Chun, P. B. Organista, & G. Marín (Eds.), *Acculturation: Advances in theory, measurement, and applied research* (pp. 17–37). Washington, DC: American Psychological Association. doi:10.1037/10472-004

Blimling, G. S. (1998). Navigating the changing climate of moral and ethical issues in student affairs. In D. Cooper and J. Lancaster (Eds.), *Beyond law and policy: Reaffirming the role of student affairs* (New Directions for Student Services, No. 82, pp. 65-76). San Francisco, CA: Jossey-Bass.

Council for the Advancement of Standards in Higher Education. (2006a). CAS characteristics of individual excellence for professional practice in higher education. In Council for the Advancement of Standards in Higher Education (Ed.), *Professional standards for higher education* (6th ed.). Washington, DC: Author.

Council for the Advancement of Standards in Higher Education. (2006b). CAS statement of shared ethical principles. In Council for the Advancement of Standards in Higher Education (Ed.), *Professional standards for higher education* (6th ed.). Washington, DC: Author.

Cuyjet, M. J., & Duncan, A. D. (2013). The impact of cultural competence on the moral development of student affairs professionals. *Journal of College and Character, 14*(4), 301–310. doi: 10.1515/jcc-2013-0039

Dalton, J. C., Crosby, P. C., Valente, A., & Eberhardt, D. (2009). Maintaining and modeling everyday ethics in student affairs. In G. S. McClellan & J. Stringer (Eds.), *The handbook of student affairs administration* (pp. 166–186). San Francisco, CA: Jossey-Bass.

Fried, J. (1997). Changing ethical frameworks for a multicultural world. In J. Fried (Ed.), *Ethics for today's campus: New perspectives on education, student development, and institutional management* (New Directions for Student Services, No. 77, pp. 5–22). San Francisco, CA: Jossey-Bass.

Fried, J. (2003). Ethical standards and principles. In S. R. Komives & D. B. Woodard (Eds.), *Student services: A handbook for the profession* (pp. 107–127). New York, NY: Wiley.

Gilligan, C. (1982). *In a different voice: Psychological theory and women's development.* Cambridge, MA: Harvard University Press.

Hamrick, F. A., & Benjamin, M. (Eds.). (2009). *Maybe I should . . . Case studies in ethics for student affairs professionals.* Lanham, MD: American College Personnel Association.

Hellmich, D. M. (2007). Considerations of power, influence, and cultural norms for the ethical community college leader. In D. M. Hellmich (Ed.), *Ethical leadership in the community college: Bridging theory and daily practice* (pp. 23-32). Bolton, MA: Anker.

Hoffman, J., & Bresciani, M. J. (2012). Identifying what student affairs professionals value: A mixed methods analysis of professional competencies listed in job descriptions. *Research & Practice in Assessment, 7.* Retrieved from http://www.rpajournal.com/dev/wp-content/uploads/2012/07/A2.pdf

Holland, J. L. (1985). *Making vocational choices.* Englewood Cliffs, NJ: Prentice-Hall.

Humphrey, E., Janosik, S. M., & Creamer, D. G. (2004) The role of principles, character, and professional values in ethical decision-making. *NASPA Journal, 41*(3), 675–692.

Janosik, S. M., Creamer, D. G., & Humphrey, E. (2004). An analysis of ethical problems facing student affairs administrators. *NASPA Journal, 41*(2), 356–374. doi: 10.2202/1949-6605.1338

Kidder, R. M. (1995). *How good people make tough choices.* New York, NY: Morrow.

Kidder, R. M., & McLeod, B. (2005). *Moral courage.* New York, NY: Morrow.

Kitchener, K. S. (1985). Ethical principles and decisions in student affairs. In H. J. Canon & R. D. Brown (Eds.), *Applied ethics in student services* (pp. 17–29). San Francisco, CA: Jossey-Bass.

Klein, D., Aldana, M., & Mattera, W. (2013). Developing an ethical framework for student affairs. *ACPA Developments, 11*(1). Retrieved from http://www.myacpa.org/article/developing-ethical-framework-student-affairs

Kohlberg, L. (1981). *The philosophy of moral development: Essays on moral development* (Vol. 1). San Francisco, CA: Harper & Row.

Komives, S. R., Lucas, N., & McMahon, T. R. (1998). *Exploring leadership*. San Francisco, CA: Jossey-Bass.

Lewin, K. (1938). *The conceptual representation and measurement of psychological forces*. Durham, NC: Duke University Press.

Magolda, P. M., & Baxter Magolda, M. B. B. (Eds.). (2011). How do professionals navigate situations when their professional beliefs clash with their supervisors' or organizations' beliefs? Engaging in dialogues about difference in the workplace. In P. M. Magolda & M. B. B. Magolda (Eds.), *Contested issues in student affairs: Diverse perspectives and respectful dialogue* (pp. 453–465). Sterling, VA: Stylus.

Mattchet, N. J. (2008). Ethics across the curriculum. In S. L. Moore (Ed.), *Practical approaches to ethics for colleges and universities* (New Directions for Higher Education, No. 142, pp. 25–38). San Francisco, CA: Jossey-Bass.

Nash, R. J. (1997). Teaching ethics in the student affairs classroom. *NASPA Journal, 35*(1), 3–17. doi: 10.2202/1949-6605.1038

National Association of Student Personnel Administrators Professional Standards Division. (2012). *NASPA ethics statement*. Washington, DC: Author.

Noddings, N. (1984). *Caring: A feminine approach to ethics and moral education*. Berkeley, CA: University of California Press.

Noddings, N. (1999). *Justice and caring: The search for common ground in education*. New York, NY: Teachers College Press.

Pope, R. L., Reynolds, A. L., & Mueller, J. A. (2004). *Multicultural competence in student affairs*. San Francisco, CA: Jossey-Bass.

Rebore, R. W. (2001). *The ethics of educational leadership*. Upper Saddle River, NJ: Merrill Prentice Hall.

Saunders, S. A., Cooper, D. L., Winston, R. B., & Chernow, E. (2000). Supervising staff in student affairs: Exploration of the synergistic approach. *Journal of College Student Development, 41*(2), 181–192.

Sternberg, R. J. (Ed.). (2002). *Why smart people can be so stupid*. New Haven, CT: Yale University Press.

Strike, K. A., & Moss, P. A. (2008). *Ethics and college student life: A case study approach* (3rd ed.). Upper Saddle River, NJ: Pearson.

Sundberg, D. C., & Fried, J. (1997). Ethical dialogues on campus. In J. Fried (Ed.), *Ethics for today's campus: New perspectives on education, student development, and institutional management* (New Directions for Student Services, No. 77, pp. 67–79). San Francisco, CA: Jossey-Bass.

Talley, E. J. (1997). Ethics in management. In J. Fried (Ed.), *Ethics for today's campus: New perspectives on education, student development, and institutional management* (New Directions for Student Services, No. 77, pp. 45–66). San Francisco, CA: Jossey-Bass.

Thomas, W. (2002). The moral domain of student affairs leadership. In J. C. Dalton & M. McClenton (Eds.), *The art and practical wisdom of student affairs leadership* (pp. 61–70). San Francisco, CA: Jossey-Bass.

Tull, A. (2006). Synergistic supervision, job satisfaction, and intention to turnover of new professionals in student affairs. *Journal of College Student Development, 47*(4), 465–480. doi: 10.1353/csd.2006.0053

Vaccaro, A., McCoy, B., Champagne, D., Siegel, M. (2013). *Decisions matter: Using a decision-making framework with contemporary student affairs case studies.* Washington, D.C.: National Association of Student Personnel Administrators.

Vaughan, G. B. (1992). Preface. In G. B. Vaughan (Ed.), *Dilemmas of leadership: Decision making and ethics in the community college* (pp. 3–29). San Francisco, CA: Jossey-Bass.

Whitt, E. J. (1993). Making the familiar strange: Discovering culture. In G. D. Kuh (Ed.), *Cultural perspectives in student affairs work* (pp. 81–94). Washington, DC: American College Personnel Association.

Winston, R. B., & Hirt, J. B. (2003). Activating synergistic supervision approaches: Practical suggestions. In S. M. Janosik, D. G. Creamer, J. B. Hirt, R. B. Winston, S. A. Saunders, & D. L. Cooper (Eds.), *Supervising new professionals in student affairs* (pp. 43–83). New York, NY: Brunner-Routledge.

SUPERVISORY STYLE

CHAPTER FOUR

Kevin W. Bailey and Jenny Hamilton

S upervision is an exciting component of student affairs administration. It's also a challenging responsibility. Helping shape the professional and personal growth of another person is not a responsibility to be taken lightly. For many people, the supervisory role is the most rewarding facet of their professional career. As exciting and rewarding as this role can be, it can also be a source of anxiety for a new professional. However, the mindset of this recent master's graduate will help put the job of supervisor in context:

> *I've supervised students in the past, but as a new professional I think I'm nervous because you want to make a strong connection with students right off the bat. You want to feel successful in your new job. As student affairs professionals, a lot of the time we want to be life changers and one component of that is being a*

good supervisor and mentor. That doesn't happen overnight. It may not happen in one year either. You sometimes don't have the best students, best structure, or a supportive supervisor to guide you. Realizing this will help us grow to our full potential as supervisors.

Making the transition into a role that involves supervising others can—and probably should—give us reason to think about our readiness for the challenge. Rest assured that this sense of readiness does not begin or end with your first professional position. It is such an important skill, yet few administrators receive training in the art of managing people (Hirt & Strayhorn, 2011). Although this book primarily addresses the issues associated with being a new professional, even student affairs officers farther up the career ladder might have concerns about supervising veteran personnel.

There is no one-size-fits-all approach to supervision. Scores of books have been written about the best approaches, and each one is likely to have some nuggets of invaluable guidance that in a given situation on a given day could be the key to success in a difficult situation. Hirt and Strayhorn (2011) suggested that supervision goes beyond the management of people: "It involves a full spectrum of duties from recruiting and hiring new staff to training them, providing them with development opportunities and evaluating their performance" (p. 372).

There is no one-size-fits-all approach to supervision.

In this chapter, we rely on Bolman and Deal's (2013) four-frame organizational model. Like the lens of a camera, each frame offers a new set of ideas, values, and emphases from which to view the many issues a supervisor faces. The *structural frame* looks at formal roles and responsibilities, including rules, policies, and management hierarchies. Although some people believe that highly bureaucratic systems are out of sync with today's primary leadership paradigm, understanding them can help you succeed in your organization. The *human resources frame*—the focus of this chapter—considers the needs of individuals within the organization. (This chapter focuses on human resource priorities.) The *political frame* examines how people and groups interact and compete in the organization for scarce resources. The *symbolic frame* analyzes the symbols, myths, and rituals that provide the roots for much of what happens in an organization. The four frames can be discussed separately, but it's the combination of the four perspectives that constitutes the dynamics of the workplace.

Supervisors as Architects

The leader who sees the organization primarily through a *structural frame* is considered an architect. This type of leader focuses on the design and analysis of the organizational infrastructure (Bolman & Deal, 2013). In organizations, responsibilities are allocated to participants (division of labor), and rules, policies, and management hierarchies are created to coordinate diverse activities. Structures are the organizational elements that can be seen (such as an operations manual), the things that are measured (such as quantitative data), and the things that can be defined (such as a policy or the chain of command). All effective supervisors must be architects to some extent.

Whether you supervise peer educators, resident assistants, orientation leaders, support staff, graduate assistants, interns, or seasoned professionals, your obligation is to provide and use the structures that support success even if those same structures aren't used to support your own success.

> *I am the only one who supervises the interns. The assistant director supervises other student employees. I report to the assistant director and we both report to the director. The director's supervising style is very different than mine. He's very hands off but not relational. There's not a lot of feedback. He'll give you different tasks but gives no expectations that are deliberately communicated. It can be a struggle for me. The assistant director has a hard time giving critical feedback. So the two people I directly report to give me little direction and expectations so I never know if I'm on the right track. For one of my interns, I say these are my expectations so she knows what I'm expecting with quality. With her I'm clear on how projects need to be prioritized, something lacking in my own supervision.* —New professional in career services at a midsize regional public university

Distributing a position description and an organizational chart helps staff members understand their roles in the organization and how those roles fit into the department. A supervisor must also articulate basic expectations for successfully accomplishing a particular job (Career Press, 1993). Employees want to know how a job description translates into the day-to-day performance of their job (Andersen, 2006). Performance guidelines help reduce the ambiguity that staff members feel in a new job or with a new supervisor. The supervision issues of documentation, working with unionized employees, and hiring staff require many skills, including those that are embedded in the role of the architect.

Documentation

An essential element of structure is documenting organizational and supervisory activity. Documentation plays many roles in an organization, from maintaining records of important conversations to providing needed information for program planning. Although a supervisor's emerging style and the organization's history will dictate when it's appropriate to document personnel concerns, the role that documentation plays in performance reviews should not be underestimated. Maintaining adequate documentation and completing required forms can help avoid misunderstandings in personnel decisions. In extreme cases—when performance leads a supervisor to consider disciplinary action—proper documentation saves time and frustration. Without documentation, supervisors must recreate history and might be unable to take disciplinary action because of the lack of a proper paper trail. Documentation also provides an excellent written record of support for salary increases and promotions. Sending a letter, note, or e-mail to document a behavioral problem or simply to say thanks is also part of good supervision. The balance between "good cop" and "bad cop" is not always easy for new professionals.

> *I have more autonomy in my decision-making when it comes to documenting my student staff than I have had in past supervisory roles. I am certainly learning how to navigate trying to maintain relationships with the student staff while also holding them accountable. Rewarding and praising them is, of course, much easier for me.* —New professional in fraternity and sorority life at a large public college

If the department's tradition does not include documentation, emphasizing it might be seen as untrusting or overzealous. Likewise, a supervisor who has a low need for documentation can be perceived as lazy or irresponsible in an organization where it is expected. If the organizational motto is "If it's not in writing, it didn't happen," supervisors who rely on informal verbal communication might become frustrated.

Personnel files are different from *personal files*. Personnel files are usually the university's formal repository for documents and information about an employee, including hire letter, performance appraisals, merit letters, disciplinary actions, and salary information. Employees are free to inspect their personnel file, which is usually kept in the human resources department.

Personal files, on the other hand, are usually kept in a secure location in the supervisor's office. They might contain private notes about an employee—including behaviors to monitor—leadership roles held on and off campus, involvement in professional associations, a list of presentations, awards received, and vacation or sick days taken. Some of this information can be used as part of the narrative in the performance evaluation, which gives meaning to the numerical score. A personal file might also contain copies of documents contained in the personnel file, such as disciplinary action and merit letters.

One of the most interesting documentation issues to emerge in recent decades is managing electronic communication. E-mail can be a documentation and communication tool, or it can be a nuisance. Organizations that rely heavily on documentation sometimes overuse electronic communication. Learning how to archive messages and sort them in folders can help prove that you complied with a specific request or objected to a particular course of action.

Labor Unions

Among the most structured supervisory relationships are those involving members of labor unions. Even for supervisors trained in labor relations, the potential for conflict is significant. Some new supervisors resist the structures that are firmly in place for union-affiliated employees, but it's incumbent upon them to become educated about the collective bargaining agreements involving their staff. Supervisors of unionized employees must understand that the policies and procedures negotiated into the labor contract are designed to protect those covered by the agreements. Two of the most basic values underlying labor agreements are due process and individual rights (Carnevale & Stone, 1995); both are also values underpinning higher education (Carnegie Foundation, 1990). Contracts are often strictly enforced; ignorance of the rules is not an excuse for noncompliance. There is little room for ambiguity in the interpretation of a labor contract.

> *The hardest things I deal with are in relation to the two rec repair guys. They have very specific job titles and responsibilities. If I ask them to do something outside of their job responsibilities, they can file a complaint with the union. I had to figure out what I can and can't ask them to do. I get jumpy about getting the brunt of the union if I ask them to do something wrong. The ones I oversee are not a motivated workforce. There's no buy in. They're not here for*

an education. They're here for a job, whereas we're here for a career.
—Assistant manager of a campus recreation facility at a midsize research university

To avoid grievances, supervisors should understand union contracts, promote good relationships with the union steward and staff, maintain a fair work environment, keep an open mind when conflicts arise, and use appropriate investigation skills in resolving conflicts (Career Press, 1993). When a unionized employee is not performing up to expected standards, it can seem difficult to work within the labor contract to hold the employee accountable. A supervisor with just cause to confront a unionized staff member must be ready to deal with the bureaucracy and the conflict. It's easy to fall into an "us versus them" mentality when dealing with unionized staff, particularly in times of conflict, but that attitude just creates another barrier. Unions exist to protect their employees, and professionals must work with them accordingly.

Hiring Practices and Policies

Hiring new staff is the most important way to shape the future of an organization. Part of supervision is participating in search and selection procedures; part of hiring is knowing the expectations and practices outlined by law, organizational policy, and our profession's ethical standards. A new professional must be aware of the laws and policies related to hiring. For instance, supervisors must consider institution- and unit-specific hiring policies. If a department has a personnel officer, that person often will have a working knowledge of how the hiring procedures fit into the framework of legal practice. This person is important to know, especially for a new professional who is involved in hiring for the first time in a particular organization. If there is no human resources officer or supervisor with knowledge of proper practice and the new supervisor has questions about the hiring process (time lines, forms, documentation, letters, etc.), the campus human resources or affirmative action office can help by reviewing hiring plans. On some campuses, the hiring and firing of student staff are considered of minor importance compared with issues related to professional staff and faculty, but new professionals who supervise student staff must ensure that the practices they follow align with the ethical standards of the field. (See Chapter Three for a discussion of ethics.)

Supervisor as Catalyst

Bolman and Deal's (2013) second organizational frame is *human resources*. Supervisors who are good managers of human resources are seen as catalysts, because they promote high performance among staff members. The human resource frame, based on the concepts and research of organizational and social psychology, starts with the premise that organizations are made up of individuals who have needs, feelings, prejudices, skills, and limitations. From a human resource perspective, the key to effectiveness is to tailor organizations to people while addressing these underlying issues (Bolman & Deal, 2013). The effective supervisor empowers and supports people so they can reach the highest levels of personal and professional achievement. An effective catalyst knows how to lead and serve people within the framework of expectations, procedures, and policies established by the organizational architects.

Although the architect's metaphor for an effective organization is that of the well-oiled machine, the catalyst sees the organization as organic— alive and growing. In student affairs, building effective teams is a process of bringing out the best in the people who work in the organization. Effective supervisors know that the individual personalities of their staff members are as important as their job descriptions. The catalyst recognizes that when there's a good fit between the person and the organization, both benefit. A supervisor who leads from this metaphor is often perceived as someone who cares very much about employees.

> *I'm definitely more relational in my supervisory style now. I use my own experience as a resident assistant (RA) to share their burden and show that I care. I reward the best bulletin board of the month with baked goods; just a little something outside of my job description. The emphasis is on the personal versus in graduate school when I tried to be all business with the RAs I supervised. I think that age plays a big role in that. In graduate school I was only a year or two older than some of them, so I wanted to be viewed as their supervisor and not their friend. But you have to build that rapport and trust with your staff. There is a line, though, that I try to keep. I'm still close in age, but it's easier now to show that I care but remain professional.*
> —New professional in housing at a large southern research university

An effective relationship between supervisor and supervisee is crucial to the success of both professionals. The relationship exists on a continuum between directive and laissez faire approaches; the supervisee should have space to demonstrate competence, ask questions, discuss expectations, and receive feedback about performance. Supervision is one of the most complex activities in the organization, and it requires certain skills and knowledge about staff development (Tull, 2006).

Communication

Effective communication skills are among the greatest assets of a supervisor—or any employee. Paying attention to and effectively communicating with staff members is a foundational skill in supervision. Staff members have important things to say, usually know more about what is happening in the organization (or with students) than their supervisor, and often feel much better about their role in the organization if they know their supervisor is listening. Communication, when carried out effectively, is a two-way street.

All supervisors face various difficult conversations with staff, whether they relate to disciplining an employee or sharing information that will make the employee unhappy. Rather than avoid the fear, anger, or hurt of the interpersonal interaction by sending an e-mail, a supervisor needs to be confident and direct.

In their book *Difficult Conversations: How to Discuss What Matters Most*, Stone, Patton, and Heen (1999) suggested that these conversations have a certain structure. The authors explained that each conversation is really three conversations in one. The first conversation is the "What happened?" conversation, which is about determining the interpretations and perceptions of how the parties arrived at the current situation. It's not about getting the facts right or who is right or wrong. The second conversation is about understanding and sharing feelings. Each of us has developed an "emotional footprint . . . whose shape is determined by which feelings we believe are okay to have and express and which are not" (p. 91). This perception of emotions manifests itself in several ways, including the idea that we should not hurt someone's feelings or that we should not disagree or question our senior colleagues. If we change our thinking, our feelings will change and we can say what's on our mind. The third conversation is the identity conversation—about how we see ourselves. What self-doubts do we harbor? What is the narrative or story that plays in our heads when we are about to enter a difficult conversation? In terminating an employee, the tendency might be to question our own competence or goodness because we bear news that hurts other people. There's no quick way to resolve the identity conversation; you must pay attention to the self-talk and try to keep the negativity from affecting your sense of self-worth.

Synergistic Supervision

Synergistic supervision is a holistic approach that emphasizes two-way communication and a mutual investment in organizational goals, in which supervisees are actively involved in the process (Tull, 2006; Winston & Creamer, 1997). As a concept, synergistic supervision falls into the organizational frame of the catalyst. Because of its collaborative approach, synergistic supervision positively correlates with greater job satisfaction in new professionals (Tull, 2006). The synergistic supervision scale (Saunders, Cooper, Winston, & Chernow, 2000) can help determine the extent to which a supervisor exhibits the traits described.

With a synergistic framework as the foundation for the supervisory relationship, performance expectations can be mutually shaped to match organizational goals and staff professional development plans. Issues such as granting compensatory time (whether formal or informal), vacation time, or flex time during the workday for doctors appointments or balancing out late night meetings and events with students are clearly articulated and understood. Appropriate communication methods between supervisor and supervisee should be discussed and agreed upon, and not just assumed in today's e-mail, text messaging, and instant messaging world. The method might have less to do with available technology and more to do with the nature of the information that needs to be communicated. One-on-one and departmental meetings are sometimes best for sharing information, resolving problems, and charting a direction. They also avoid the problems of inadvertently hitting "reply all" when you really need to communicate with only one person or having to read from the bottom up to understand the flow of conversation that precedes your input.

Delegation as Staff Development

Most professionals want their jobs to provide autonomy, variety, challenge, and enjoyment. Supervisors must learn how to delegate interesting projects to staff members who are ready for new challenges. Often, the only way to find out who's ready is to ask or to provide the challenge and monitor the results. Delegating a project is particularly difficult for supervisors

> **Supervisors should remember that the more people they have doing innovative and interesting work, the more productive their staff and department will be.**

who like to maintain a high level of control. Providing appropriate guidance on a project based on the skill level of the staff without being too controlling is a difficult balance to achieve but an important skill to learn. Supervisors should remember that the more people they have doing innovative and interesting work, the more productive their staff and department will be, which reflects positively on the supervisor and provides excellent experience for the staff. If the supervisor is the only person doing innovative projects, the whole team suffers.

Staff Training and Development

Kaufman (1994) viewed the human resources of an organization as *human capital*. This idea parallels traditional notions of organizational capital—the financial resources available to corporations and other organizations. Kaufman wrote that investing in human capital is important in order to have a high-quality labor force and an effective organization. When supervisors invest in their employees—helping them gain greater skills, increase their knowledge, and maintain good health—the result is a happier, more highly skilled, more motivated, and more effective workforce. Investment involves allocating time for education and training (Kaufman, 1994). For new supervisors, this investment means that staff training programs should include helping people improve their job performance (e.g., how to program, how to advise a student group, how to handle a disciplinary referral) and grow in areas outside their jobs (e.g., personal wellness, career advancement). Good training and development programs take into consideration the needs of the organization and the needs of the individuals. Training and development can occur in group settings (e.g., formal time for staff development in the weekly schedule) or individually. Allow time during one-on-one supervision meetings to discuss ways that you, as a supervisor, can enhance the professional development of each staff member by creating individualized learning opportunities.

Performance Review

Investing in human capital means more than providing training and development opportunities for staff members; a supervisor must also find ways to assess employees' ongoing performance. The ability to review performance fairly is an important skill to develop. Student affairs professionals who plan a career path that includes supervision must learn the key skill of giving both positive and constructive feedback to staff.

Performance review does not mean the same thing to everyone. A student affairs professional who once worked in a corporate setting said she was evaluated there on purely measurable criteria: "If I made my goals, I was a good employee." In student affairs, a performance review is often less quantifiable; at its best, it blends qualitative and quantitative measures. A numerical score—even with a description of what the numbers indicate—does not sufficiently describe an employee's strengths, accomplishments, or challenges, and the little comment box underneath each rating does not provide adequate space to be thoughtful about your narrative. It's frustrating to be new to the institution and review an employee's past performance appraisals only to see numbers circled on the page with no context. A narrative description that supports the numerical ratings enhances the overall evaluation by providing greater understanding of an employee's performance, noting improvements from previous years and articulating employee strengths on which the supervisor can build.

Different supervisors use evaluation as a tool to achieve different ends. A supervisor can use the performance review to exercise power in appropriate (to reward and influence) or inappropriate (to manipulate) ways. A review can be an important yearly ritual or a requirement that supervisors (and staff) learn to dread. The supervisor must communicate the purpose of performance review and the criteria used to evaluate performance to staff members. What staff members believe about evaluation is very important. Even the simple rating scale used in a performance review process can cause stress. Supervisors should provide staff members with the knowledge they need to understand the "grading" scale. For example, on a scale of 1 to 5, it is important to define what a 3 represents. Of course, it is imperative that supervisors use the grading scale consistently with all members of the staff. "Processes that lead supervisors to assign equal ratings to all employees or that prohibit any staff member from excelling are destined to fail" (Hirt & Strayhorn, 2011, p. 379).

Evaluating performance should be transparent and ongoing rather than episodic (Hirt & Strayhorn, 2011). The evaluation does not begin at the performance review. In a synergistic supervisory style, the loop begins on the day staff tasks are defined and expectations are mutually negotiated, continues at most supervisory meetings, leads to the formal performance review, and culminates with the articulation of new staff expectations and a plan for professional development, which then begins the performance cycle anew. Staff members should be given an opportunity to provide feedback on the expectations of the organization and to appraise their own performance through a self-evaluation.

The annual performance appraisal might be a time to review previous feedback discussions, but it should not be a time for surprises. If the staff member is surprised by the evaluation, it means the supervisor has not given enough ongoing feedback. Supervisees need to learn to take some responsibility for not being surprised by periodically asking for feedback if it is not regularly forthcoming from the supervisor. And, although supervisors are busy providing constructive ways for staff members to improve performance, they should also be providing appropriate positive feedback. If giving constructive criticism is difficult, supervisors should consider finding at least one positive for each constructive issue presented. If there's nothing positive to say in a performance review, supervisors should ask themselves, Why is this person still working for me? The answer could be political (e.g., a person cannot be fired because he or she is related to a senior administrator), but it could just as easily be that the supervisor is not providing sufficient structure and feedback.

New professionals should determine whether their departments provide opportunities for staff members to evaluate them as supervisors. Giving staff members a process through which they can provide feedback to the supervisor is invaluable. If there's no formal mechanism for this type of feedback, one should be created. Few people know the skills, foibles, and vulnerabilities of supervisors quite like their own staffs. This type of evaluation also sets a positive example for ongoing evaluation and self-development.

One mechanism that allows supervisor feedback is 360-degree feedback. In this process, supervisors receive feedback from staff members at various levels: their supervisor, staff who report to them, and peers with whom they work. For example, a hall director would receive feedback from an immediate supervisor, RAs and desk staff, and peers such as other hall directors and staff in other departments where the hall director has significant peer relationships because of job responsibilities. The feedback is usually anonymous and is given to the supervisor in the aggregate from each of these groups. Usually coordinated by the person's supervisor, 360-degree feedback can be a time-consuming process because of the dissemination, collection, sorting, and aggregating of data; however, it provides a holistic view of the person's impact on multiple constituencies in his or her sphere of influence.

Supervisor as Advocate

A new supervisor who views organizational activity through the *political frame* realizes that all action is not dictated by policy and all decisions are not made in formal meetings, as would be assumed by someone viewing the world strictly through the structural frame. Seeing the organization through the political frame encourages a focus on how different people and interest groups compete for power and scarce resources to influence action and focus energy in an organization. The advocate, or the political supervisor, builds coalitions, serves as spokesperson for staff, and works the formal and informal systems for the benefit of the staff and the whole institution (Bolman & Deal, 2013). All members of an organization interact as political beings. Being apolitical or choosing to remain outside the political arena is practically impossible and professionally irresponsible given the multiple obligations of a supervisor. The political frame encourages recognition of informal ways of influencing action in the organization, in contrast to the structural frame, which focuses on formal means to ends and goals (e.g., through written policies).

In the political frame, supervisors work within systems composed of different interest groups that are constantly bargaining, negotiating, compromising, and, occasionally, coercing. Virtually all decisions of consequence offer many possibilities for the dynamic interplay of organizational politics. Professionals in the supervisory role for the first time might be uncomfortable with conflict. Wanting to be liked and to feel good about your environment and relationships might exacerbate the discomfort; when conflict arises, the new supervisor might wonder, What have I done wrong? In the political frame, however, conflict is seen as inevitable, a natural and necessary element in the growth of the organization. When conflict is faced openly and honestly, relationships can build on trust, and individual and organizational performance can be enhanced.

The Advocate and Power

Some professionals dislike the word, but *power* can be good or bad, used or abused. Power is the ability to perform or act effectively, to exercise influence or control. Supervisors need to be aware of the various types of power they have or have access to—and the power that others have—so they can enhance their ability to influence organizational action and obtain necessary resources.

The most obvious power available to an organizational member is the power of position; that is, the formal authority associated with a position in an organizational hierarchy. Even persons higher in the hierarchy—such as directors, deans, and vice presidents—recognize that this type of power is limited and that other forms of power are necessary to influence the staff members they supervise. These include the powers associated with rewards, information, and access.

The power of rewards. In some organizations, supervisors don't control formal rewards, such as salary and benefits, but other types of rewards are available, such as positive feedback, public recognition, professional development opportunities, job enrichment, and advancement. As previously stated, some of these rewards can be tied to the performance review process. All employees are motivated by some type of reward. Understanding which employee responds to what type of reward can lead to increased productivity, higher retention rates, and change in behavior. "Changes in the reward and punishment system are also one of the easiest ways to begin to change behavior. . . ." (Schein, 2010, p. 108).

The power of information. Information is the lifeblood of an organization and of the people in it—information about resources, budgets, expectations, perceptions, outcomes, goals, changes, organizational history, and priorities. Having, controlling, and filtering information are inevitable aspects of organizational life. Supervisors are conduits for information flowing through an organization. Although flow might be seen as a structural matter—information flows up and down the hierarchy—all information is filtered in the process of communication. When information is selectively disseminated to influence decisions, it becomes a political tool. New professional supervisors must seek out information if they expect to enhance their performance and the performance of their staff. When supervisors recognize that all information is, inevitably, filtered and incomplete, they become more proactive in clarifying the data they receive and seeking the data they do not have. Supervisors are better able to do their jobs when they obtain and pass on necessary information to their staff members.

Consider the plight of the complex director who is concerned about the volume of e-mail. Some of that mail, in the eyes of the director, is a documentation nightmare, while central office staff sees it as the fastest way to empower staff with knowledge. Here are some thoughts to consider when making choices about electronic communication:

☞ E-mail is not confidential or private. E-mail is never truly deleted from your files. Electronic correspondence can be requested through sunshine laws, subpoenaed, or used as official university documentation in the same way any other document can be used.

☞ Electronic communication sent and received from a personal e-mail account can be subpoenaed or produced in a sunshine law request if the information is work related.

☞ Be concise. Be mindful of the receiver's time.

☞ Use e-mail subject lines that help the reader prioritize and organize—as if you were providing a hint about which file folder the e-mail should be stored in.

☞ Do not overuse "reply all" or mass mailings when a targeted e-mail suffices.

☞ Respond to e-mails in a timely fashion. If you need time to provide adequate information, offer a quick response that includes a timeline for getting the requested information.

☞ Request delivery receipts only if documentation is essential. Use the "high priority" option in your e-mail program sparingly.

☞ Civility is as important in electronic communication as it is in face-to-face communication. If you're angry, frustrated, or hurt, reconsider your impulse to send an e-mail.

☞ E-mail can be a reflection of professional writing skills. Be careful to differentiate between circumstances that permit informality and those that are more formal or that require attention to detail.

☞ Be mindful of the chain of command in the organization when sending e-mail. Political issues are the same in any form of communication when you use the carbon copy or the blind carbon copy function on a memo.

☞ Communicate supervisory expectations about e-mail, instant messaging, chatting, tweeting, or text messaging to staff members.

☞ Attend training or read policies associated with how the legal counsel or human resources personnel at your institution view electronic correspondence, particularly with regard to supervisory documentation.

The power of access. Having access to individuals and groups with power is one way new supervisors can influence the effectiveness of their staff and garner the resources they need. The first step is to determine which persons and groups in the organization wield influence in a particular area of interest (e.g., budgeting, policy making). Access can be formal (e.g., getting appointed to the budget planning committee) or informal (e.g., establishing a relationship with the chair of the policy and procedures committee). In addition to information, rewards, and access, power might include personality (charisma) and expertise. Viewing the supervisory role through the political frame means being aware of the bases of power in the organization (including your own) and learning how to use them effectively.

Team Development

Whether in the private or public sector, the value of working collaboratively is well documented. Corbin (2000) wrote, "The power of teamwork remains true today. Multiple people working in unity are so much more powerful than the same number of people working independently" (p. 133). Katzenbach and Smith (1993) added that teams are more flexible because they can easily be assembled and disbanded for the task at hand. When the right group of people is assembled, team performance is unbeatable.

Supervisors are often in the position to select staff members to participate on or lead a team. In selecting someone for a team, supervisors should match the needs or purpose of the team with the skills or interest of the staff member. A team assembled to select a new student conduct database requires different skills and expertise than a team assembled to plan the division's holiday party. In leading a team, a supervisor must manage the team dynamics, which includes understanding and dealing with multiple personality traits, various levels of skill and experience, and different levels of willingness to work collaboratively. Conflicts in the group over power and resources can make the role of team leader and supervisor particularly challenging. Some groups are easier to mold into teams than others. Corbin (2000) offered this caution regarding supervising groups of people:

> Because of the power of teamwork in organizational success, leaders must arrange workspace for collaborative efforts and arrange the work itself so that each person, when making his or her most expert contribution, produces a necessary part of the whole. Additionally, rewards are given for the team's projects at completion. Ideally, competition is fostered between organizations, not within organizations, which is why rewards are given for individual improvement and not on the basis of comparative performance. The greater reward, however, must be given on a team level—something that can be achieved only through cooperation. (p. 120)

Supervisor as Interpreter

The fourth frame of reference is that of *organizational culture* or *symbolism*. Probably the most elusive of the four frames, it is a significant influence in campus and personnel issues (see Chapter Two). Although organizations can be viewed as machinelike (structural frame), they also have qualities of a culture similar to those of the cultures of racial, ethnic, or religious backgrounds; that is, they have patterns of shared values, beliefs, assumptions, and symbols. Every organization develops distinctive patterns of beliefs and behaviors over time. Many of them are subconscious—reflected in myths, stories, rituals, ceremonies, and other symbolic forms. Managers who can interpret and make use of the meaning of symbols have a better chance of influencing their organizations than those who focus only on the other three frames (Bolman & Deal, 2013).

Institutions of higher education are loaded with very powerful messages about who their members are and what they believe. Consider why people cry when they sing the alma mater or why they paint their faces at football games. They don't do this because there's a campus policy mandating emotional displays at football games, but because rituals, heroes, and myths are powerful ways to share common meaning and experience within a culture. Faculty, students, alumni, donors, staff, legislators, administrators, parents, and others compete to have their voices heard on campus, but on fall Saturday afternoons, the crowd—composed of all these groups—cheers for the football team. It's not accidental that college athletics has symbolic power in higher education.

The cultural frame takes the focus away from what the organization does and how it does it. Instead, it focuses on *why* it does the things it does: on the meaning of organizational and individual action. The culture of the organization and institution often dictate how supervisors should behave. The "shoulds" that begin as part of the formal structure become part of the culture. For example, the issue of documentation varies in emphasis and meaning depending on the culture of the particular organization. To the new assistant dean, following up a meeting with a memo means that he's ensuring accurate communication. To his supervisor, it means that the assistant dean doesn't trust him to do what he said he would; formally documenting meetings and agreements is just not part of that organization's culture.

As a supervisor, interpreting and understanding the culture as soon as possible increases the new person's chances of success. Time in the position helps, but so does careful and sensitive observation of practices, reactions, language, and priorities. A new supervisor should observe what people do and listen to the stories they tell about the organization. Who are the departmental heroes, and what did they do to gain such fame? On any campus, you can look around and identify the department or staff groups that seem to be the tightest knit teams.

What are the department's special rituals? What are the inside jokes and special stories that make the team seem cohesive? Skilled supervisors learn how to manage and shape the culture of their staff and of the organization. Practical examples of culture management are special banquets, award ceremonies, regular social gatherings, slogans, T-shirts, songs, and mission statements. You must, however, go beyond the surface meaning of activities to their underlying, more powerful subconscious meanings.

Supervisors work within the context of an historically based institutional culture. Supervision does not occur in a vacuum. Supervisors need to be aware of the culture of the department, of the overall organization, and of the various constituency groups within the organization.

Integrating the Frames

It is unlikely that as a new supervisor you will be a skilled architect, catalyst, advocate, and interpreter in your first position. You'll probably be most comfortable and effective with one, perhaps two, of the four frames. Be careful to not overestimate the use of frames. As a supervisor you might think you're using one frame, yet no one else perceives the use of that frame (Kezar, 2011). The organizational setting will have a significant impact on the emphasis you can or will place on one or more of the frames.

One supervisor might be structure oriented and thrive on budgets, operational calendars, and the development of policy and procedures; another might be oriented toward the people in the organization and thrive on collaborative projects, relationships, and committee work. Regardless of how the supervisor is most comfortable, it's wise to view the organization and a supervisor's role in it through multiple perspectives. The supervisory role requires skills from each of these perspectives; focusing on one frame will mean missing out on important information or actions.

> The supervisory role requires skills from each of these perspectives; focusing on one frame will mean missing out on important information or actions.

As an example of the need to integrate perspectives, an analysis of a typical RA staff meeting provides a useful scenario. You can raise questions about structure (e.g., purpose, agenda, outcomes, degree of formality, required attendance), human resources (e.g., role of RAs, degree of collaboration), and politics (e.g., working together to influence departmental policy). From a cultural perspective, you can ask, Why are staff meetings important? Are they weekly rituals that enhance the performance of the group as a whole? Are they weekly requirements to pass along memos from the central administration? Does the group's culture support change, or does the status quo usually prevail? Considering all four of Bolman and Deal's (2013) frames not only raises different questions but also might lead to different outcomes and more effective decisions.

Integrating the Frames to Build a Coherent Style

We have presented many different concepts in this chapter, representing the different perspectives, or frames, with which we can approach a topic. In any given organization or situation, different approaches or different perspectives can be brought to bear, and, in all likelihood, none of them would be incorrect. That is the crux of the complexity of being a leader and a supervisor: One situation can be dealt with using many different approaches. The discussions in this section take a few issues and approach them from different frames of reference.

Generational Issues

Defining a generation is controversial in and of itself. The defining characteristics attributed to a boomer or an Xer might or might not be appreciated by a member of the labeled group. Boomers think Xers lack loyalty, work ethic, and commitment. Nexters think boomers are stuck in the past.

> Like death and taxes, defining characteristics are assumed to be immutable and irreparable, and consequently, they are never openly addressed. In the "old" rigid, highly regimented organization, that may not have mattered. In the "new" organization, they can be devastating. They nonetheless fester, cause tension, and lead to unnecessary, at times disabling, personal, departmental, and organizational conflict. (Zemke, Raines, & Filipczak, 2000, p. 12)

An example of a generational conflict is embedded in the following quote:

> *Technology is what I rely on. I can text all of them with mass text or e-mail. It's not as personal as I'd like it to be, but sometimes it's the only way. We have mid-semester meetings, and they have to come to one of the four sessions where we talk about general things, good or bad. When possible I think face to face is best. And these kids need practice. They've been in tech since they were knee-high to a grasshopper, and I think it's only getting worse. They have no critical thinking. When they have questions, I tell them to go look it up first and then if they can't find it, I'll help them.* —Recreation professional at a public northeastern university

Some people might think of technology as a generational issue between boomer and Xers, between those who had no technology growing up versus those who have adapted to the use of technology in their daily lives, although they weren't born with tablets in their hands. What this recreation professional described is the rift between two technology-oriented generations—one that is totally immersed in it and the other who understands the limits of technology and uses it appropriately. The implication is that the former is lazy and relies on an electronic resource instead of logically reasoning through an issue. Strategies for facing generational issues cannot just be given lip service; we encourage reading up on this topic. *Generations at Work*

(Zemke et al., 2000) includes a cross-generational workplace assessment embedded with many concepts regarding how you and your organization relate to generational differences. Consider these examples, taken directly from the Zemke et al. (2000) assessment:

- ☞ There is no one successful type in this organization. Managers, leaders, and those in the most desirable jobs are a mix of ages, sexes, and ethnicities.

- ☞ When a project team is put together, employees with different backgrounds, experiences, skills, and viewpoints are consciously included.

- ☞ There is lots of conversation, even some humor, about differing viewpoints and perspectives.

- ☞ Our atmosphere and policies are based on the work being done, the customers being served, and the preferences of the people who work here.

- ☞ There is behind-the-back complaining, passive–aggressive behavior, and open hostility among groups of employees.

- ☞ There is an element of fun and playfulness about most endeavors here.

- ☞ Managers adjust policies and procedures to fit the needs of individuals and the team.

- ☞ We are concerned and focused, on a daily basis, with retention.

- ☞ Work assignments here are broad, providing variety and challenge, and allowing each employee to develop a range of skills.

- ☞ We market internally, "selling" the company to employees and continually looking for ways to be the employer of choice. (pp. 253–257)

This list represents 10 of the 20 items on the assessment; it shows the types of organizational and supervisory priorities that get to the heart of cross-generational issues. Each item offers a clue to the theoretical framework that is the bedrock of the assumption. For instance, in this group of 10 items, some issues are associated with the organizational architect (policy, procedure, hiring policy); the catalyst (variety, challenge, playfulness); the advocate (selling, employee behaviors); and the interpreter (development of organizational culture through retention of employees).

Discipline

Disciplining an employee—from a verbal reprimand to termination—is one of the most difficult things student affairs professionals do. Even with synergistic supervision, ongoing feedback, and opportunities to improve, sometimes there's no alternative but to terminate an employee. Some people believe that terminating an employee is a recognition that both the supervisor and the employee have failed, but the reality is that good supervision is not always sufficient.

> Some employees lack and cannot gain the necessary skills to perform their jobs. Some seek to obfuscate and deny any responsibility for failure. Worse, some engage in personal diatribe and denial in which they adopt a vitriolic attitude toward the supervisor and the organization. (Zemke et al., 2000, p. 416)

Your direct supervisor should be in the loop on your plan to terminate an employee, to make sure the documentation supports the outcome. The human resources department should also support your decision in case legal action is taken against the university. The process should be done humanely, with attention to the employee's dignity. The employee is not a bad person, just not a good fit for the job. The conversation should be brief but direct, stating the opportunities you gave the employee to improve, the fact that the employee did not act on those opportunities, and that the next step is termination. In some cases you can give the employee the option to resign instead of termination, as it is kinder and has implications for unemployment benefits.

> *I was faced with the decision three weeks before the end of the semester about whether or not to terminate a high-performing RA. He was a staff and resident favorite but had an unfortunate incident which impacted the safety of our students. Because we had such a good relationship and because he came to me knowing that this would cost him his job, I was empowered by my supervisors to give him the option of resigning. It allowed him to save face and us to*

keep our relationship intact. It was a best-case scenario of a terrible situation. —Hall director at a large southern research university

You should be absolutely clear in your mind that the termination is the direct result of the employee's lack of performance and that you did not contribute in any way to getting him or her fired. The termination should occur with a witness in the room and be fairly short; the employee should be given a time frame for vacating the office and turning in keys and ID card, and for when access to e-mail and other systems will be deactivated (student record and financial data contain the most sensitive data where access should be deactivated immediately). Issues of the last paycheck and unused vacation hours can be referred to the human resources department or explained in a letter that you hand the employee. Do not set yourself up for a hostile exchange with the employee by debating the issue, devaluing contributions made to date, or making the termination personal. Consult your supervisor or the human resources department on what you should or shouldn't say about the departure of the staff member. Obviously, if there's a party being thrown in his or her honor, the person is leaving on good terms. Anything else that is of a jarring here-today-gone-tomorrow scenario leads to speculation and rumor-mill gossip that shouldn't be left to fester.

Less severe disciplinary measures include a formal letter of warning or reprimand, a performance action plan, or a reduction in merit pay. In each instance, you should refer back to job expectations, provide specific examples of expectations that were not met, give the reason for the corrective action, and state what both parties need to do in the future so that the employee can be successful in the job. If you write a letter or develop an action plan, review it carefully to ensure that the feedback is clear and concise and that improvement can be easily measured.

Multicultural Issues

Cross-cultural supervision can be challenging. If a supervisor is uncomfortable because of a cultural (e.g., racial, ethnic, international) or other (e.g., sex, disability, sexual orientation) difference, it's the supervisor's responsibility to identify the root of the discomfort and take appropriate steps to address it. Being selected to supervise others does not eliminate a person's experience, biases, or stereotypes. In fact, to assume that one does not have biases is perhaps the greatest obstacle to self-learning and effective

> The combination of self-awareness, knowledge, and practical skills enables us to serve at the highest levels of our profession with regard to multicultural competence.

cross-cultural supervision. Pope, Reynolds, and Mueller (2004) challenged practitioners to achieve competence in three distinct categories in student affairs: exemplary multicultural awareness, exemplary multicultural knowledge, and exemplary multicultural skills. The combination of self-awareness, knowledge, and practical skills enables us to serve at the highest levels of our profession with regard to multicultural competence. Although having an intellectual command of multicultural issues might be a good attribute, knowledge alone does not provide the basis of good supervision in a multicultural environment. Being aware of our own biases and issues associated with oppression is helpful, but awareness alone is not enough.

In recognizing the need to learn more about a particular difference (e.g., supervising a deaf staff member for the first time), the supervisor should not place responsibility solely on the staff member but must take the initiative to learn about those who are different. New professionals—both members of majority groups and those who are marginalized or underrepresented in the institution—should reflect on their experiences and assumptions regarding supervision of people they perceive as culturally or otherwise different.

> By reexamining the core competencies of student affairs professionals and infusing the multicultural attitudes, knowledge, and skills that are needed to create a more multiculturally sensitive campus, both practitioners and scholars provide more ethical and effective programs and services. Multicultural awareness, knowledge, and skills are core competencies that all student affairs professionals need regardless of their job responsibilities and level of training. (Pope et al., 2004, p. 28)

Turning the Table: Supervisor as Supervisee

Regardless of how many years of experience supervisors have in the profession, most have a mix of strengths, areas for development, and major skill deficiencies. What if you find yourself working with a bad boss? First, you should understand that, for example, an extraordinary architect who is not a strong catalyst is probably not a bad boss. Nor is the supervisor who is a skilled catalyst but a weak architect necessarily a bad boss.

A laundry list of traits that describe a bad boss should not just be traits that are the opposite of our preferred style of leadership. Look for ways to capitalize on your similarities with your supervisors for the betterment of the organization. Are you coming from opposite perspectives? Learn how to incorporate the supervisor's perspective to enhance your personal skill and job effectiveness. Even when differences are extreme, try to develop a relationship grounded in mutual respect. Once respect is established between two people, possibilities arise for sharing concerns about weaknesses and areas for improvement. Accept differences and learn from them.

There are times when a supervisor's lack of skill or inappropriate behavior warrants concern. A supervisor might be unable to manage job responsibilities or might exhibit uncivil or unethical behavior. The subordinate must make some choices when a supervisor's behavior goes beyond a few underdeveloped skills and starts to seriously and negatively affect the professional or personal environment on the job. The sensitive nature of any relationship that has a power and authority differential calls for case-by-case analysis.

The ideal course of action to deal with conflict is to directly address the problem. If appropriate, address specific issues with the supervisor directly and request for a change in behavior. Use civil language and behavior. If the behavior changes and the outcomes are satisfactory, the story has reached an ideal ending. If the behavior is so extreme that a one-on-one confrontation is not possible, or if the behavior does not change after an initial confrontation, seek assistance. If mentors are available to help develop a strategy, talk with them. Additional campus resources include human resources personnel, an ombudsman, harassment officers, and the direct supervisor of the person causing concern. Coworkers with more experience can offer perspective and suggest strategies to work through difficult situations. But, again, always look first for ways to capitalize on similarities and differences with supervisors for the betterment of the organization.

Being a Good Supervisee

Although this chapter's focus is on supervision, being a good supervisee also requires certain skills.

> *A lesson I learned from my first supervisor that has exponentially increased in value now that I supervise professionals is the "same team" mentality. It can be really easy to create an "us-versus-them" dichotomy between entry-level and managerial staff responsible for*

different things in the organization. Remember that supervisors are just as invested as the rest of the team in the success of students and the organization. This is the best way to maintain a positive per- spective and reduce frustration when supervisors question, disagree, critique, or deny.—Assistant director of housing and residence life at a large public university

We must all remember that we are a part of larger systems. The choices we make as supervisees are as important as those we make as supervisors. Perhaps the lessons of civility statements are among the most important we can bring to our supervisory relationship. A strong work ethic and a commit- ment to civility are a winning combination for both supervisor and supervisee.

Conclusion

Understanding and integrating the four frames does not mean that all super- visory decisions will be popular and perfect; however, supervisors increase the probability of making a good decision when they tap a deep understand- ing of the organization. Additionally, supervisors might have more empathy with persons who are opposed to a decision if they can see that the opposi- tion is based in a particular way of viewing the situation. Improved decision making, working relationships, and performance provide ample justification for trying to understand and view the organization through multiple lenses.

There's no question that the most rewarding part of my job is supervision of staff. With each passing year, I learn as much about myself through the role of being a supervisor as I do about the people I supervise. I have always believed that supervision is a two-way street. There was a time when I tried to make everyone happy. I have learned through experience that making people happy isn't always the best path. It may be the path of least resistance, but it is often not the path that will maximize my team or the individual. The joy in supervision often comes many years later at a conference, when someone you may have butted heads with says thank you for caring enough to be critical or being bold enough to face conflict. As I have gotten older, I admit that I still do enjoy those supervisory relationships that fit like a glove. However, I am genuinely grateful for the supervisory relationships that force me to be a little uncomfortable. —Veteran supervisor in residence life at a large southern university

It's one thing to read about supervision and quite another to actually do it. Each new professional has a unique style that, initially, will be a good fit for some individuals, staffs, and organizations and not such a great fit for others. Strive to weave the principles of lifelong learning and civility, and the perspectives of the architect, catalyst, advocate, and interpreter into your skills as a practitioner.

References

Andersen, E. (2006). *Growing great employees: Turning ordinary people into extraordinary performers*. New York, NY: Penguin.

Bolman, L. G., & Deal, T. E. (2013). *Reframing organizations: Artistry, choice, and leadership* (5th ed.). San Francisco, CA: Jossey-Bass.

Career Press. (1993). *The supervisor's handbook* (2nd ed.). New York, NY: Author.

Carnegie Foundation for the Advancement of Teaching. (1990). *Campus life: In search of community*. Princeton, NJ: Author.

Carnevale, A. P., & Stone, C. S. (1995). *The American mosaic: An in-depth report on the future of diversity at work*. New York, NY: McGraw Hill.

Corbin, C. (2000). *Great leaders see the future first: Taking your organization to the top in five revolutionary steps*. Chicago, IL: Dearborn.

Hirt, J. B., & Strayhorn, T. L. (2011). Staffing and supervision. In J. H. Schuh, S. R. Jones, & S. R. Harper (Eds.), *Student services: A handbook for the profession* (5th ed., pp. 372–384). San Francisco, CA: Jossey-Bass.

Katzenbach, J. R., & Smith, D. K. (1993). *The wisdom of teams: Creating the high performance organization*. Cambridge, MA: Harvard Business School Press.

Kaufman, B. E. (1994). *The economics of labor markets*. Fort Worth, TX: Dryden Press.

Kezar, A. (2011). Organizational theory. In J. H. Schuh, S. R. Jones, & S. R. Harper (Eds.), *Student services: A handbook for the profession* (5th ed., pp. 226–241). San Francisco, CA: Jossey-Bass.

Pope, R. L., Reynolds, A. L., & Mueller, J. A. (2004). *Multicultural competence in student affairs*. San Francisco, CA: Jossey-Bass.

Saunders, S. A., Cooper, D. L., Winston, R. B., Jr., & Chernow, E. (2000). Supervising in student affairs: Exploration of the synergistic approach. *Journal of College Student Development, 41,* 181–192.

Schein, E. H. (2010). *Organizational culture and leadership* (4th ed.). San Francisco, CA: Jossey-Bass.

Stone, D., Patton, B., & Heen, S. (1999). *Difficult conversations: How to discuss what matters most*. New York, NY: Penguin.

Tull, A. (2006). Synergistic supervision, job satisfaction and intention to turnover of new professionals in student affairs. *Journal of College Student Development, 47,* 465–480.

Winston, R. B., & Creamer, D. G. (1997). *Improving staffing practices in student affairs*. San Francisco, CA: Jossey-Bass.

Zemke, R., Raines, C., & Filipczak, B. (2000). *Generations at work: Managing the clash of veterans, boomers, Xers, and Nexters in your workplace*. Toronto, Canada: Amacom.

COLLABORATION WITH ACADEMIC AFFAIRS AND FACULTY

CHAPTER FIVE

Camille Consolvo and William H. Arnold

I n efforts to establish campus environments that support "learning and development as intertwined, inseparable elements of the student experience" (American College Personnel Association [ACPA] & National Association of Student Personnel Administrators [NASPA], 2004, p. 1), many student affairs administrators often find an organizational and functional gap between academic affairs and student affairs. To bridge the gap, collaboration with faculty is a logical and oft-prescribed solution (American Association for Higher Education [AAHE], ACPA, & NASPA, 1998; ACPA, 1994; ACPA & NASPA, 1997; Frost, Strom, Downey, Schultz, & Holland, 2010; Johnson & Cheatham, 1999; Schroeder, 1999b).

Collaboration is defined as "to work jointly with others . . . in an intellectual endeavor" and "to cooperate with [someone] with [whom] one is not immediately connected" ("Collaboration," n.d.). Extending this definition to the work in student affairs, our intellectual endeavor with faculty is to design and deliver learning environments and opportunities for students. Because we are not immediately connected with faculty in most institutions, and because faculty tend to see only the formal curriculum as the core of education, we must intentionally cross organizational lines and work with faculty to develop a shared vision—a common agenda—for student learning and success. In addition, we must be willing to work together both in and outside the classroom to create systems and assessment practices that promote these learning outcomes. Colleges and universities must work as a single system (especially academic affairs and student affairs) to successfully educate students in the 21st century (Cook, Ghering, & Lewis, 2007). A first step in working toward this common agenda requires faculty and student affairs professionals to identify and recognize their different assumptions.

Understanding Both Cultures

To build bridges between students' experiences—both in and out of class—new professionals must first understand and appreciate the cultures of both the faculty and student affairs. A simple comparison of values of the two groups illustrates inherent cultural differences. Faculty tend to share four values: (a) a pursuit and dissemination of knowledge; (b) professional autonomy, including academic freedom; (c) collegiality through self-governance; and (d) an emphasis on thinking and reflecting over doing (Winter, 2009). Student affairs professionals tend to share four different values: (a) an interest in holistic student development; (b) collaboration over autonomy; (c) teamwork; and (d) an emphasis on doing over thinking and reflecting (Love, Kuh, MacKay, & Hardy, 1993). Understanding both cultures and sets of values helps student affairs professionals and faculty work together to create an institutional culture that encourages student learning and development. Both groups can fill the gaps created by their diverse knowledge, values, and roles (Price, 1999).

> To build bridges between students' experiences—both in and out of class—new professionals must first understand and appreciate the cultures of both the faculty and student affairs.

Although academic freedom, independence, scholarship, and cultivation of knowledge are likely shared values among faculty across institutions, faculty members are not a homogeneous group. Student affairs professionals must view each faculty member as an individual. Faculty members who work at the same institution might not necessarily communicate regularly with each other, have common goals, or value undergraduate education in the same way (Eimers, 1999). In addition, faculty tend to identify more with their disciplines than their institution (Love et al., 1993; Winter, 2009) As a result, a faculty member's closest colleague might work at another institution. To understand the faculty at a particular institution, you must consider the type of institution, the history, traditions, and culture of that institution, and the socialization process for faculty (Hirt, 2006). All of these elements coalesce to create a system in which the expectations that influence how and where faculty devote their attention, including those associated with promotion and tenure or merit, are likely to be quite different from those in student affairs.

Learning about your own professional cultures and that of other constituents is a prerequisite for any successful collaboration (Philpott & Strange, 2003). Developing a sense of the assumptions, values, norms, and expectations that influence how we view students and the learning process will promote common goals, a shared commitment to student success, and a seamless educational environment (Frost et al., 2010).

> *After building strong relationships with faculty, they were more willing to take time to understand my responsibilities and the developmental work I do with students. After I formed those relationships, they were much more likely to collaborate and work closely with me.* —Hall director at a large public university

> *I know a bad experience with one faculty member can make other relationships very difficult. So, I make sure that I'm constantly thanking them for their time, reminding them how important their feedback is, and making sure that I'm not unduly burdening them. I give them specific, manageable requests with very clear goals and tasks so that the task becomes as easy for them as possible.* —Assistant director for supplemental instruction at a large public university

> *I like to reach out to individual faculty regarding student questions or concerns because faculty appreciate providing their expertise to help students, and it gives me a chance to learn more about that faculty member.* —Academic advisor at a small 2-year public college

Conditions for Collaboration

Collaboration between student affairs and academic affairs on most campuses has grown, resulting in a greater sense of shared commitment to student success (Bourassa & Kruger, 2001). Finding common values, goals, and a commitment to student success and a seamless educational environment can enhance this collaboration (Frost et al., 2010). Expanded collaboration depends on several conditions (Brown, 1990). Of these, agreement on the core institutional mission, respect for faculty appointments, adoption of an educator identity, and active involvement in broad institutional activities are highlighted here as particularly salient for new student affairs professionals.

Primacy of Mission

Student affairs professionals (new and seasoned) must understand and acknowledge that the mission of colleges and universities—academics—comes first. Barr (2000) went so far as to say, "Failure to understand, appreciate, and translate the mission of the institution into programs and services can rank among the biggest mistakes a student affairs administrator can make" (p. 25). Research on college student success continues to demonstrate the positive contributions of properly planned student affairs-related programs in terms of desired college outcomes including: cognitive development, moral and ethical development, and persistence that leads to degree completion (Kuh, 2009). In this regard, student affairs professionals should clearly articulate the relationship between current research, program development, and institutional mission.

Nature of Faculty Appointments

To increase collaboration with faculty, student affairs professionals should understand the nature of faculty preparation, priorities, and daily activities. In most institutional contexts, the faculty, individually and collectively, are charged with establishing and maintaining the formal curriculum. In addition, faculty appointments have historically been constructed and, in turn, evaluated on a combination of research and scholarship, teaching, and service. Within this mix, research and scholarship and teaching are weighted significantly greater than service. Faculty naturally prefer to direct their energies toward activities they perceive to align with these expectations (Schroeder, 1999b). Fortunately, certain environmental conditions are emerging in academe that likely support collaboration. Professional development for faculty has expanded, and as a result, faculty's conception of their role and obligation to students and their learning has broadened (Austin & Sorcinelli, 2013). Broader definitions of scholarship with a focus on teaching, learning, and assessment of student outcomes are likely to favor collaboration (Banta & Kuh, 1998). In addition, the next generation of faculty brings new perspectives and interests and assumes a broader range of appointments (i.e., nontenure track, part-time) that might lead them to be more open to collaboration.

Educator Identity

Keeling (2004) stated that it is realistic to consider the entire campus as a learning environment that includes both in- and out-of-class experiences. Student affairs professionals must view themselves as an integral part of the academic experience and active contributors to student learning (Sandeen, 2004). They must also ensure their actions align with these ideals, which means student affairs administrators need "to bring more to the table than insight on student learning outside the classroom. They need tools and expertise in teaching and learning" (Johnson & Rayman, 2007, p. 19).

As student affairs professionals, we should be confident that we make a difference in students' lives and be comfortable living in the breach between being just a service provider and a faculty member (Hossler, 2001). We need to let go of the weak self-identity that leads to ineffectiveness, an anti-intellectual culture, concern that territory will be gained or lost, and a need to be seen at the center of the institution. Instead, we should recognize our value as educators and include a focus on learning. We should reimagine our work and develop relationships without borders across campus (ACPA & NASPA Task Force on the Future of Student Affairs, 2010). Initiation of collaboration may have to come from us, however, because often it will not be faculty who reach out to collaborate.

> *I anticipated that I would encounter a lot of resistance, and I approached the relationship with faculty members with the idea that I was in a less powerful position, rather than entering into the relationship as an equal. There's definitely a power differential but I've encountered very little resistance, so that's a pleasant surprise.*
> —Assistant director for supplemental instruction at a large public research university

Opportunities for Collaboration

A broad range of interactions occur with some frequency between faculty and student affairs professionals (Brown, 1990), including standing committees or councils, institutionwide programs and functions (e.g., admissions, orientation, commencement, honors programs, academic support programs), cultural programming, and campus diversity initiatives. With national disasters, such as college shootings and hurricanes, faculty members see how student affairs staff handle campus crises and are beginning to view their importance differently (Manning, Kinzie, & Schuh, 2014).

Brown (1990) and Schroeder (1999b) described several areas where increased collaboration between student affairs and academic affairs professionals can improve undergraduate education, such as reshaping curricular and cocurricular opportunities, establishing integrative learning communities, expanding assessment practices, and enhancing intercultural and global awareness. Each of these areas represent unique opportunities for student affairs professionals to utilize Engstrom and Tinto's (2000) three-phase continuum of involvement: (a) serve as a clearinghouse of information; (b) work cooperatively with faculty while maintaining traditional roles; and (c) work cooperatively with faculty in which the roles and expertise of both parties are appreciated and utilized.

> *I think what made collaboration successful was the idea that we were working together and utilizing our knowledge and expertise to meet a common goal: serve our students.* —Coordinator for new student orientation at a midsize urban public university

Curricular and Cocurricular Reform

With a renewed emphasis on learning, the academic community needs to focus on different methods of teaching and on how to help students learn more effectively. Curricular reform with a particular emphasis on general education is another collaboration opportunity. The general education curriculum (e.g., psychology, history, philosophy, the natural sciences, literature) promotes student development and contributes to the development of identity, competency, autonomy, appreciation for diversity, and the clarification of values. Gaff (1983) noted that student affairs professionals and other administrative staff should be included in the debate about general education, stating that they can help establish expectations and advance learning goals for students outside the classroom.

Coupled with a focus on active learning, general education curricular reform provides an opportunity for student affairs professionals to serve as advocates, facilitators, and reinforcers in helping students understand the developmental aspects of the core academic disciplines (Brown, 1990). Methods for improving outcomes include freshman-year integration and transition programs (Banta & Kuh, 1998; Garland & Grace, 1993), leadership training (Martin & Murphy, n.d.), service–learning (Engstrom & Tinto, 1997; Fried, n.d.), residential-life programs that incorporate vocational or career interests of faculty (Garland & Grace, 1993), cooperative education and internships, new-faculty orientation (Finley, 1996), academic support programs (e.g., study skills labs, writing labs, tutoring), academic advising, honors programs (Brown, 1990), early warning systems for students in academic difficulty, and living–learning communities (Schroeder, 1999a). Values education, cultural diversity, and teaching social responsibility are additional opportunities for collaboration (Brown, 1990). Student affairs professionals can design cocurricular experiences to reinforce course content, identify high-risk classes, and work with instructors to improve success rates, as well as organize discussion groups for students enrolled in common courses. Recently, many campuses have begun to realize the need to have both faculty and student affairs staff participate in teaching first-year experience courses and the benefit of tapping into the expertise of both (Kezar, 2009).

In the past 25 years, many institutions have focused on integrating service–learning across the curriculum, which encourages students to make tangible relationships between classroom content and real-life experiences. Furthermore, Engstrom and Tinto (1997) argued that service–learning provides ideal opportunities for collaborative activities between academic and student affairs where both parties can make significant contributions. They cited several institutions that are creatively and effectively forging partnerships in this area. Service–learning is an excellent opportunity to bring students, faculty, staff, and community agencies together to build effective, collaborative, and reflective learning experiences (Stein, 2007).

Integrative Learning Communities

A great way to collaborate with faculty is through residential learning communities, such as faculty-in-residence programs, faculty fellows who coordinate regular programs with specific halls, first-year programs, classes that meet in a residence hall, students living in proximity and taking the same courses, and themed halls with affiliated faculty. Residence halls are particularly productive settings in which to integrate academic and social life by bringing faculty and students into regular contact with one another. In residential learning programs, students can have more meaningful conversations with faculty outside the classroom, which makes students more comfortable when interacting with faculty (Nesheim et al., 2007) and feel a greater satisfaction with the overall college experience (Astin, 1985). Faculty also benefit from these interactions. By getting to know students better, some faculty members improve their teaching (Kuh, Schuh, & Whitt, 1991). Thus, student affairs professionals should broker opportunities for connections between students and faculty when possible.

> *I do not believe there is any type of deep understanding between our faculty and the staff. I am not sure many faculty members see the connection between our cocurricular work and learning opportunities with the students and their academic work.*—Residence life director at a small private liberal arts college

Because residential students have a continuous presence on campus, faculty and staff need to create truly seamless learning environments. Student affairs staff, however, aren't always trained to build academic collaborations, and faculty often don't think about addressing student learning from a broader institutional perspective. Looking at how to create learning environments, not in isolation but in collaboration, is essential. We must look for components of partnerships that already exist on campus (e.g., pairing service–learning with residence-hall community-service programs). Successful pilot projects using existing resources demonstrate that ongoing partnerships can be tapped into (Masterson, 2008). Increased student centeredness and a more holistic understanding of students are examples of the benefits to faculty in collaboration, but there are drawbacks as well in partnering in living–learning programs: reduced time for research and a possible impact on promotion or tenure. Good candidates for becoming involved in such residential partnerships are faculty members at transition points in their careers, for example, those who just completed an administrative appointment or those who are a few years away from retirement, are looking for a different experience, or are between research projects (Stewart, 2008).

Assessing Learning Outcomes

Banta and Kuh (1998) described outcomes assessment in higher education as "one of the most promising but underused opportunities for collaboration" (p. 42). They argued that it's one of the few activities on campus in which student affairs professionals and faculty can participate equally. Programs addressing needs of new students as well as cocurricular transcripts are examples of working collaboratively to focus institutional effort on student learning. Especially at larger, more research-oriented institutions, student affairs professionals can demonstrate their ability to collect and analyze outcome data to faculty immersed in research culture.

The Council for Higher Education Accreditation and several regional accrediting agencies want evidence to validate the assessment of learning outcomes in and outside the classroom (Newman, Couterier, & Scurry, 2004). They emphasize an organizational structure and culture in which the chief academic and student affairs officers work closely to create a learning-centered environment. The call from external constituents for accountability, increased graduation rates, employable graduates, and evidence of learning outcomes emphasizes the need for collaborative partnerships between faculty and student affairs staff (Cook & Lewis, 2007). Keeling, Wall, Underhile, and Dungy (2008) stressed the importance of a collaborative use of all campus resources in promoting student success. Both student affairs professionals and faculty members must reconsider assessment policies, patterns, and practices in colleges and universities and respond to greater expectations for institutional accountability. Academic and student affairs faculty and staff can use this method of addressing common concerns to focus on engaging in evidence-based, reflective practice and supporting one another in doing their best work.

Collaborative assessment of overall learning should become part of the campus culture. Student affairs has the opportunity to take the lead in collaborating with faculty on assessments to build evidence of learning in and out of the classroom. Sharing the results of these assessments can promote discussion and empower both faculty and staff to continue assessment of student learning. Faculty–staff partnerships can help students who need additional support and also help broaden the learning of all students (Eaker & Sells, 2007). Using student surveys, focus groups, observations of student engagement, and other assessment methods might provide useful data for assessing the effectiveness of collaboration and improving the learning environment. For more about assessment as a new professional, see Chapter Six.

Intercultural and Global Awareness

In the last decade, colleges and universities have increasingly addressed the demands of preparing individuals for a diverse, pluralistic, and globalized society (Engberg, 2007; Twombly, Salisbury, Tumanut, & Klute, 2012). As a result, greater numbers of faculty and students engage in programs, courses, and initiatives that involve travel, both domestic and international. The number of U.S. college students engaging in study-abroad opportunities has more than tripled in the last two decades (Institute for International Education, 2013), much of it because of the increase in short-term, faculty-led programs that spring from individual, faculty-initiated activities (Amey, 2010; Barr, 2013). In taking on responsibility for directing these activities, faculty often have to manage multiple roles they're not generally accustomed to. This is an ideal opportunity for collaboration. Goode (2008) identified four distinct dimensions of the role faculty must fulfill in short-term study-abroad programs: logistics, intercultural, academic, and dean of students (which includes elements traditionally addressed by a dean of students office on campus, including social life, physical and mental health, safety, and alcohol use). Of these, faculty view the dean of students dimension as most challenging. Because student affairs professionals are educated, trained, and hired to work with students on campus in these out-of-classroom aspects of the college experience, it makes sense that they function in a similar capacity for off-campus programs as well. According to Barr (2013), "Having staff support from professionals trained to contend with such matters can be paramount to making study abroad programs successful, safe, and positive experiences for everyone involved" (p. 140).

As the number and variety of off-campus study opportunities increase, institutions are deliberately integrating pre- and post-travel components into the entire college learning experience. Although initially intended to help students make the transition to and from their off-campus experience, these elements can also enhance the learning experience. According to Twombly et al. (2012), "Study abroad should fit into the college or university's over-all conception of student learning and development. This means that the experiences in which students engage before and after studying abroad cannot be ignored, minimized, or left to chance" (p. 113). The authors further state,

"We would be remiss to minimize the potentially critical role that student affairs programming could play toward these educational goals" (p. 114).

Table 5.1 summarizes additional intentional ways student affairs professionals can collaborate with their academic colleagues, all of which provide seamless learning environments where students make the most of learning resources that exist both inside and outside of the classroom, and where the curricular and the cocurricular appear to be one whole, continuous experience (ACPA, 1994).

Table 5.1. Opportunities for Collaborative Efforts Between Student Affairs and Academic Affairs

Enrollment management, retention, recruitment, and admissions (Brown, 1990; Martin & Murphy, n.d.)
Precollege enrichment courses, learning support centers
Undergraduate research and other creative opportunities with faculty (Cook & Lewis, 2007)
Freshman-year integration and transition programs, team-taught first-year seminars, linked or clustered courses, common reading programs (Banta & Kuh, 1998; Fried, n.d.; Frost et al., 2010; Garland & Grace, 1993; Kezar, 2009)
Faculty's vocational or career interests incorporated into residential-life programs (Garland & Grace, 1993)
Cooperative education, internships, field experiences (Stein, 2007)
Residential-life programs: Theme housing, freshman-interest groups, living–learning communities, residential communities, faculty-in-residence efforts (Brown, 1990; Fried, n.d.; Martin & Murphy, n.d.; Schroeder, 1999b)
Student conduct and discipline (Dannells, 1997; Garland & Grace, 1993)
Faculty included on unit or departmental advisory boards (Brown, 1990)
Participation in "awareness" events (e.g., Women's History, Alcohol Awareness, Black History)

Table 5.1. Opportunities for Collaborative Efforts Between Student Affairs and Academic Affairs *(Continued)*

Cocurricular transcripts or portfolios (Banta & Kuh, 1998)
Advising student organizations (Brown, 1990)
Involvement with student newspaper and radio (Brown, 1990)
Assessments (Banta & Kuh, 1998)
International and study-abroad programs
Service on faculty governance committees (Brown, 1990)
University day-care centers (Brown, 1990)
New-faculty orientation (Finley, 1996)
Academic support programs, such as study skills labs, writing labs, tutoring, supplemental instruction (Brown, 1990)
Honors college or honors program involvement and involvement with academic honor societies connected to specific majors (Brown, 1990; Cook & Lewis, 2007)
Faculty development workshops (Finley, 1996)
Individual or team teaching (e.g., freshman-experience course, graduate course in college student personnel, undergraduate course) (Cook & Lewis, 2007; Martin & Murphy, n.d.)
Protection of human subjects committees
Early warning or alert systems for students in academic difficulty
Connections between academic programs and course and career choices

Table 5.1. Opportunities for Collaborative Efforts Between Student Affairs and Academic Affairs *(Continued)*

Adventure learning or outdoor programs (e.g., ropes course, wilderness experiences) (Cook & Lewis, 2007)
Response to increased violence and decreased civility on campus (Garland & Grace, 1993)
Long-range planning groups (e.g., space, resources)
Joint appointments in student affairs and on the faculty
Leadership training and coursework on leadership efforts
Community service and service–learning
Consultants for each other
Joint research, joint publications, or joint professional presentations

Collaboration in the Community College Setting

Approximately 50% of all college students attend 2-year and community colleges (American Association of Community Colleges, 2014). Because of their missions, open admissions policies, proximity to the student's home, and affordability, community colleges tend to have the most diverse student populations among postsecondary institutions, including students of color and first-generation students (Cook & Lewis, 2007). Because of this diversity and the need to help these students be successful, faculty and student affairs professionals should collaborate in designing services, programs, and systems to put these students at the center of learning (Shenk & de la Teja, 2007). The results from the 2013 Survey of Entering Student Engagement (SENSE), designed for community and technical colleges, emphasized the importance of engaging students in their first term on campus as a key to retention from first to second term (Center For community Colleges Student Engagement, 2013). Effective collaboration between faculty and student affairs staff helps students feel more supported and engaged (Frost et al., 2010). Therefore, working with faculty in the community college setting to engage students is essential.

With learners at the center of the community college culture, Keeling (2006) suggested it is essential to engage all campus community members in creating experiences that support learning. Student affairs staff can become "dialogue experts" to help bring diverse groups together, stimulate discussion, and promote student learning (Keeling, 2006). The need for intentional collaboration in this environment to identify and assess student learning outcomes among diverse community college learners is critical to addressing student success in a holistic manner. Student affairs staff can help make meaning of the data collected and advocate for students with faculty.

> *Although faculty might not know exactly what I do in my job, the majority of faculty seem willing to work toward a common goal with my department. My experience has been that when they understand the role of student affairs, they are very willing to work with my department.* —Academic advisor at a small 2-year college

In a survey of community college best practices, O'Banion (1997) found that assessment of learning outcomes, involvement of key staff on joint committees, and shared responsibilities are essential elements of successful collaboration. A commitment to ongoing professional staff development, and to identifying ways academic affairs and student affairs might collaborate on student learning are keys to successful collaborations.

Another way to partner with faculty is to help community college students transition from 2-year to 4-year institutions through collaborative advising and orientation programs. New professionals have an opportunity to join faculty in helping students understand how classes, registration, advising, internship, job search, and involvement opportunities might differ at 4-year institutions.

Advice for Building Collaborative Relationships

As *The Student Learning Imperative* (ACPA, 1994) implored, we should attempt to bridge the "functional silos on campus, make seamless what are often perceived by students to be disconnected experiences, and develop collaborative partnerships with faculty and others to enhance student learning. Student affairs staff offer expertise in student characteristics, development and learning, program development, supervision, administration, policy development, networking with diverse groups, conflict mediation, and student conduct (Dannells, 1997; Engstrom & Tinto, 1997). This knowledge and how it benefits students should be promoted to faculty as an incentive to engage in collaborative efforts. Student affairs professionals should emphasize their expertise as educators along with their administrative skills. As Magolda (2005) stated, to be successful these partnerships must be "meaningful, reciprocal, and responsive" (p. 17). Creating effective, collaborative relationships with faculty requires student affairs professionals to connect, find common ground, share a linked vision, develop an action plan, see their perspective, be on their side, and engage in honest self-critique (Ellis, 2009).

> *I expected collaboration to come a lot easier being that I work at a small campus, but that was not the case. There are certain faculty that I interact with a lot more than others so I learned that I needed to make much more of an effort to establish relationships with those that I do not work with regularly.* —Academic advisor at a small 2-year public college

To build effective relationships, we must assess the environment and identify institutional issues that cross the boundaries between academic affairs and student affairs (e.g., retention, assessment). We facilitate collaboration, for example, by building relationships with colleagues in learning centers and advising offices that straddle the functional silos and by developing a shared vision with academic colleagues. By creating cross-functional teams with diverse skills and experiences, we can understand that faculty are people like ourselves and find ways to connect with them. Persistent attempts to connect with faculty, recognizing them publicly for their collaborative efforts toward student learning, and continually identifying those major issues that lend themselves to collaboration will increase our opportunities to work effectively together. We must leave the comfort and security of organizational boundaries and take some appropriate risks (Schroeder, 1999a).

> **To build effective relationships, we must assess the environment and identify institutional issues that cross the boundaries between academic affairs and student affairs (e.g., retention, assessment).**

With faculty and staff, I've found that the variety of train-
ing between administrators and faculty requires that we share a
common thread (that of education). —Assistant director of student
conduct at a private urban liberal arts college

To create seamless environments we should start collaborating on
small projects to achieve some success and then build on them. We should
demonstrate how student affairs programs promote personal and academic
development and engage faculty in discussions about how to make this
an outcome of the academic curriculum as well (Brown, 1999). As Cleary
(2014) described it for the community college setting, strong institutional
leadership can inspire faculty and staff toward the common goal of increasing the number of students who complete college.

Kuh (1996) suggested several ways to create seamless learning environments with faculty: invite faculty members to present research findings at
student affairs staff meetings; have student life and academic deans, as well
as other faculty, attend annual professional conferences together; and hold
occasional joint meetings of senior staff. Finley (1996) recommended finding
faculty allies who appreciate what student affairs brings to the educational
experience by participating in new-faculty orientation and following up,
writing articles for faculty newsletters about services and programs, sending
brief e-mails to keep faculty informed about what's happening in student
affairs, and offering to guest lecture in their classes. Helping faculty access students as research participants and serving on institutional review boards for
the protection of human subjects is another way of developing faculty allies.

Much of the initial interaction with faculty is done by my supervi-
sor as he is well known and well liked across the campus. This
helps tremendously to gain access to departments or individuals
that might otherwise dismiss or ignore me. For new student affairs
professionals, I think it is extremely important to identify an ally
that can help vouch for you when trying to initiate conversations
with faculty and departments. —International programs coordinator at a large public university

Cook and Lewis (2007) offered several tips to help student affairs
practitioners build collaborative partnerships with faculty. Learn to accept
an unequal partnership, for example. New professionals in particular often
expect projects to be carried out on a 50–50 basis, but this is unrealistic. Identify yourself as an educator and not just a logistics person. Be a

spokesperson for active student involvement in academic life (e.g., service–learning, cooperative education, academic honor societies, undergraduate research, field experiences). Ask students which faculty members have influenced them, and use these recommendations to engage those members. Keeling (2004) suggested mapping out where learning opportunities occur to find the intersection of academic affairs and student affairs as an opportunity to discuss partnering on projects and programs.

The opportunities to engage with faculty are numerous. Get involved with the academic side of the institution by taking a class, teaching or co-teaching a class, serving on a committee, participating in joint research, writing, or giving professional presentations. Join activities such as playing "noon ball" or running. Personally invite faculty to be involved in structured, daytime, time-limited tasks in student affairs (e.g., orientation planning, staff screening and selection, conduct boards). Make experiences comfortable for faculty by structuring events so they'll know what to expect, providing an escort to introduce them and show them what to do, or having more than one faculty member present. View every interaction as an opportunity to introduce faculty to the values and goals of your unit and the profession (e.g., serving on advisory boards to your unit or program). Follow through and have fun (Love et al., 1993).

> *I give them specific, manageable requests with very clear goals and tasks so that the task becomes as easy for them as possible.*
> —Assistant director for supplemental instruction at a large public research university

Student affairs professionals often object that they're the ones who always have to approach the faculty; they wish faculty would initiate contact. Considering faculty culture and values, the size of some institutions, or campus culture, that's not likely to happen. We must approach faculty using language they understand and value to build bridges and create effective learning environments for our students. The key to this involvement is persistence.

> *I've learned to take time to explain certain processes so that those in academic affairs develop an understanding of what I do and why I do them to get their support. This also means explaining why things can or cannot be done a certain way due to politics or limitations.* —Coordinator for new student orientation at a midsize urban public university

Although comprehensive research has not been conducted to assess the outcomes of collaboration on student learning, the desired results of improved cognitive, interpersonal, and organizational skills, responsibility for self and community, increased leadership and citizenship, self-understanding, and academic success and retention are worth the effort (Bloland, Stamatakos, & Rogers, 1996).

> **Persistence and optimism with faculty, while maintaining a focus on issues and themes around student learning, will pay big dividends in the end.**

Persistence and optimism with faculty, while maintaining a focus on issues and themes around student learning, will pay big dividends in the end. Although historical, organizational, and cultural obstacles might impede easy progress, the greatest barrier to collaboration with faculty, and the one most within our control, is attitude.

Whitt et al. (2008) researched academic and student affairs partnerships at 18 colleges and identified seven principles of effective collaborations. They should: (a) reflect and advance the institution's mission; (b) embody and foster a learning-oriented ethos; (c) build on and nurture relationships; (d) recognize, understand, and attend to institutional culture; (e) value and implement assessment; (f) use resources creatively and effectively; and (g) demand and cultivate numerous expressions of leadership. New professionals should know the context within which they work, focus on student learning, create partnerships with those faculty they view as allies, participate in assessment, and expect partnerships to require sustained effort. With a focus on these principles in your work, you can create successful, enduring collaborative relationships.

References

American Association of Community Colleges. (2014). Students at community colleges. Retrieved from http://www.aacc.nche.edu/AboutCC/Trends/Pages/studentsatcommunitycolleges.aspx

American Association for Higher Education, American College Personnel Association, & National Association of Student Personnel Administrators. (1998). *Powerful partnerships: A shared responsibility for learning.* Washington, DC: Author.

American College Personnel Association. (1994). *The student learning imperative: Implications for student affairs.* Washington, DC: Author.

American College Personnel Association & National Association of Student Personnel Administrators. (1997). *Principles of good practice for student affairs.* Washington, DC: Authors.

American College Personnel Association & National Association of Student Personnel Administrators Task Force on the Future of Student Affairs. (2010). *Envisioning the future of student affairs.* Retrieved from http://www.naspa.org/images/uploads/main/Task_Force_Student_Affairs_2010_Report.pdf

Amey, M. J. (2010). Administrative perspectives on international partnerships. In P. L. Eddy (Ed.), *International collaborations: Opportunities, strategies, challenges* (New Directions for Higher Education, No. 105, pp. 57–67). San Francisco, CA: Jossey-Bass.

Astin, A. (1985). *Achieving education excellence: A critical assessment of priorities and practices in higher education.* San Francisco, CA: Jossey-Bass.

Austin, A. E., & Sorcinelli, M. D. (2013). The future of faculty development: Where are we going? In C. W. McKee, M. Johnson, W. F. Ritchie, & W. M. Tew (Eds.), *Special issue: The breadth of current faculty development: Practitioners' perspectives* (New Directions for Teaching and Learning, No. 133, pp. 85–97). San Francisco, CA: Jossey-Bass.

Banta, T. W., & Kuh, G. D. (1998). A missing link in assessment. *Change, 30,* 40–46.

Barr, M. J. (2000). The importance of institutional mission. In M. J. Barr & M. K. Desler (Eds.), *The handbook of student affairs administration* (2nd ed., pp. 25–36). San Francisco, CA: Jossey-Bass.

Barr, T. F. (2013). Utilizing student affairs professionals to enhance student and faculty experiences and mitigate risk in short-term, faculty-led study abroad programs. *Journal of International Education in Business, 6*(2), 136–147. doi:10.1108/JIEB-05-2013-0019

Bloland, P. A., Stamatakos, L. C., & Rogers, R. R. (1996). Redirecting the role of student affairs to focus on student learning. *Journal of College Student Development, 37,* 217–226.

Bourassa, D. M., & Kruger, K. (2001). The national dialogue on academic and student affairs collaboration. In A. Kezar, D. J. Hirsch, & C. Burack (Eds.), *Special issue: Understanding the role of academic and student affairs collaboration in creating a successful learning environment* (New Directions for Higher Education, No. 116, pp. 9–38). San Francisco, CA: Jossey-Bass.

Brown, R. D. (1999). Shaping the future. *ACPA Developments, 25*(1), 16.

Brown, S. S. (1990). Strengthening ties to academic affairs. In M. J. Barr & M. L. Upcraft (Eds.), *New futures for student affairs* (pp. 239–269). San Francisco, CA: Jossey-Bass.

Center for Community Colleges Student Engagement. (2013). *Survey of entering student engagement.* Retrieved from http://www.ccsse.org/sense/survey/survey.cfm

Cleary, K. (2014). Realizing the promise of community colleges: From access to completion. *Leadership Exchange, 12,* 20–24.

Collaboration. (n.d.) In *Merriam-Webster's online dictionary* (11th ed.). Retrieved from http://www.merriam-webster.com/dictionary/collaboration.

Cook, J. H., & Lewis, C. A. (Eds.) (2007). *Student affairs and academic affairs collaboration: The divine comity.* Washington, DC: National Association of Student Personnel Administrators.

Cook, J. H., Ghering, A. M., & Lewis, C. A. (2007). Divine comity: The basics. In J. H. Cook & C. A. Lewis (Eds.), *Student affairs and academic affairs collaboration: The divine comity* (pp. 1–15). Washington, DC: National Association of Student Personnel Administrators.

Dannells, M. (1997). *From discipline to development: Rethinking student conduct in higher education* (ASHE-ERIC Higher Education Report, 25[2]). San Francisco, CA: Jossey-Bass.

Eaker, R. E., & Sells, D. K. (2007). Circle five: Mutual understanding through frequent communication. In J. Cook & C. Lewis (Eds.), *Student affairs and academic affairs collaboration: The divine comity* (pp. 105–116). Washington, DC: National Association of Student Personnel Administrators.

Eimers, M. T. (1999). Working with faculty from diverse disciplines. *About Campus, 4,* 18–24.

Ellis, S. (2009). Developing effective relationships on campus and in the community. In G. McClellan & J. Stringer (Eds.), *The handbook of student affairs administration* (5th ed., pp. 455–457). San Francisco, CA: Jossey-Bass.

Engberg, M. E. (2007). Educating the workforce for the 21st century: A cross-disciplinary analysis of the impact of the undergraduate experience on students' development of a pluralistic orientation. *Research in Higher Education, 48*(3), 283–317. doi:10.1007/s11162-006-9027-2

Engstrom, C. M., & Tinto, V. (1997). Working together for service learning. *About Campus, 2,* 10–15.

Engstrom, C. M., & Tinto, V. (2000). Developing partnerships with academic affairs to enhance student learning. In M. Barr & M. Desler (Eds.), *The handbook of student affairs administration* (4th ed., pp. 425–452). San Francisco, CA: Jossey-Bass.

Finley, D. (1996, March). Faculty and student services: Friends or foes. Paper presented at the annual convention of the American College Personnel Association, Baltimore, MD.

Fried, J. (n.d.). *Steps to creative campus collaboration* [Invited paper]. Washington, DC: National Association of Student Personnel Administrators.

Frost, R., Strom, S., Downey, J., Schultz, D., & Holland, T. (2010). Enhancing student learning with academic and student affairs collaboration. *Community College Enterprise, 16*(1), 37–51.

Gaff, J. G. (1983). *General education today: A critical analysis of controversies, practices, and reforms.* San Francisco, CA: Jossey-Bass.

Garland, P. H., & Grace, T. W. (1993). *New perspectives for student affairs professionals: Evolving realities, responsibilities, and roles* (ASHE-ERIC Higher Education Report, Vol. 2, No. 7). San Francisco, CA: Jossey-Bass.

Goode, M. L. (2008). The role of faculty study abroad directors: A case study. *Frontiers: The Interdisciplinary Journal of Study Abroad, 15,* 149–172.

Hirt, J. B. (2006). *Where you work matters: Student affairs administration in different types of institutions.* Washington, DC: American College Personnel Association.

Hossler, D. (2001). Reflections on the scholarship of application in student affairs. *Journal of College Student Development, 42,* 356–358.

Institute for International Education. (2013). *Open doors 2013: Fast facts.* Retrieved from http://www.iie.org/Research-and-Publications/Open-Doors

Johnson, C. S., & Cheatham, H. E. (Eds.). (1999). *Higher education trends for the next century: A research agenda for student success.* Washington, DC: American College Personnel Association.

Johnson, G., & Rayman, J. R. (2007). e-Portfolios: A collaboration between student affairs and faculty. In J. W. Garis & J. C. Dalton (Eds.), *Special issue: e-Portfolios: Emerging opportunities for student affairs* (New Directions for Student Services, No. 119, pp. 17–30). San Francisco, CA: Jossey-Bass.

Keeling, R. P. (Ed.). (2004) *Learning reconsidered: A campus-wide focus on the student experience.* Washington, DC: American College Personnel Association and National Association of Student Personnel Administrators.

Keeling, R. P. (Ed.). (2006) *Learning reconsidered 2: A practical guide to implementing a campus-wide focus on the student experience.* Washington, DC: American College Personnel Association, Association of College and University Housing Officers–International, Association of College Unions International, National Academic Advising Association, National Association of Campus Activities, National Association of Student Personnel Administrators, and National Intramural–Recreational Sports Association.

Keeling, R. P., Wall, A. F., Underhile, R., & Dungy, G. J. (Eds.). (2008). *Assessment reconsidered: institutional effectiveness for student success.* Washington, DC: International Center for Student Success and Institutional Accountability.

Kezar, A. (2009). Supporting and enhancing student learning through partnerships with academic colleagues. In G. McClellan & J. Stringer (Eds.), *The handbook of student affairs administration* (5th ed., pp. 455–457). San Francisco, CA: Jossey-Bass.

Kuh, G. D. (1996). Guiding principles for creating seamless learning environments for undergraduates. *Journal of College Student Development, 37,* 135–148.

Kuh, G. D. (2009). What student affairs professionals need to know about student engagement. *Journal of College Student Development, 50*(6), 683–706. doi:10.1353/csd.0.0099

Kuh, G. D., Schuh, J. H., & Whitt, E. J. (1991). *Involving colleges: Successful approaches to fostering student learning and development outside the classroom.* San Francisco, CA: Jossey-Bass.

Love, P., Kuh, G. D., MacKay, K. A., & Hardy, C. M. (1993). Side by side: Faculty and student affairs cultures. In G. D. Kuh (Ed.), *Cultural perspectives in student affairs work* (pp. 37–58). Washington, DC: American College Personnel Association.

Magolda, P. M. (2005, January/February). Proceed with caution: Uncommon wisdom about academic and student affairs partnerships. *About Campus, 6,* 16–21.

Manning, K., Kinzie, J., & Schuh, J. (2014). *One size does not fit all: Traditional and innovative models of student affairs practice* (2nd ed.). New York, NY: Routledge.

Martin, J., & Murphy, S. (n.d.). *Building better bridges: Creating effective partnerships between academic affairs and student affairs* [Invited paper]. Washington, DC: National Association of Student Personnel Administrators.

Masterson, J. (2008). Academic/student affairs partnerships in residential settings: Principles and practices. In G. Luna & J. Gahagan (Eds.), *Learning initiatives in residential settings* (Monograph No. 48, pp. 19–28). Columbia, SC: University of South Carolina, National Resource Center for the First-Year Experience and Student in Transition.

Nesheim, B., Guentzel, M., Kellogg, A., McDonald, W., Wells, C., & Whitt, E. (2007). Outcomes for students of student affairs–academic affairs partnership programs. *Journal of College Student Development, 48*(4), 435–454. doi: 10.1353/csd.2007.0041

Newman, F., Couturier, L., & Scurry, J. (2004). *The future of higher education: Rhetoric, reality, and the risks of the market.* San Francisco, CA: Jossey-Bass.

O'Banion, T. (1997). *A learning college for the 21ˢᵗ century.* Phoenix, AZ: Oryx Press.

Philpott, J., & Strange, C. (2003). "On the road to Cambridge": A case study of faculty and student affairs in collaboration. *Journal of Higher Education, 74*(1), 77–95. doi: 10.1353/jhe.2003.0003

Price, J. (1999). Merging with academic affairs: A promotion or demotion for student affairs? In J. H. Schuh & E. J. Whitt (Eds.), *Creating successful partnerships between academic and student affairs* (New Directions for Student Services, No. 87, pp. 75–83). San Francisco, CA: Jossey-Bass.

Sandeen, A. (2004). Educating the whole student: The growing academic importance of student affairs. *Change: The Magazine of Higher Learning, 36*(3), 28–33. doi: 10.1080/00091380409605577

Schroeder, C. C. (1999a). Forging educational partnerships that advance student learning. In G. S. Blimling & E. J. Whitt (Eds.), *Good practice in student affairs: Principles to foster student learning* (pp. 133–156). San Francisco, CA: Jossey-Bass.

Schroeder, C. C. (1999b). Partnerships: An imperative for enhancing student learning and institutional effectiveness. In J. H. Schuh & E. J. Whitt (Eds.), *Creating successful partnerships between academic and student affairs* (New Directions for Student Services, No. 87, pp. 5–18). San Francisco, CA: Jossey-Bass.

Shenk, E. J., & de la Teja, M. H. (2007). Collaboration in the community college. In J. Cook & C. Lewis (Eds.), *Student affairs and academic affairs collaboration: The divine comity* (pp. 201–238). Washington, DC: National Association of Student Personnel Administrators.

Stein, J. (2007). Circle six: Service–learning as crossroads. In J. Cook, & C. Lewis (Eds.), *Student affairs and academic affairs collaboration: The divine comity* (pp. 117–154). Washington, DC: National Association of Student Personnel Administrators.

Stewart, D. (2008). The role of the faculty in the residential setting. In G. Luna & J. Gahagan (Eds.), *Learning initiatives in residential settings* [Monograph No. 48, pp. 55–62]. Columbia, SC: University of South Carolina, National Resource Center for the First-Year Experience and Student in Transition.

Twombly, S. B., Salisbury, M. H., Tumanut, S. D., & Klute, P. (2012). *Special issue: Study abroad in a new global century—renewing the promise, refining the purpose* (ASHE Higher Education Report, Vol. 38, No. 4). San Francisco, CA: Jossey-Bass.

Whitt, E. J., Nesheim, B., Guentzel, M., Kellogg, A., McDonald, W., & Wells, C. (2008). "Principles of good practice" for academic and student affairs partnership programs. *Journal of College Student Development, 49*(3), 235–249. doi: 10.1353/csd.0.0007

Winter, R. (2009). Academic manager or managed academic? Academic identity schisms in higher education. *Journal of Higher Education Policy and Management. 31*(2), 121–131. doi:10.1080/13600800902825835

ASSESSMENT IN STUDENT AFFAIRS PRACTICE

CHAPTER SIX

Matthew R. Wawrzynski, Ashleigh Brock, and Austin Sweeney

Although it might be a developing skill, assessment should be a familiar term to new student affairs professionals. The field of student affairs has long placed value on assessment as an important part of good practice. For more than 75 years, *The Student Personnel Point of View* (American Council on Education [ACE], 1937), one of student affairs' seminal documents, has explicitly called on student affairs educators to research and evaluate the programs and services offered under their umbrella. More recently, the American College Personnel Association (ACPA) and the National Association of Student Personnel Administrators (NASPA) jointly created *Professional Competency Areas for Student Affairs Professionals* (ACPA & NASPA, 2010) that outlines the knowledge, skills, and competencies expected of student affairs professionals today. Anyone who has worked in student affairs or is graduating from a student affairs graduate program knows that student affairs educators are expected to have a basic knowledge and understanding of assessment. That the two largest student affairs organizations jointly advocated for basic student affairs assessment skills is a telling sign of its importance today. Yet, professionals beginning their journey in the student affairs field, anxious to apply what they have learned in graduate school, are often surprised that not everyone is enthusiastic or knowledgeable about conducting student affairs assessment.

Take, for example, the following story. After their student affairs summer internships, second-year master's students reflected on their summer experiences in their professional development class. Many recounted the positive experiences they had applying theory to practice, but at the same time, they were surprised that after the first few days of their internship discussing student learning outcomes for their events, most of their time was spent on logistics of events and programs and much less on assessing the learning. One posed the following question to the rest of the group:

> *So, if assessment is such a vital component of measuring student learning, why don't more student affairs professionals engage in assessing student learning and outcomes?*

Student affairs educators engage in assessment for two main purposes: accountability and the need to improve the cocurricular experiences for students who use the programs and services. Student affairs, similar to other parts of higher education, is accountable to accrediting agencies and stakeholders who seek justification for the resources used and to demonstrate the value added to the student experience (Hoffman & Bresciani, 2010). Unfortunately, when top-level administrators mandate assessment activities only for accountability measures, these efforts appear to be afterthoughts to student affairs professionals, rendering assessment of student learning secondary or tertiary. When assessment is initiated via mandate, rather than organically within a student affairs unit, educators might retrofit activities and programs to a prescribed set of desirable outcomes for accreditation purposes. Certainly, collecting evidence to demonstrate accountability to stakeholders is important (Schuh, 2013), but we believe assessing in order to understand and improve the quality of student learning is of equal value for student affairs professionals.

Student affairs assessment must be a part of student affairs culture.

To this second purpose, student affairs assessment must be a part of student affairs culture. Assessment should be as much a component of every student affairs professional's *daily* (yes, daily!) activities as meetings and other responsibilities. Those fortunate to work in environments where assessment is a valued part of the student affairs culture realize the benefits. A recent graduate from a student affairs master's program shared the following story after a student life and activities departmental retreat:

> *At the retreat, the director of our department (who was also newly hired) informed me and the other six assistant directors (ADs) that the office would be engaged in assessing the learning outcomes for our office (a task that seemed to be a new concept based on everyone's reaction). I was told that ADs needed to keep count of students who attended programs, and that seemed to work just fine for previous assessment efforts. I was dumbfounded when my seasoned colleagues met the director's announcement with blank stares. When I was a graduate student, I was engaged in the assessment efforts for the office where I held my graduate assistantship. So, I was really excited about building on my knowledge of assessment here, but as I looked around at my colleagues seated at the table, everyone was afraid of making eye contact with the director because they might be asked to conduct the assessment.* —Student activities professional at a large public university

Some student affairs professionals, like the six ADs in this scenario, view student affairs assessment as a daunting task that might be found under the "other duties as assigned" clause of many job descriptions, thus becoming just one more responsibility in an already overloaded schedule. Still other student affairs professionals view assessment as making sense of large, nationally collected data that isn't helpful, doesn't assess student affairs efforts or effectiveness, and isn't directly relevant to student affairs practice.

Such skepticism, though not common, hinders necessary engagement in student affairs assessment, which is at the core of this chapter's message. We begin with a definition of student affairs assessment. We then discuss common reasons assessments are not implemented, followed by the benefits of assessments. The chapter concludes with a set of practical tips for successful assessment, case studies to consider, and resources to use in your assessment efforts.

What is Assessment?

Many scholars have tried defining assessment and have noted confusion over various terms such as *research, evaluation,* and *assessment* (see, e.g., Schuh & Upcraft, 2001). Student affairs professionals need not be concerned about the nuances of each differing definition of these terms but should focus on demonstrating the value their programs and services add to student learning and other outcomes. For the purposes of this chapter, we adopted Blimling's (2013) definition of assessment in student affairs: "the process of collecting and analyzing information to improve the conditions of student life, student learning, or the quality and efficiency of services and programs provided for students" (p. 5). Using this definition to guide assessment efforts will most likely result in collecting data that can be used in other endeavors (e.g., accountability and accreditation). Data can be collected in as varied means as there are people doing the collecting. Assessment must go beyond developing questions at the last minute and talking to a few students or e-mailing students a Web address to complete a survey. Perhaps most important in conducting assessment is the intentionality you have for what is to be assessed. Student affairs assessment efforts must be purposeful and strategic, guided by the needs, interests, or outcomes being measured.

Reasons Student Affairs Professionals Do Not Engage in Assessment

In a 1978 article, which is still relevant almost four decades later, Louis Stamatakos cautioned new professionals from doing things just because they have always been done. In the same manner, we caution new professionals not to fall into the "we just don't do assessment here" trap. Avoiding this trap requires awareness of its signs and symptoms. Following are 10 reasons we have heard over the years that student affairs professionals do not engage in assessment.

1. **It takes too much time.** Perhaps the most frequently cited reason for not implementing student affairs assessment is the lack of time. If you're unable to think of how you could possibly fit one more responsibility into your already packed work week, then it could be beneficial to explore strategies for altering your professional time commitments. For example, talk to your supervisor about shifting committee responsibilities in order to devote more time to assessment initiatives. If you supervise a staff, delegate responsibilities

that aren't absolutely necessary for you to handle directly, freeing up time for assessment. Most student affairs educators agree they spend an exorbitant amount of time implementing programs and services for students. Yet, failing to assess programs and services makes it challenging, if not impossible, to demonstrate whether students are learning or that student affairs professionals add value to the student experience. Be intentional and schedule time to develop a plan for student affairs assessment on a weekly basis.

2. **I don't know where to begin.** Beginning any new professional experience can be daunting at first. On the bright side, you're not the first student affairs professional to face this dilemma. At the end of this chapter is a list of resources to engage you in your assessment efforts. You might also find the 11-step process for assessment developed by Schuh and Upcraft (2001) helpful for your assessment efforts (see Table 6.1).

3. **I don't know how to decide what to assess.** The learning outcomes and domains found in the most recent edition of *Professional Standards for Higher Education* (Council for the Advancement of Standards in Higher Education [CAS], 2012), *Learning Reconsidered* (Keeling, 2004), and *Learning Reconsidered 2* (Keeling, 2006) serve as excellent foundations for developing specific outcomes for almost any experience you might assess. Seek out and read existing literature; stay abreast of what's happening in the student affairs field. Whether through your membership in a student affairs professional organization or by using databases at your institution's library, you can access countless articles and reports on useful assessments and their results.

4. **I don't know the best way to collect the data.** There isn't always a "best way" but rather multiple ways you can accomplish your assessment goals. Different methods are likely to yield different types of results, which might be needed to holistically assess your programs or services. When multiple strategies for collecting data are employed, results can be triangulated, meaning that you're able to confirm what you have found through more than one method (e.g., focus group, reflection paper, survey).

5. **I don't know what to do next.** Collecting the data you need might be the easiest part of the student affairs assessment process. The real challenge is deciding what to do after the data are collected.

Many student affairs divisions and departments sit on mountains of data collected with good intentions but never analyzed, reported on, or used to implement or improve programs and services. When you set out to conduct an assessment, make sure you have developed a plan for what comes next: how you'll share the data and results, with whom, and for what purposes.

6. **What if I can't prove our programs are making the difference that I believe they are making?** Assessment doesn't always yield the outcome you hoped for. The data that you do collect, however, still have meaning. Analysis is a key component of Blimling's (2013) definition of student affairs assessment. When your results don't align with student learning outcomes or goals set prior to assessing, review your methods and consider why your predictions don't line up with the data. Consider assessing the same program or student group using different methods (e.g., moving from a quantitative survey collection approach to a qualitative focus-group approach). Utilizing multiple assessment methods for the same population or program allows you to triangulate your results. You can also collect data during more than one year or cycle, which enables you to examine trends in your data and draw additional conclusions not possible with a single assessment effort.

7. **My supervisor doesn't value student affairs assessment efforts.** Assessment is a political process that you'll need to learn to navigate. You are in the process of developing your professional identity and philosophy for your career in student affairs. In doing so, you'll be exposed to a number of different philosophies and you'll need to decide whether you want to adopt, adapt, or negate them as part of your developing philosophy. Consider the sphere of influence you have—remember, you were probably not hired to maintain the status quo, but that doesn't mean that you were hired to change an entire department's culture, either. You can still work to assess the programs and services you oversee. Additionally, ask several people how student affairs assessment is valued, supported, and conducted in your on-campus interview. If you've already landed your first full-time position, talk with your colleagues, both in and outside your office, about where or if assessment fits into your shared work.

8. **The results won't be used, so what's the point?** If the point of conducting assessment is to collect and analyze information to improve student learning and programs, then assessment efforts "count," even if you're not being held immediately accountable for the data you collect. Depending on what you find or how busy your office is when you collect and analyze the data, not everyone will eagerly seek your results. That's okay! There's still value in assessing a program or the learning outcomes tied to your programs, because ultimately *you* will use the results to grow and improve in the work that you do.

9. **It's not my job!** It's true. Assessment might not have been directly stated as one of the requirements in your job description. But knowing the value and influence of your efforts and being able to support your work with data shows your supervisor, department, or division what you bring to the team. Although you might not be required to assess your work as dictated by your job description or supervisor, accreditation requirements, changes in campus leadership, or other mitigating factors might come into play during the tenure in your position. Collected data can be helpful or even vital to proving your value or your department's value within student affairs or your institution more broadly.

10. **I am not trained to "do" assessment.** The emphasis graduate programs, internships, and assistantships place on the importance of assessments might vary widely for new student affairs professionals. As a result, student affairs professionals enter the field with varying levels of comfort about and knowledge of assessment processes and practices. If you're in a role where assessing your work would be valuable but you're not equipped with the skills or knowledge to do so effectively, seek assistance. Many professional colleagues can help get you started. (See p. 142 for a list of useful resources.)

Benefits of Assessment

Have you ever seen a sensible program or policy change get turned down, even though you instinctively or anecdotally knew it would benefit students? Oftentimes good ideas don't come to fruition because decision makers say there isn't enough evidence. Working past any initial fears and engaging in assessment practices helps give professionals at all levels the data often needed to bring about meaningful change.

In addition to better understanding and serving students, conducting assessments has many other benefits in gaining valuable professional experience. We hope the following benefits serve as motivation to keep persisting in your efforts.

Conveying Value and Promoting Intentional Practice

In order for student affairs to remain an essential and relevant piece of the increasingly complex higher education puzzle, student affairs professionals must consistently convey that they improve on the work they do (Keeling, 2006; Schuh & Gansemer-Topf, 2010). Engaging in assessment simultaneously allows student affairs professionals to convey their merit through data and be more intentional in their student development work. Assessment can promote intentional practice by creating learning outcomes that infuse purpose, goals, and direction into what we do. Just as helpful as data that convey we're meeting goals are results that convey we're falling short. Information serves as a platform from which to improve on prior efforts.

Effectively Managing Fiscal Resources

In a time when departments are often challenged to support students while being fiscally efficient (Dungy & Gordon, 2010), assessment can serve as a tool for identifying areas that merit more or less funding. For example, if a TRIO program were to create and assess learning outcomes for all of its academic support initiatives, it would likely discover which initiatives were successful and which fell short of meeting desired outcomes. Such assessment results can inform departmental decisions on the most sensible resources to discontinue or reallocate if put in a position to cut expenses.

Becoming an Expert on Students and Campus Culture

Assessment is an effective way for professionals to become experts on students and their needs. Student affairs professionals at all levels share the responsibility of knowing and supporting students personally and holistically, which contributes to their persistence and success in college (Sedlacek, 2004). Assessing students' learning, sense of belonging, and motivation allows for a comprehensive understanding of how they are succeeding and where greater challenge or support is needed. Assessment can enhance what is known about students' successes and failures and allow student affairs professionals to communicate valuable information to other campus divisions.

Assessment also provides insight into important details about students' experiences and can convey their perceptions of campus culture (e.g., how students feel included or excluded, feeling of connection to the institution, student–faculty relationships). To this end, assessment initiatives can help new professionals develop strong insights into the culture of their department or campus, which is important when working with students, colleagues, and campus partners. For example, a professional working with health and wellness education would benefit from using a campus climate survey to inform decisions on what programs and topics to offer with certain student populations and the most effective means of content delivery (e.g., social media, a peer education workshop, posters).

Skills for Strategic Planning

Developing skills in assessment gives you the ability to establish and evaluate goals and to make informed decisions rooted in data. Having this ability to create and improve departmental or campus initiatives is a key aspect of effectively participating in strategic

> **Developing skills in assessment gives you the ability to establish and evaluate goals and to make informed decisions rooted in data.**

planning. Depending on the size of the institution, you might not always sit at the table as part of the strategic planning for your department, division, or institution; however, if you become involved with and convey an aptitude for assessment at any level, you'll be a logical choice to be selected to contribute to important initiatives.

Providing Purpose for Students

Student affairs professionals often work with bright and inquisitive student leaders who regularly ask challenging questions and seek to make well-reasoned decisions. To this end, analyzing assessment results, using them to make decisions, and intentionally sharing this process and reasoning with student leaders lend deeper meaning and purpose to what the organization and staff want to accomplish.

Take the following example of how analyzing results from assessment can be helpful in student affairs practice. A residence hall director (RD) assesses his residence hall students' comfort with approaching their resident assistant (RA) with an issue. The RD learns that the one meeting that RAs are required to have with their residents doesn't develop the support net for students who have transition concerns and issues. The RD proposes to the RA staff that they increase their required one-on-one meetings with residents from one meeting per semester to two. If the RD mandates the meetings without collecting the data and providing some context, the RAs could understandably become frustrated and confused. However, if assessment results convey that residents feel most supported when interacting one-on-one with their RAs, then this evidence helps secure RA buy-in for the change in expectations. In addition to better engaging with student leaders, assessment results also can help new professionals better understand who the uninvolved students are and how to better engage them.

Setting and Improving on Goals

Developing learning outcomes allows a department to establish and use measurable goals. Assessing learning outcomes and analyzing results help student affairs professionals go beyond anecdotal evidence to determine whether goals are being actualized. Once student affairs professionals know whether their goals are being met, they can improve those areas that fall short of desired expectations.

Improving Processes and Policies

The need to alter processes and policies or develop physical spaces on campus often seems obvious. However, such ideas can be easily rejected if they're not grounded in substantial reasoning. Along with understanding and supporting student learning, assessment can help a department develop the reasoning needed to improve its processes and policies.

For example, a residential life department considering gender-inclusive restrooms should assess students' value of inclusivity to identify the possible effects such an initiative might have. In this sense, assessment can be a tool for guiding policy improvements. Assessment results give professionals information for making a meaningful change or deciding that a change isn't necessary.

Becoming a Leader Early

New professionals who effectively practice and promote assessment in their department might be invited to lead or serve on committees at a much earlier stage in their career, especially if the culture of assessment is not developed. If you choose to take the initiative with assessment in your department, though, start at a manageable level. For example, if you're a career counselor and want to implement assessment of advising meetings in your department, start with piloting the assessment in your own meetings. Such an assessment could gauge whether students are feeling heard, supported, challenged, and better able to articulate their vocational goals. From there, you can improve your assessment methods and work to expand them in your department.

Aligning Programs and Services With Missions

Earlier we mentioned that when student affairs assessment is done only for the sake of accreditation, programs and activities are often retrofitted to align with a set of desirable outcomes, which presumably align with the institution's mission. Make no mistake: Conducting assessment is important for resource allocation and accreditation. But how would student affairs assessment be perceived if all programs and services in your office were aligned with your student affairs functional area department mission, student affairs division mission, and institutional mission, rather being retrofitted to conform to them? The authors of *The Student Personnel Point of View* have long argued a guiding principle of student affairs educators is to support the academic mission of the institution (ACE, 1937). The thoughtful and intentional alignment of our programs to the various missions is one way of supporting the academic mission.

Practical Tips for Successful Assessment

We believe you can and should incorporate assessment into your day-to-day work, thus establishing a personal commitment to assessing your efforts throughout your career in the field. We do not, however, expect you'll become an assessment whiz overnight! The following tips and suggestions will help you begin your assessment journey and continue to build skills and knowledge in student affairs assessment methods in your first job.

Start Small and Manageable

Don't feel as though you need to immediately assess the entire out-of-class student experience. Aim for small successes; success builds confidence.

If you don't yet have major programs or initiatives to assess, begin by reviewing your department, division, and institutional mission, vision, and values. These documents provide key terms and foundations for developing learning outcomes and help you think strategically about how your work connects to each level of your institution.

Start With You

Early in your career, assessment might not be a central feature of (or even in) your job description. But your own performance is one of the most important things you can assess, and doing so will help you develop key skills for using assessment methods throughout your career.

☞ Create annual goals for yourself and phrase them as learning outcomes, making sure they are measurable and mix both quantifiable and qualitative methods.

☞ Ask your supervisor about performance measures and consider how you can develop methods for determining whether you've met or exceeded expectations in your role.

☞ Sometimes not being *required* to assess learning makes the process easier and takes away some of the pressure. Consider a program or event you manage. How can you develop a simple assessment technique to gauge its success?

Theory to Practice

You have spent countless hours reading articles and books and writing papers in your graduate program. When it comes to assessment, don't forget about the literature. Chances are good that if you're considering assessing a particular aspect of student learning or a type of program, someone else has asked similar questions in research. Gaining a sense of whether similar work has been done by reviewing the literature can greatly inform your methods.

Ask About Available Assessment Tools

Some colleges and universities have offices or departments devoted to institutional effectiveness or assessment. If such a department exists on your campus, ask whether online assessment tools are available for your use.

Such resources are often accompanied by free training programs to teach faculty and student affairs professionals how to use assessment tools effectively. In addition, your institution might collect campuswide data using a national survey, such as the National Survey of Student Engagement or the Cooperative Institutional Research Program's Freshman Survey. If surveys like these are already in use, you might be able to add institution-specific questions so as not to invent new surveys that compete with students' time.

> **As you adapt to your new department and institution, network with people on your campus who take assessment seriously and do it well.**

Find an Assessment Mentor

Adopting a robust assessment agenda is daunting for a new professional. As you adapt to your new department and institution, network with people on your campus who take assessment seriously and do it well. Foster connections with professionals who integrate assessment into their professional practice and seek their mentorship as you get started.

Attend Assessment-focused Programs and Presentations

Assessment is a highly discussed and featured topic in higher education. Many professional organizations and institutions alike offer webinars, drive-in conferences, and program presentations during annual meetings and conventions to explore and explain the many types, tools, and ways assessment is used in student affairs. Seek opportunities to engage in professional development through professional organizations, both inside your institution and outside, to learn about assessment techniques and tools that fit your needs and role.

Take the Initiative

Despite the many resources that prepare student affairs professionals to use assessment tools effectively, many professionals avoid taking on assessment-related projects. Getting involved in how your department or division assesses its work—from individual programs to large-scale, campuswide climate studies—is one of the best ways to know your student population, your assessment-focused colleagues, and your institution. When opportunities arise within your department or student affairs division to support assessment efforts, volunteer to collect data, or participate in committee work related to assessment initiatives, take the initiative.

Share Your Results and Seek Feedback

One step in assessment that student affairs educators often overlook is making results known. One successful strategy in disseminating results comes from an assistant director of residence life who had specific responsibilities for assessing the residential experience for students. The department engaged in multiple assessments throughout the year, starting with assessing expectations for college from first-year students in their first week on campus. After each assessment, the AD provided the highlights (and lowlights) of the data in a newsletter report to other student affairs professionals (e.g., admissions counselors), academic staff (e.g., academic advisors), faculty, and members of the president's cabinet. The goal was to provide a snapshot of students' experiences in the residence halls to other interested parties on campus. Informing others was a win–win situation for the department: First, the AD was able to discuss what students expected of their college experience. Second, the institution learned valuable information about its students. At the end of the spring semester, one assessment asked students to list individuals at the university who had a positive influence on their experiences. The AD looked up the names and campus addresses of everyone who was named (more than 3,000!) and sent them and their supervisor a letter explaining they were one of the individuals mentioned by students. Now that is a powerful way to share results. Unfortunately, when the AD retired, the culture of assessment wasn't embedded with other colleagues to carry on the dissemination of results.

Look for Collaborators

We cannot underscore enough the importance of collaboration with colleagues on campus both in and outside of student affairs. Partnering with colleagues within your department or division means more than one person is reviewing assessment methods, noting missing items, highlighting needed changes, and seeing the possibility of bias. Working with others on assessment projects can also help make initiatives more manageable within a hectic work schedule. Assessment projects can help you build bridges across campus and into other functional areas. A career advisor assigned to work with first-year students, for example, recognized that a needs assessment among this population resulted in lots of interesting information about students' academic advising experiences. Sharing results with colleagues in academic advising and with academic deans allowed the career advisor to strengthen existing partnerships between the career center and those offices and to forge new relationships with professionals on campus.

You Will Make Mistakes

As with any new skill you develop, the only universal truth about student affairs assessment is that you'll certainly make mistakes. All of us do! Don't let the fear of "messing up" or not going about assessment in the "right" way stop you from making the effort. As you gain experience with assessment and the many methods and processes therein, you'll gain confidence, learn from mistakes, and develop habits for your own best practices.

Developing Learning Outcomes

In the spirit of addressing the fear of making assessment mistakes, one aspect of the evaluation process that can be particularly scary is developing learning outcomes. Fear not, as any professional with the ability to do a little bit of planning and reflection can create high-quality outcomes to work toward and achieve. Additionally, numerous resources and examples pertaining to learning outcomes already exist, among them the learning domains found in CAS's (2012) *Professional Standards for Higher Education*. You should never be in a position to create outcomes without guidance. The following are some tips and valuable resources for creating learning outcomes in your work.

Before wading into this information, though, have a clear definition of what a learning outcome is. We define a learning outcome as a written statement that specifically communicates what the successful student or learner is expected to know or be able to do as a result of a learning experience (e.g., module, course, training, leadership role). Like assessment in general, learning outcomes should support the mission of the institution and department, embed the work of student affairs in learning, and be measurable.

Know What You Want To Know

As emphasized by Schuh and Upcraft (2001), it's important for the assessment process to start assessment initiatives by asking, What do we want to know and achieve, and how will we know if we have achieved it?

Once this question is answered, you should be able to articulate your learning outcomes and the means for assessing them. Each goal should have its own outcome; having more than one goal in an outcome hinders your ability to clearly assess the outcome and interpret results. For example, potential learning outcomes for a student leadership retreat you facilitate might include: Students will enhance their ability to facilitate group conversations as leaders and develop one long-term goal for an organization in which they are involved. When each of these goals are tied to its own learning outcome, assessing whether the students achieved none, one, or both of the outcomes allows you to effectively discern which outcomes are or are not achieved.

Learning outcomes in student affairs vary as widely as the functional areas that comprise our profession and might focus more on non-cognitive outcomes or variables (i.e., nonacademic performance characteristics that contribute to student learning, success, and persistence). Examples of these variables are being connected to a community on campus, ability to apply knowledge in one area of involvement to another, ability to articulate one's strengths and weaknesses, and having access to a strong support person (Wawrzynski & Beverly, 2012; Wawrzynski, Heck, & Remley, 2012; Wawrzynski & Sedlacek, 2003). As student affairs professionals, these non-cognitive variables are often at the core of our efforts to support students. Therefore, being mindful of these variables when creating learning outcomes is logical.

Which Comes First?

A critical question in developing learning outcomes and planning programs is, Which comes first, the outcome or the program? Do we tailor our initiatives to our outcomes, or do we craft our outcomes after the groundwork for a program has been laid? The answer is that either works. What is most important in the assessment process is to develop outcomes, whether they are for new programs or for existing ones. Assessment is beneficial because it involves creating goals that provide clear purpose and guidance in our work.

Established Resources

As mentioned, you're not left to your own devices in creating learning outcomes. Several resources rooted in extensive research and student development theory already exist that can serve as the basis for the outcomes you craft (e.g., drawing from CAS for learning outcomes applicable to student learning and engagement). CAS calls student affairs professionals at all levels to be intentional about moving assessment efforts beyond satisfaction to focusing on student learning. Table 6.1, "Steps in Assessment," from CAS, provides a framework for the kind of learning-centered approach that professionals engaged in assessment should strive for.

Table 6.1. Steps in Assessment

1. Define the problem. • What information do you need? • Why do you need it?
2. Determine the purpose for the assessment. • What are your goals? • What do you hope to achieve with your assessment project?
3. Determine where to get the information needed. • Does the information you need already exist on campus or in the literature, or do you need to collect it? • Where will you gather the data you need?
4. Determine the best assessment methods. • What are the most appropriate and efficient assessment methods to fulfill your needs given your problem and the information you hope to gather?
5. Determine whom to study. • Whom does your assessment need to target? • Does the problem you seek to solve require you to examine the entire campus population; a small, specific subset; or a particular group?
6. Determine how data will be collected. • Will you gather data by using an online survey tool, talking to focus groups, or conducting individual interviews?
7. What instruments will be used? • Will you use an existing assessment instrument or create one yourself? • Has your office used instruments in the past? • Do you have access to any national test or survey instrument publishing houses?

Table 6.1. Steps in Assessment *(Continued)*

8. Who should collect the data?

- Are you closely connected to or have strong feelings about the subject that might bias your assessment efforts?
- Is there another student affairs professional who's unconnected with your project that can review your assessment tools and approach?
- Is there a trusted colleague with assessment experience who can implement parts of your process if you determine your personal connections or biases might affect the results?

9. Determine how the data will be analyzed.

- Does your sample provide a good representation of the problem or population you intend to study?
- What are appropriate procedures for analyzing your results, given the instruments and methodology you used in your assessment?

10. Determine implications for policy and practice.

- How does what you have learned from your assessments affect your work?
- Did you find what you expected to?
- How do your results help improve your programs and inform your future efforts?

11. Report the results effectively.

- What plans do you have for disseminating relevant findings and implications?
- How will you package the findings and implications given which audiences (if any) might benefit from your results?
- Who should receive the full report, and who needs a one-page executive summary of your main findings or an in-person debrief of them?

Note. The 11 steps are a summary of key points from Schuh and Upcraft's (2001) applications manual for student affairs professionals. Each step represents important considerations when preparing to engage in assessment, even if all 11 steps are not always followed.

Additionally, two of our profession's guiding documents, *Learning Reconsidered* (Keeling, 2004) and *Learning Reconsidered 2* (Keeling, 2006), effectively outline why it's imperative for our work to center on student learning and outcomes—and similarly to CAS, *Learning Reconsidered 2* details specific outcomes that serve as a valuable tool for informing assessment efforts. *Beyond the Big Test* (Sedlacek, 2004) provides helpful insight into the noncognitive variables that we should strive to incorporate into students' experiences. Sedlacek included a variety of detailed examples on how to intentionally incorporate non-cognitive variables into a wide range of functional areas and how to assess these initiatives.

Assessment in Action

To help you think about your assessment efforts, we provide the following case studies, which prompt you to connect theory to practice.

Case Study 1

Less than a month after you begin your first job in student affairs, your institution's president announces that every department will need to tighten its fiscal belt. Everyone must make tough decisions about the budget. The president emphatically contends that despite the budget concerns, student learning cannot be compromised and that every department and program must be scrutinized. The vice president for student affairs announces that each department in the division must identify student learning outcomes associated with the various programs offered. Identify the student learning and development outcomes that are important for your specific department and then identify the programs and activities that align with these programs. Develop a plan for assessing these outcomes across the various programs and department.

Case Study 2

You have just accepted your first full-time job in student affairs. Your supervisor informs you that at the end of your first 6 months (your probationary period as a new hire), you'll undergo a performance review to determine the extent of your acclimation to your role and your progress in its responsibilities. Review your current job description, along with any performance standards available through your office and human resources department. Develop a set of learning outcomes for yourself that reflect what you intend to achieve in your first 6 months. Determine how you could assess your progress along each learning outcome, using both quantitative (e.g., Likert-scale satisfaction surveys administered to student leaders you work with) and qualitative measures (e.g., monthly written reflections on your progress).

Conclusion

From this chapter, we hope you see that assessment is a doable and necessary component of your student affairs work. You undoubtedly will interact with some assessment naysayers during your time as a student affairs professional and will probably hear some of the 10 reasons they're not engaged in assessment. We hope that, rather than adopt their stance on assessment, you'll see the benefits of assessment and be able to put to task the practical tips we provided. As a student affairs professional, you have a responsibility to assess the programs and services you offer. After all, assessment has always been, and continues to be, a part of the philosophical underpinnings of the student affairs profession for good reasons—to understand and improve the quality of student learning.

References

American College Personnel Association & National Association of Student Personnel Administrators. (2010). *Professional competency areas for student affairs practitioners*. Washington, DC: Authors.

American Council on Education. (1937). *The student personnel point of view*. Washington, DC: Author.

Blimling, G. (2013). Challenges of assessment in student affairs. In J. Schuh (Ed.), *Special issue: Selected contemporary assessment issues* (New Directions for Student Services, No. 142, pp. 5–14). San Francisco, CA: Jossey-Bass.

Council for the Advancement of Standards in Higher Education. (2012). *Professional standards for higher education* (8th ed.). Washington, DC: Author.

Dungy, G., & Gordon, S. A. (2010). The development of student affairs. In J. H. Schuh, S. R. Jones, & S. R. Harper (Eds.), *Student services: A handbook for the profession* (5th ed., pp. 61–79). San Francisco, CA: Jossey-Bass.

Hoffman, J. L., & Bresciani, M. J. (2010). Assessment work: An exploratory study of assessment-related job requirements and skills in student affairs. *Journal of Student Affairs Research and Practice, 47*(4), 495–512. doi: 10.2202/1949-6605.6082

Keeling, R. P. (Ed.). (2004). *Learning reconsidered: A campus-wide focus on the student experience*. Washington, DC: American College Personnel Association and National Association of Student Personnel Administrators.

Keeling, R. P. (Ed). (2006). *Learning reconsidered 2: A practical guide to implementing a campus-wide focus on the student experience*. Washington, DC: American College Personnel Association, Association of College and Housing Officers–International, Association of College Unions–International, National Academic Advising Association, National Association of Campus Activities, National Association of Student Personnel Administrators, & National Intramural–Recreational Sports Association.

Schuh, J. H. (2013). Challenges of assessment in student affairs. In J. Schuh (Ed.), *Special issue: Selected contemporary assessment issues* (New Directions for Student Services, No. 142, pp. 89–98). San Francisco, CA: Jossey-Bass.

Schuh, J. H., & Gansemer-Topf, A. M. (2010, December). *The role of student affairs in student learning assessment* (NILOA Occasional Paper No.7). Urbana, IL: University of Illinois and Indiana University, National Institute for Learning Outcomes Assessment.

Schuh, J. M., & Upcraft, M. L. (2001). *Assessment practice in student affairs: An applications manual*. San Francisco, CA: Jossey-Bass.

Sedlacek, W. E. (2004). *Beyond the big test: Non-cognitive assessment in higher education*. San Francisco, CA: Jossey- Bass.

Stamatakos, L.C. (1978). Unsolicited advice for new professionals. *Journal of College Student Personnel, 19*, 325–330.

Wawrzynski, M. R., & Beverly, A. (2012). Realized benefits for first-year student peer educators. *Journal of the First Year Experience and Students in Transition, 24*(1), 45–60.

Wawrzynski, M. R., Heck, A., & Remley, C. (2012). Student engagement in South African higher education. *Journal of College Student Development, 53*(1), 106–123. doi: 10.1353/csd.2012.0007

Wawrzynski, M., & Sedlacek, W. (2003). Race and gender differences in the transfer student experience. *Journal of College Student Development, 44*(4), 489–501. doi: 10.1353/csd.2003.0045

Additional Resources

American College Personnel Association. (2007). *ASK standards: Assessment skills and knowledge content standards for student affairs practitioners and scholars.* Washington, DC: Author.

Banta, T. W., Lund, J. P., Black, K. E., & Oblander, F. W. (Eds.). (1996). *Assessment in practice: Putting principles to work on college campuses.* San Francisco, CA: Jossey-Bass.

Bresciani, M. J., Zelna, C. L., & Anderson, J. A. (2004). *Assessing student learning and development: A handbook for practitioners.* Washington, DC: National Association of Student Personnel Administrators.

Bresciani, M. J., Gardner, M. G., Hickmott, J. (2010). *Demonstrating student success: A practical guide to outcomes-based assessment of learning and development in student affairs.* Herndon, VA: Stylus.

Collins, K., & Roberts, D. (2012). *Learning is not a sprint: Assessing and documenting student leader learning in cocurricular.* Washington, DC: National Association of Student Personnel Administrators.

Keeling, R. P., Wall, A. F., Underhile, R., & Dungy, G. J. (2008). *Assessment reconsidered.* Washington, DC: International Center for Student Success and Institutional Accountability.

Schuh, J. H. (2008). *Assessment methods for student affairs.* San Francisco, CA: Jossey-Bass.

Suskie, L. (2009). *Assessing student learning: A common sense guide* (2nd ed.). San Francisco, CA: Jossey-Bass.

*WHAT **IS** THE CRISIS MANAGEMENT PLAN*
AT MY NEW INSTITUTION?

CRISIS MANAGEMENT FOR
NEW PROFESSIONALS

CHAPTER SEVEN

Eugene L. Zdziarski II and Dawn Watkins

Many people in a college or university community feel somewhat responsible for managing campus crises, but in a true crisis, they typically look to student affairs professionals for leadership. A recent survey of provosts in higher education found that the person most frequently identified as integral to the management of a crisis was the vice president for student affairs (Mitroff, Diamond, & Alpaslan, 2006). Therefore, having a framework in place for understanding crisis management is key for all student affairs professionals and, in particular, new professionals.

The skill set for handling crises is required throughout the careers of student affairs professionals. Although the crises most often discussed are major or catastrophic events, in reality it's the smaller events—those that most people in the college or university community never even hear about—that student affairs professionals deal with on a regular basis. These

> **The skill set for handling crises is required throughout the careers of student affairs professionals.**

day-to-day crises make up the majority of the work of student affairs professionals and, in particular, new professionals who are on the front line. Understanding how to manage small incidents prepares a student affairs professional to manage day-to-day crises as well as the large-scale incidents that, sadly, often make national news. In this chapter, we introduce some theoretical crisis management concepts, apply them to higher education, and then relate them to specific events that new professionals in student affairs might face in their work.

Crisis Management as a Process

> *No matter what, you can't stop crazy; you just have to be prepared for the worst, but I worry that I'm not prepared.* —Hall director at a research university

Crisis management planning is not something that is done once, involving a pretty notebook that sits on a shelf, to be used in the event of an incident. Crisis management is a continuous process that evolves as higher education administrators move through both small- and large-scale events. Many authors (Coombs, 1999; Federal Emergency Management Agency [FEMA], 1996; Koovor-Misra, 1995; Mitroff, Pearson, & Harrington, 1996; Pauchant & Mitroff, 1992; Ogrizek & Guillery, 1999) have described the process as a series of stages or phases. On a fundamental level, it's often viewed as a three-phase process: pre-crisis, crisis, and post-crisis (Birch, 1994; Coombs, 1999; Guth, 1995; Koovor-Misra, 1995; Meyers, 1986; Mitchell, 1986; Ogrizek & Guillery, 1999). In this three-phase model, certain actions and steps are taken before, during, and after the crisis event to effectively manage the incident. With the advent of FEMA and the Department of Homeland Security, additional models have been introduced.

The current emergency management model adapted to institutions of higher education is a five-phase model: prevention, protection, mitigation, response, recovery (U.S. Department of Education, 2013). The *prevention* phase includes all actions taken to avoid, deter, or stop a potential crisis from occurring. Student affairs professionals frequently manage prevention programs (e.g., alcohol education programs, instruction for the use of college or university vehicles for sport clubs, fire drills in residence halls), although they're often not recognized as part of the overall crisis management process. Such prevention efforts are key to institutional crisis preparedness and need to be acknowledged as essential elements of the crisis management system.

In the *protection* phase, all actions taken to protect students, faculty and staff, visitors, and institutional property and systems are considered part of the crisis management process. Such measures may include card access systems, emergency notification procedures, "blue phones," and video cameras, as well as other institutional policies designed to protect members of the campus community from harm.

The *mitigation* phase focuses on actions taken to eliminate or reduce the physical harm or damage caused by a particular crisis event. Typical actions in this phase include sandbagging to prevent water damage; intentional shutdowns of various systems such as gas, water, and electricity; and procedures for sheltering in place.

Crisis *response* includes actions taken to stabilize the situation once a crisis has occurred and to create a safe and secure environment that facilitates recovery. This phase is the one most people focus on when they discuss or analyze crisis management. A key question student affairs professionals need to plan for during this phase is how to account for students and ensure their safety and well-being as other emergency responders are addressing the specific threat.

The *recovery* phase addresses the actions taken to return the institution to normal operations. Crisis managers must understand that the recovery phase may last days, weeks, months, or—as with the aftermath of Hurricane Katrina on the U.S. Gulf Coast—years. This phase is often both overlooked and underestimated for its importance in responding to individual needs as well as restoring the affected community. Sometimes people are so anxious to get back to business as usual that they overlook the needs of individuals and of the affected community as a whole. Student affairs professionals are frequently the ones who attend to the human needs; they're adept at recognizing and responding to persons in crisis.

The Crisis Matrix

> *The reality is that my coursework and field experience throughout graduate school prepared me for the profession to a certain extent. When it comes to handling crises, all of that was learned on the job.* —Coordinator of Greek Life at a regional public university

A matrix provides a conceptual framework for examining crisis management. It allows the student affairs professional to capture an understanding of a crisis and how to respond following predetermined steps for each phase. The Crisis Matrix (Zdziarski, Dunkel, & Rollo, 2007) involves three dimensions: type of crisis, level of crisis, and intentionality of crisis (see Figure 7.1).

Crisis events in higher education can generally be grouped into three types: environmental, facility, and human. *Environmental* crises include weather-related events such as hurricanes, tornados, earthquakes, and floods. *Facility* crises include such events as fires, power outages, structural collapses, and computer failures. *Human* crises include death, serious injury, and mental health issues. Understanding the differences between types of crises entails distinct ways of responding to the varying crises.

Figure 7.1. Crisis Matrix

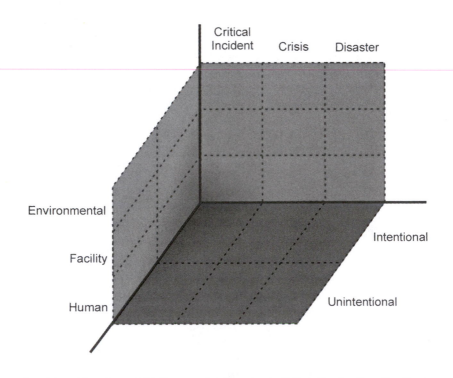

The second dimension in the Crisis Matrix is the level of the crisis. Generally, a campus *crisis* is defined as an event, often sudden or unexpected, that disrupts the normal operations of the institution or its educational mission and threatens the well-being of the personnel, property, financial resources, or reputation of the institution (Zdziarski, 2006). In this context, crises affect the entire institution, disrupting normal operations.

Some crises affect not only the institution but the surrounding community as well—these events are usually considered *disasters* and typically place significant demands on community resources. For example, in the case of a hurricane, everyone in the area is affected by high winds and flooding, and support must go to the entire community. Colleges and universities must be aware of the availability of support should a disaster strike.

Another level of crisis affects only a segment of the campus community. These crises, called *critical incidents*, affect a residence hall, a student group, or a subset of a student population. Institutional plans typically operate at the level of campuswide crises and major disasters; student affairs professionals typically deal with critical incidents on a daily basis. As a new professional, you should focus your learning in this area and hone your crisis management skills. This experience will serve you well in the future as you move into senior roles within student affairs, where you're likely to lead the response to major crises.

The third dimension of the Crisis Matrix is the intentionality of the crisis, which refers to the continuum from an act of God to an intentional act by or toward someone. When someone dies from natural causes or in an accident, people are more likely to understand and accept the death. However, when a person dies as the result of an act of violence—such as terrorism or a shooting—the psychological impact on people is much more significant, as are the level and nature of the immediate response, the investigation, and the follow-up.

The Crisis Matrix allows student affairs professionals to develop and enhance their understanding of existing crisis management plans. Then they can take the events listed in a crisis audit and fully explore and understand the resources and response modalities that can be set in motion for a critical incident, a campuswide crisis, or a disaster. The student affairs professional can see how the management of the crisis changes depending on whether the event is intentional or not.

The student affairs professional must understand the difference between crisis management *plans* and crisis management *protocols*. In putting together a plan, a basic outline for managing a crisis is created. The outline defines: (a) the purpose of the plan; (b) who has the authority to initiate the plan; and (c) which aspects of the plan remain the same regardless of the type or nature of the crisis event. The plan includes sets of protocols: situational protocols and functional protocols. Situational protocols provide a series of actions to address a specific kind of crisis event (e.g., active shooter, bomb threat, hurricane, etc.). Functional protocols provide a series of actions to perform certain functions during a crisis (e.g., notification process for serious injury or death, building fire watch procedures, campus evacuation, etc.). Minimally, the crisis portfolio includes a situational protocol for each type of crisis and functional protocols to effectively address each situation. Both sets of protocols would be scalable in order to address each level of crisis.

Crisis Management and Institutional Type

What IS the crisis management plan at my new institution?
—Financial aid counselor at a small liberal arts college

Crisis management is more than just responding to a set of circumstances, and a one-size plan does not fit all. Everyone who might be involved in crisis response should be included in the institution's crisis management planning. Whether at a large university, a small college, or a community college, students and their families expect that a crisis response will include personal attention. Larger institutions have more resources. For example, most large colleges and universities have their own commissioned police officers, while smaller institutions are more likely to rely on local law enforcement. On the other hand, student affairs professionals at smaller colleges and universities might know most students on an individual basis, which can make it easier to respond to individual needs in a crisis.

There are no hard and fast rules associated with managing a crisis at a smaller or larger institution. Student affairs professionals must understand the strengths of their institution and maximize them in times of crisis; they must understand the limitations of their institution and minimize them in a crisis. For example, as part of the planning process, a small college that relies on local law enforcement should have detailed discussions about the type and level of support. Will institutional managers have access to campus buildings if local law enforcement is handling a crisis? If so, how will this work? Should college personnel have badges to alert local law enforcement of their role in assisting with an institutional crisis? Will local law enforcement provide information to college or university personnel in the midst of a crisis? In a large university, "while there may be a desire for personal attention, there is also likely a realization that students will be more anonymous on campus" (Rollo & Zdziarski, 2007, p. 5); thus, student affairs professionals should plan how to respond to students individually with the available staff resources. These kinds of discussions must occur during the planning process.

The challenge to the new professional is how to put all this information together. Managing a crisis might sound overwhelming but, to a certain extent, student affairs professionals do it every day. Applying sound management principles is the key to resolve both daily incidents and large-scale events.

Title IX

I started working for this university 9 months ago. From the day I started, there have been a plethora of Title IX-specific conversations detailing the process and my role as a staff professional. I value the rigid framework around Title IX investigations and hearings, but I find myself wondering what series of events led to Title IX today?
—Area coordinator at a midsize private university

Title IX and sexual misconduct issues are not new to college campuses; however, there has been continued emphasis on issues of sexual violence by the federal government and the U.S. Department of Education. Although this chapter does not delve deeply into any particular crisis event, addressing sexual violence in a comprehensive manner is of key importance to all institutions, and we would be remiss if we didn't include this topic in a chapter about crisis management. The following section is intended to provide some broad and general information new professionals should know about sexual violence and how it relates to crisis communications and crisis management.

Title IX of the Education Amendments of 1972 prohibits sex discrimination in federally funded education programs. The driving force behind the creation of Title IX was to mitigate the disparity between male and female athletic programs in K–12 and higher education (a disparity that to a lesser extent still exists) by ensuring equal access for girls and women to athletic programs. In April 2011, colleges and universities across the country received a "Dear Colleague" letter from the U.S. Department of Education Office for Civil Rights (OCR) that established a link between sexual misconduct and Title IX: "[D]iscrimination on the basis of sex can include sexual harassment or sexual violence, such as rape, sexual assault, sexual battery, and sexual coercion" (U.S. Department of Education, n.d., para. 1). The letter also outlined responsibilities and procedures for every institution. The OCR is the federal agency tasked with investigating any complaints related to Title IX.

Since 2011, Title IX, OCR, and sexual misconduct have frequently been part of news and updates within higher education. With this as a backdrop, the connection to crisis management and crisis communications becomes clear. Headlines such as "55 Colleges Under Title IX Probe for Handling of Sexual Violence and Harassment Claims" (Anderson, 2014) and "White House to Press Colleges to Do More to Combat Rape" (Steinhauer, 2014) propel crisis communications teams into high gear. Colleges and universities face a myriad of complex issues that must be considered from a crisis communications perspective: legal, financial, emotional, physical, educational, reputational, operational, and behavioral. Those handling crisis communications for the institution must consider all of these angles when responding to sexual misconduct.

Although crisis communication is both important and time consuming, the emotional impact of sexual violence on a campus is certainly of greater importance to student affairs professionals and easily reaches the level of crisis management. Whether perception or reality, student affairs professionals and crisis management teams must consider:

- ☞ concerns about a lack of fairness or equity in a conduct process;

- ☞ inadequate sanctioning;

- ☞ inconsistency within or unequal access to appeals process;

- ☞ retaliation concerns;

- ☞ inadequate education programs;

- ☞ accepted institutional culture; and

- ☞ lack of communication and coordination that affect involved students. (Smith, 2014)

Likewise, crimes of sexual violence present a wide variety of student responses about which student affairs professionals and those involved in crisis management must understand, including but not limited to:

☞ the nature of victimization;

☞ counterintuitive victim behaviors;

☞ delays in reporting;

☞ the role of alcohol and other drugs;

☞ that most sexual violence is committed by someone known to the victim;

☞ that most assaults are achieved through threats, intimidation, and exploiting vulnerabilities;

☞ the likelihood of repeat offenders and undetected predators;

☞ concerns over false reports;

☞ little to no physical or forensic evidence;

☞ that the most common defense is consent;

☞ that decisions are often based solely on credibility;

☞ the inability to completely eliminate occurrence; and

☞ the emotionally charged and incendiary nature of the issues. (Smith, 2014)

Faced with an exceedingly complex issue, with no easy answers for anyone involved, student affairs professionals and crisis management teams must be familiar with Title IX and its implications and work closely with college and university communications professionals to manage institutional concerns while also working closely with conduct professionals and health care and counseling staff to achieve best possible outcomes. These situations are incredibly complex and challenging. Therefore, proactive education, as required by law, should also be a part of a comprehensive approach to sexual misconduct.

Student affairs professionals and crisis management teams must be familiar with Title IX and its implications and work closely with college and university communications professionals to manage institutional concerns while also working closely with conduct professionals and health care and counseling staff to achieve best possible outcomes.

Crisis Events

My campus is as safe as it can be, but how do I teach students not to take that for granted but not live in fear? —Coordinator for student activities at a small liberal arts college

The case studies that follow illustrate the kinds of critical incidents that new student affairs professionals encounter in their work and how they can apply crisis management principles to resolve them.

Case Study 1

You're an area coordinator at a midsize university. One of your hall directors reports that a custodian has noticed vomit in the community bathroom area on a regular basis. You have the resident assistant ask a few questions in that particular hall, and she reports that (a) food has been disappearing out of people's individual refrigerators in that hall, (b) one woman in the hall has experienced significant weight loss since the beginning of the academic year, and (c) the same woman said she has been experiencing flu-like symptoms throughout the fall semester and has occasionally vomited in the community bathroom.

Case Study 2

You're the assistant director of student activities at a small college. Because you and the director take turns attending events, you're the sole student activities staff person overseeing an outdoor evening concert. Two hours before the start of the event, the concert chair of the activities board comes to you in a panic, because she just heard that a tornado watch has been called for your county. She asks you whether the concert should be canceled. The stage is already set and the technical crew is currently setting up microphones and speakers. To attract students to the event, dinner is currently being served on the lawn area adjacent to where the concert will occur.

Case Study 3

You're a coordinator for campus recreation at a large university and have worked closely with the lacrosse sport club to arrange their game at a university about 100 miles away. A team member calls to say that one of the vans in their caravan of four has had an accident. Local police are on the scene. The student reports that there are no injuries, but the police may be arresting the student driver. As you question the student further about why the student driver is being arrested for a minor accident, you learn that there might have been open containers of alcohol in the van at the time of the accident.

Applying the Principles

Applying some of the theoretical concepts discussed above, how does a new professional plan, prevent, respond, and recover from these kinds of crises? Case 1 involves what appears to be a hall resident with an eating disorder. As the area coordinator, you identify the situation as a human crisis and report it to the university's at-risk committee, which then helps you determine the next steps to involve the student in some sort of intervention. The at-risk committee (which has different names at different institutions) is usually a committee of college or university staff who review situations in which students are considered at risk— which can be anything from academic jeopardy to mental health concerns.

New professionals must know and understand existing institutional plans to address human crises and make sure their actions are consistent with institutional expectations. This case also illustrates the need for pre-vention planning. Have you trained residential life and custodial staff about eating disorders and the need to communicate with other student affairs professionals even for what may seem like insignificant or unrelated events? To answer such questions, you should conduct a crisis audit for your scope of responsibility.

In Case 2 involving the assistant director of student activities with a tornado watch announced shortly before the start of an outdoor concert, the planning aspect of crisis management is key. Is there a system or mechanism in place to receive such information on a regular basis, or is the department truly dependent on a student listening to the radio? Weather cannot be prevented, but action can be taken to reduce the impact of a weather emergency. As an assistant director, you must be familiar with the authority structure in place to make a decision about continuing or canceling the event. In the time available, can you research the likelihood that a tornado will occur and weigh the risks? Does

> New professionals must know and understand existing institutional plans to address human crises and make sure their actions are consistent with institutional expectations.

the department have a "rain plan"? Is a shelter specified and available if the decision is made to continue the concert outdoors and the storm hits? You must consider such questions in planning events, and when making decisions about how to prevent further escalation of crisis events and how to manage overall college risk.

In Case 3, the new professional who is advising a student over the phone about a van accident can rely on the recovery and learning aspects of the theoretical framework. The first step is to confirm the well-being of those involved; in this case, there is no loss of life or injury requiring medical treatment, and damage to the vehicle appears minimal. Should the trip continue? How would you accommodate the students who were traveling in the wrecked van? Can a colleague at a neighboring institution, who is closer to the accident, provide immediate support and assessment of the situation? Who else in the institution needs to be notified? Moving into recovery, you may have to attend to the individual needs of students who are traumatized by the accident. What should you do about the student who has been arrested? Should campus disciplinary action be considered for all the students in the van? From a learning perspective—to close the loop—what educational programs exist to stress no-alcohol policies and practices on sports club trips and during other student activities? Do the existing educational programs need to be modified?

These three cases illustrate the kinds of events you might encounter and how you might apply the crisis management cycle to develop protocols for responding to them. If you get used to applying the crisis management model to crises at every level of student affairs work, you'll be better prepared to apply it to a critical incident, campus crisis, or disaster. Although crisis events might differ in terms of scope and magnitude, the theoretical elements of crisis management remain the same. New professionals should feel empowered in their work as day-to-day crisis managers and recognize that this work is preparing them to manage serious crises in their future professional careers.

References

Anderson, N. (2014, May 1). 55 colleges under Title IX probe for handling of sexual violence and harassment claims. *The Washington Post*. Retrieved from http://www.washingtonpost.com/local/education/ federal-government-releases-list-of-55-colleges-universities-under- title-ix-investigations-over-handling-of-sexual-violence/2014/05/01/ e0a74810-d13b-11e3-937f-d3026234b51c_story.html

Birch, J. (1994). New factors in crisis planning and response. *Public Relations Quarterly, 39*, 31–34.

Coombs, W. T. (1999). *Ongoing crisis communication: Planning, managing, and responding* (Vol. 2). Thousand Oaks, CA: Sage.

Federal Emergency Management Agency. (1996). *Guide for all-hazard emergency operations planning* (State and local guide–SLG 101). Retrieved from https://www.fema.gov/pdf/plan/0-prelim.pdf

Guth, D. W. (1995). Organizational crisis experience and public relations roles. *Public Relations Review, 21*(2), 123–136.

Koovor-Misra, S. (1995). A multidimensional approach to crisis preparation for technical organizations: Some critical factors. *Technological Forecasting and Social Change, 48*, 143–160.

Meyers, G. C. (1986). *When it hits the fan: Managing the nine crises of business*. New York, NY: Mentor.

Mitchell, T. H. (1986). Coping with a corporate crisis. *Canadian Business Review, 13*(3), 17–20.

Mitroff, I. I., Diamond, M. A., & Alpaslan, C. M. (2006). How prepared are America's colleges and universities for major crisis? *Change, 38*(1), 61–67. doi: 10.3200/CHNG.38.1.61-67

Mitroff, I. I., Pearson, C. M., & Harrington, L. K. (1996). *The essential guide to managing corporate crisis: A step-by-step handbook for surviving major catastrophes*. New York, NY: Oxford University Press.

Ogrizek, M., & Guillery, J. M. (1999). *Communicating in crisis: A theoretical and practical guide to crisis management* (H. Kimball-Brooke & R. Z. Brooke, Trans.). New York, NY: Walter de Gruyter.

Pauchant, T. C., & Mitroff, I. I. (1992). *Transforming the crisis-prone organization: Preventing individual, organizational, and environmental tragedies*. San Francisco, CA: Jossey-Bass.

Rollo, J. M., & Zdziarski, E. L. (2007). The impact of crisis. In E. L. Zdziarski, N. W. Dunkel, & J. M. Rollo (Eds.), *Campus crisis management: A comprehensive guide to planning prevention, response and recovery* (pp. 1–33). San Francisco, CA: Jossey-Bass.

Smith, G. M. (2014, April). *Sexual assault prevention in higher education*. Presentation at the North-American Interfraternity Conference, Atlanta, GA.

Steinhauer, J. (2014, April 28). White House to press colleges to do more to combat rape. *The New York Times*. Retrieved from http://www.nytimes.com/2014/04/29/us/tougher-battle-on-sex-assault-on-campus-urged.html?_r=0

Title IX of the Education Amendments of 1972, 20 U.S.C. § 1681 *et seq.* (1972).

U.S. Department of Education, Office for Civil Rights. (n.d.). *Know your rights: Title IX prohibits sexual harassment and sexual violence where you go to school*. Retrieved from http://www2.ed.gov/about/offices/list/ocr/docs/title-ix-rights-201104.pdf

U.S. Department of Education, Office of Elementary and Secondary Education, Office of Safe and Healthy Students. (2013). *Guide for developing high-quality emergency operations plans for institutions of higher education*. Retrieved from http://rems.ed.gov/docs/REMS_IHE_Guide_508.pdf

Zdziarski, E. L. (2006). Crisis in the context of higher education. In K. S. Harper, B. G. Paterson, & E. L. Zdziarski (Eds.), *Crisis management: Responding from the heart* (pp. 3–24). Washington, DC: National Association of Student Personnel Administrators.

Zdziarski, E. L., Dunkel, N.W., & Rollo, J. M. (2007). The crisis matrix. In E. L. Zdziarski, N. W. Dunkel, & J. M. Rollo (Eds.), *Campus crisis management: A comprehensive guide to planning prevention, response and recovery* (pp. 35–51). San Francisco, CA: Jossey-Bass.

USING TECHNOLOGY AND SOCIAL MEDIA

CHAPTER EIGHT

Grace A. Bagunu and Danielle N. Quiñones-Ortega

A dvancements in technology and the rampant use of social media platforms arose from the creative minds of college students using the Internet and new technologies to engage in innovative ways within their college community. There has been a flood of research in recent years on the impact of social media and technology on engaging college students using various platforms (Barrett, 2003; Conway & Hubbard, 2003; Dodson & Dean, 2003; Fishman, 2012; Gruzd, Takheyev & Wellman, 2011; Heiberger & Harper, 2008; Jenness, 2011; Joosten, Pasquini, & Harness, 2013; Junco, 2012; Marklein, 2009; Moneta, 2005; Reich, 2010; Wortham, 2013).

Social media and technology serve important roles in professional growth and development in the student affairs field. In this chapter, we share research related to the use of technological advances in higher education, best practices for using social media and technology in student affairs work, and strategies for staying current with trends and maintaining professionalism. As a new professional, you'll benefit from understanding the history, advantages, and hazards of using social media and technology in student affairs work.

History and Emergence of the Social Media Culture in Higher Education

At the turn of the century, prior to the emergence of social media, technological advances shaped the way people performed their work in higher education and the way information was shared at each institution (Duderstadt, Atkins, & Van Houweling, 2002). From the rapid development of technology, a new form of community building emerged as access to the Internet increased and mobile technology became more advanced. Now a vast array of social media platforms is available to professionals. Each platform was created with a certain purpose in mind. If there's one thing each has in common, it's the ability to connect users to the global community. Because they're the most widely used, we concentrate on Facebook, Twitter, and LinkedIn in this section.

When Facebook was developed at Harvard University in 2004, its purpose was to connect students to each other at the institution. Little did the creators of this platform know how much this technology would change the way we engage with one another on a global scale. Social media have altered how individuals around the globe communicate and share information in a matter of minutes. Facebook alone has evolved and continues to grow daily. Initially, Facebook required the user to sign up with a university-sponsored e-mail account. The "edu" e-mail address was the key to this semi-privatized online world. Getting "poked" was a game, and sharing feelings or thoughts as status updates provided the Facebook community with a glimpse into the world through the user's eyes. Facebook opened the door for other social media platforms to bloom.

Parallel to Facebook's development and creation, LinkedIn was founded in 2003 as a professional social media platform for users to develop online career portfolios. At its inception, the purpose of LinkedIn was to help employed professionals connect to one another and to help unemployed professionals network for potential job opportunities. Users create LinkedIn profiles to highlight their work and volunteer experience while they engage in groups and discussions related to professional development. Only in recent years have college students been encouraged to create profiles in order to network on LinkedIn. This platform is a place for professionals to endorse each other in various areas of professional competencies, make connections, and find potential career advancement opportunities.

The emergence of Twitter in 2007 changed the way people interact with one another in a matter of seconds. "A Tweet is an expression of a moment or idea" (Twitter, 2014, para. 1). The creators of Twitter added a challenge to this concept: Share that idea in 140 characters or fewer. Twitter has been a strong social media platform revolutionizing the way information circulates. In addition to the 140-character limit, users add a hashtag so that tweets are searchable. Twitter provides a platform for commenting on a specific event from anywhere in the world, which creates a space for dialogue across a diverse population of users. Twitter users can also harness this technology to share information gathered in person to anyone, anywhere in the world, which establishes what is known as the *backchannel*. EDUCAUSE (2010) defined the backchannel as "a secondary electronic conversation that takes place at the same time as a conference session, lecture, or instructor-led learning activity" (p. 1). This virtual conversation—the ability to participate in the conversation without physically being present—has made Twitter a very popular social media platform for users on a global scale.

Understanding the original purposes of social media platforms supports the ability to effectively use them in our field. Many of the best practices and pitfalls to using social media

> **Understanding the original purposes of social media platforms supports the ability to effectively use them in our field.**

and technology apply to the multitude of options available for student affairs professionals to use. Technological advances have quickly revolutionized the way we communicate on a global scale in a matter of seconds and will continue to do so; technology has implications for our work in higher education and the way we engage with the campus community.

Competencies for Using Technology and Social Media in Student Affairs

Technology and social media are fairly new areas of research and are changing quickly and constantly. We have synthesized information from very recent literature and address current social media platforms and technology, knowing that by the time you read this, it might already be somewhat outdated. Hopefully, the best practices and pitfalls addressed in this chapter will be relevant to current as well as emerging platforms in technology and social media.

Technology and social media have had a profound impact in higher education and student affairs in a short period of time (Kleinglass, 2005; Moneta, 2005). Student affairs professionals at all levels need to be competent and prepared to use technology and social media (Barrett, 2003; Gemmill & Peterson, 2006; Joosten et al., 2013; LeDuc & Samaha, 2011; Leece, 2011; Love & Estanek, 2004; Lovell & Kosten, 2000). Many student affairs preparation programs lack courses directly related to technology and social media use in higher education (Renn & Zeligman, 2005). Student affairs professionals have had to learn on the job about many of the advancements in technology in order to adjust to the demands of tech-savvy students. Lowery (2004) argued that students come in with different desires and needs, and student affairs professionals must be flexible to respond to these changing expectations. Kleinglass (2005) said that professional organizations need to step up and provide development opportunities for professionals to attain more knowledge and capacity for using social media and technology. Since that time, the number of professional development opportunities related to technology has increased.

Student affairs has evolved over time and become an integral part of the college student experience and development of the whole student. One job responsibility of new professionals is to engage students to get involved. Without students in attendance at events, the programs that provide knowledge and opportunities for developing campus communities lose their validity. Marketing events by word of mouth or flyers is not enough anymore; social media announcements are now common practice in student affairs work. Students are engaged in social media use, and student affairs professionals can capitalize on their online engagement to increase involvement in on-campus opportunities (Heiberger & Harper, 2008). To this day, disseminating information through department-sponsored social media accounts is one way to get the word out.

In one study, experts in student affairs were asked to identify typical responsibilities related to entry-level positions; using technology, such as websites and databases, emerged as one of the 26 responsibilities (Burkard, Cole, Ott, & Stoflet, 2005). New professionals have more opportunities to use social media and technology, such as the many other commonly reported responsibilities: promoting university events, writing reports, recruiting students, and providing counseling to individual students. Many admissions counselors use social media to promote the university brand.

> *We have utilized Pinterest boards to engage our prospective students. Pinterest, amongst females, is one of the most frequently used forms of social media. You can really brand the identity of your school on Pinterest to reach out to your [student] demographics.* —Assistant director of student affairs at a small liberal arts college

Burkard et al. (2005) found 32 competencies for successful new professionals. The top six are: (a) flexibility; (b) interpersonal relations; (c) time management; (d) multitasking; (e) oral communication; and (f) written communication. Technology and social media are uniquely intertwined with each of these six competencies. New professionals who possess these competencies will be able to use technology and social media to enhance their work and, by using various platforms and devices, can enhance their ability to exhibit these six competencies. Lovell and Kosten (2000) and Burkard et al. (2005) acknowledged the growing need for student affairs professionals to be more technologically competent as applications continue to advance and become more prevalent in higher education.

Social media and technology platforms have emerged from the need to continue connecting university students to their communities. In a recent informal survey, we asked our colleagues their thoughts on using social media to build community and received a variety of insightful responses, one of which follows:

> *Facebook is on its way out. I'm a part of the generation that used Facebook, but what I'm discovering as I work with younger students (newer freshmen coming in) is that Facebook is no longer a primary means of communication for students. I am 100 times more likely to get students following me or my programs on Instagram or asking to receive my Snapchats than I am to get a request on Facebook or an RSVP to a Facebook invitation to an event.* —Resident director at a large public university

This perspective demonstrates the importance of social media use for communication, regardless of the platform, as we continue our work with and for students. Instagram and Snapchat are two of a multitude of other platforms we do not describe in detail here; many of these platforms did not exist 5 years ago. Being knowledgeable of best practices and technological advances is essential in continuing to serve students and build community through our work.

In addition to the evolution of social media, information management resources, such as OrgSync, CollegiateLink, and massive open online courses, have emerged to support our work with students. Technology has created a culture of mass communication and accessibility to information at our fingertips. As a new professional, you'll be expected to use these technologies in your work, from using a laptop or computer in your office, to using portable devices, to collecting survey data from students across the campus.

Best Practices and Benefits of Technology and Social Media

There are several best practices and benefits to using technology and social media in student affairs. Staying current and aware of new advancements through online forums and attending professional development opportunities will help you effectively use social media and technology in your work. In this section, we discuss three best practices for: (a) engaging students; (b) networking with colleagues; and (c) developing an online brand.

Engaging Students to Increase Involvement

Engaging students through technology is not a new concept, because best practices have been shared through professional organizations since the early 2000s (Conway & Hubbard, 2003). In a study on competency and skills of new professionals, Burkard et al. (2005) found that entry-level positions entail high student contact through program responsibilities and direct services. New professionals are expected to engage with students in a variety of means, and communicating through social media and technology is a best practice. As student affairs practitioners, we often face challenges to connect students to resources that enable them to thrive. Tech-savvy students are coming into higher education institutions with portable electronic devices and multiple social media accounts, which means higher education professionals need to be prepared to engage with students using social media and technology. It's important to use emerging technologies that

> Staying current and aware of new advancements through online forums and attending professional development opportunities will help you effectively use social media and technology in your work.

directly support service to students. Some of these include CollegiateLink and OrgSync, which were created to support the administration of campus organizations. Founded by student leaders, OrgSync was created as a platform that houses resources and centralizes campus organizations online. In addition to advances in technology, social media provide tools for engaging prospective and current students in the campus community.

There are also additional opportunities to increase involvement and sense of belonging for marginalized student populations through social media. Creating a sense of community using online communities is common for adolescents (Reich, 2010). Wittenberg University found that engaging students of color before they come to campus and providing opportunities for current students to use social media to engage with prospective and incoming students can be beneficial for all parties (Wortham, 2013). DeAndréa, Ellison, LaRose, Steinfeld, and Fiore (2012) found that social media can be a key factor in helping students transition into college. Twitter provides an online community for individuals to engage with one another (Gruzd et al., 2011). Student affairs professionals can be innovative in engaging students in the online and in-person campus community.

The use of social media in your position might be determined by how campus leaders and students use these platforms. Johnson (2011), a vice president for student affairs, shared his experience using Facebook and Twitter as a means of engaging with the campus community:

> I may not have met them face-to-face, but students come up to me and start talking and interacting with me as if they know me and have met with me personally. They say, "I saw your post on Facebook," or "I read your Tweet," and that's enough to get the in-person conversations started. (p. 12)

There are unwritten rules and expectations for engaging with students through social media. As a best practice, it's important to understand the code of conduct as it relates to social media usage on your campus. Engaging with students using social media and technology must be done in a professional manner and within the guidelines of your institution. Considering that more and more college students have access to mobile devices, using social media and technology to market events could be very fruitful in engaging more students.

I manage content on my department's Facebook page to share information with students regarding scholarships, fellowships, and employment opportunities that are directly aimed at them. I also use Facebook to publicize upcoming events so that they remain engaged year-round. —Assistant director of activities at a large public university

Technological advances have created a variety of ways to communicate with students beyond passive websites and e-mails. The use of mobile devices has made short messaging systems, such as text and instant messaging, a more proactive way of engaging with students. As it relates to recent events that have happened on college campuses across the country, the need to communicate with students about campus safety through alerts and emergency notifications means we're using social media and technology as mass communication systems. There are several platforms new professionals in student affairs can use to communicate information to students directly and instantly. This generation of students seems to respond to the use of these more direct means of sharing information and reminders about events. Using text messages is another way of engaging students in the campus community. Just be sure to set some clear boundaries for using this technology concerning how often and at what times.

I use texting a lot to engage students, send invitations or reminders about events, and to communicate with my student leaders. —Assistant dean of student affairs at a midsize private university

Technological advances can also be used in assessments. As new professionals, knowing how to best assess your programs is instrumental. Surveys can be administered using pen and paper, of course, but online surveys are becoming more common. Using newer technology—such as tablets and mobile polling systems—allows data to be collected at the point of contact and adjustments to be made quickly in how we engage with students on campus.

Networking and Professional Development

New professionals can use social media to engage with other professionals in the field. Meeting online can create an impression that lasts just as long as a connection you make in person (LeDuc & Samaha, 2011). As mentioned in Chapter Nine, professional connections can be made and networks can be maintained using various social media accounts and advances in technology. Schawbel (2013) wrote, "By becoming proficient in the most prominent social networks, like Facebook, Twitter, LinkedIn, and Google+, and by identifying and learning how to use ones that have not been invented yet, you'll keep yourself ahead of the curve" (p. 80).

Online engagements, in most cases, are a way to follow-up and maintain relationships with colleagues you meet through various professional development opportunities. In addition, as one student affairs professional shares, connecting through social media and technology prior to in-person networking events can ease the anxiety of professionals who find it difficult to speak up.

> *As an introvert, it's easier for me to engage in dialogue and be involved online. Whereas, in person, I would absolutely sit or stand back and be more of an observer, but participating online, in meaningful dialogue, there has already been an introduction. Therefore, when I see a colleague in person, we have some form of rapport established.* —Program coordinator at a community college

Using social media and technology can help make networking easier for different personality types as well as for those who can't afford to travel to conferences or to workshops.

New professionals have several ways to share knowledge using social media. Similar to the way information can be shared at professional development conferences across the country, social media platforms, such as Twitter and YouTube, allow student affairs professionals to share and obtain knowledge and best practices. An example of how we, the authors, actively participate in knowledge sharing is by engaging in #SAChat, which is short for "Student Affairs Chat" through Twitter. Junco et al. (2010) explored the hashtag further and explained how "#SAChat is a weekly, focused, online conversation for student affairs practitioners and graduate students to share, learn, and connect with each other" (p. 252). Each #SAChat session provides us an opportunity to share what we know about a given topic or share something we heard that supports learning in our field. Gruzd et al. (2011) argued that Twitter creates an online community that allows individuals to form new relationships as well as maintain any existing relationships. These personal learning networks create online learning opportunities that bring together professionals at all levels and in different institution types, which enhances our knowledge and range of use.

Professionals can also use social media to share job opportunities that are not yet posted on university websites. As an example, Torres (2012) discussed how she used social media and various technologies to find her first job after graduate school. Many online forums and professional networking groups actively post job and professional development opportunities in student affairs. If you're interested in getting involved in a professional association or landing a job in a specific geographic or functional area, consider joining a social media group related to your interests. Engaging in online professional development activities and searching for prospective job opportunities are part of networking and developing as a new professional in student affairs.

Developing an Online Brand and Persona

Social media offers student affairs professionals the opportunity to develop an online brand and persona that reflect their individual professional expertise and personality. Authenticity in social networking is related to online branding, in which a new professional can have an online presence that authentically represents the person and the professional.

> *Social media are a representation of yourself. Whatever is shared by you and exchanged among friends and colleagues markets who you are. If you thought the world was small by people-to-people degrees of separation, it becomes much smaller via social media.*
> —Director of student activities at a large public research university

Keeping this in mind, new professionals need to pay attention to the way they represent themselves through various social media platforms as well as in electronic communications (i.e., e-mails, text messages). The way you communicate with others is all part of your branding and a demonstration of your competency and skills. Personal branding is not a new practice, but creating an online brand is an emerging best practice. You can build your brand by integrating several outlets, including online, in person, and on paper to positively represent you and the work you do.

Information you share through your social media feed can both positively and negatively affect your digital reputation.

Information you share through your social media feed can both positively and negatively affect your digital reputation. Be mindful of the image you're creating to build your brand. Whatever social media platform you use, it's important to fill out your profile entirely. Consider these three main tips to maximize your personal branding creation.

☞ **Invest the time and money to get a professional head-shot taken.** It's good to use this same profile picture across all platforms to create a personal brand. Your social network connections can associate your name with your picture.

☞ **Share your professional biography.** Where applicable, fill in your employment and education history and include relevant information consistent with the image you want to convey. Keep your network informed about your professional experience and accomplishments.

☞ **Own your name.** Using your full name on your social media accounts binds them to your brand. Wherever possible, use your name in your customized URL or in your user name or handle.

Technology is advancing rapidly, and social media platforms are becoming more integrated in daily conversations and tasks in the educational setting. Student affairs professionals need to be knowledgeable and prepared to meet the demands from students, parents, and the community who expect to access information and professionals at their fingertips. Kleinglass (2005) argued that student affairs professionals need to find balance in the way they engage a community of learners, which includes adapting privacy settings per platform. As your network continues to grow, make sure your settings allow connections to easily find you and access resources you share. Although content must be available at all times, student affairs professionals need to set boundaries in the use of social media and technology.

Hazards and Pitfalls

Hazards and pitfalls abound in using technology and social media in student affairs work. Lovell and Kosten (2000) discussed the uncertain impact technology will have on interpersonal relationships in the educational setting. However, the use of social media and technology should not take away from the human and personal interactions new professionals have with students on their campus. Technological advances allow the university and higher education professionals to be accessible at any given moment. How we, as student affairs professionals, choose to use the various platforms and devices has implications in accessibility and engagement with students. Three areas addressed in this section are: (a) lack of professionalism; (b) overuse of technology and social media; and (e) limited interactions for authentic networking.

Lack of Professionalism

New professionals must be aware of how they engage through social media. As discussed in Chapter Three related to professional ethics, new professionals must make ethical decisions related to social media and technology. Some images and statements posted through social media might be viewed as lacking professionalism. Retweeting an image that might be offensive or posting in all capital letters—which is interpreted as shouting—are just two examples of unprofessional behavior using social media. The way you communicate through social media and technology might also be interpreted as a representation of the institution where you're employed. A simple rule of thumb is to add a disclaimer statement on each of your accounts. One example is: "Disclaimer: The personal views, content, and opinions expressed in my profile are my own and do not necessarily represent those of my department or the university." As a new professional, you must be aware of how your level of professionalism and communication skills might be viewed by potential employers looking at your online posts. Thoroughly read all your retweets and posts to ensure the impact of your social media communication positively reflects your brand.

To mitigate some of the errors that come with using social media "on the fly," create a plan for using social media. Hagler (2011) and LeDuc and Samaha (2011) suggested creating individual and departmental plans to meet job expectations regarding social media and to maintain a consistent schedule for posting content. Further, Cabellon (2010) explained how to create a student affairs social media plan (including a strategy for measuring whether the department reached its goals of student engagement), going beyond everyday technologies to incorporate new social media platforms and executing social media to create a professional brand.

Although technology is useful in certain situations, it can also be a distraction and can take away from face-to-face interactions that are necessary when working with others and serving students. The Internet is helpful in many situations, but using technology in a meeting can be disrespectful to those around you. Some positions in student affairs require you to be accessible at all hours or while on duty, but being on your phone while in a meeting can be viewed as unprofessional. If you do need to use a cell phone, be sure it's in silent mode in order to reduce interruptions. Not all communications that come to your phone are emergencies. Finding a balance for using technology allows you to be accessible and connected to the online community while also fully engaging in the environment with the people around you.

Overuse of Technology and Social Media

Because of the increasing number of social media platforms and technological devices, their use can become detrimental to the effectiveness of new professionals. Time spent using social media might take away from time spent working on face-to-face interactions with students and colleagues. The negative impact cell phone technology has on interactions between students on college and university campuses can potentially have the same negative impact on new professionals (Barnard, 2003). Although handheld devices have made information easily accessible, they can be used at the cost of human interactions and building authentic relationships. Overuse of social media and technology can have a negative impact on your ability to network and build professional relationships with students and colleagues. There is a limit to how effective an individual can be when there are too many social media accounts to maintain.

It can be challenging to keep up with the program, Facebook, Twitter, and Instagram accounts. Sometimes I feel like I can barely keep up with my e-mails. —Dean of students at a large public research university

Gemmill and Peterson (2006) found a relationship between high levels of technology use, disruptions from technology, and perceived stress for professionals. As stated earlier, finding balance using social media and technology is important for new professionals as they develop their professional practice. Social media and technology are meant to enhance the programs and services offered to students, not to take away from our impact on students. Use them and manage them effectively. As technology continues to advance and social media platforms continue to be developed, how can we, as professionals, avoid overusing these tools? Consider quality over quantity and how to manage the use of social media and technology to maximize your reach to students and colleagues. Assess what tools work best for you to meet the needs of your job responsibilities.

Limited Interactions for Authentic Networking

Using social media and technology to develop professional relationships with students and colleagues can be very helpful when developing a network and online support system. One limitation with developing relationships through electronic communications is that most platforms and media have privacy settings that either allow users to hide parts of their profiles or prohibit other users from finding their profile. Although privacy settings are helpful in many cases, one pitfall is that people who are not in your online network won't be able to see what you're posting.

> *I realized that by having a private account I was not fully engaging in these online discussions.* —Program coordinator at a midsize public university

Hagler (2011) discussed the lack of sincerity in how users of social media and technology platforms communicate with other users. Some users develop an online brand or persona that is not completely congruent with their personal values and actions. Although this can be beneficial for building an online relationship in the short term, it might present challenges to building authentic long-term professional relationships. Student affairs professionals can uniquely communicate with various campus constituents to increase accessibility and build community by sharing about family, meetings, university-related events, and even personal workouts (Johnson, 2011). The more authentic and personal you can be, while maintaining your professionalism in your online interactions with others, the more you'll have meaningful interactions and authentic networking relationships.

Using Technology and Social Media in Student Affairs

Technology and social media in higher education continue to evolve with new advances and platforms. New professionals need to be proactive in learning the history, best practices, and hazards related to social media and technology in student affairs work.

> *It may take some time to adjust to social media platforms initially; however, after that initial investment of time and resources, it becomes more feasible to manage. I'd suggest asking for help to maximize the potential of technology; I was reluctant to use Twitter for many years, then realized how much useful information is out there.* —Vice president of student services at a community college

As the literature and personal accounts have demonstrated, new professionals need to develop competencies in technology and social media. The following six strategies will help you maximize your technology and social media use in student affairs.

1. **Decide what technology works best for your job responsibilities.** Several social media and technology platforms are available to you as a professional. Not all platforms make sense for the work you're responsible for in your position. Stay on top of innovative technology and choose a few platforms that work best for you and the work you do with students.

2. **Develop a social media plan.** Although social media and new technology can be overwhelming to coordinate and implement, creating a plan helps keep you organized and on top of all the Facebook liking, Twitter following, and LinkedIn posting. Consider delegating tasks and creating a team to disburse the workload. Strategically using social media and technology helps you serve your constituents and build a campus community.

3. **Connect and share information with students and colleagues in person and online.** Not only can you use social media and technology to build community on your campus, you can also use various platforms to connect with colleagues and share best practices related to your work in student affairs. Participate in #SAChat or post content that builds capacity for students and colleagues in higher education.

4. **Embrace ambiguity, be flexible, and continue to seek out professional development opportunities to learn more about new technology.** Technological advancement will not come to a halt any time soon. There is a new application or device that improves on the technology that existed before it nearly every month. New professionals should be ready to learn the newest technology and how students are using it to engage in the campus community.

5. **Know how to be a digital citizen.** It is the user's responsibility to know the law, best practices, and security concerns related to technology use. In order to be a knowledgeable digital citizen, regularly check online sites such as Digital Citizenship (http://www.digitalcitizenship.net) and Digital Media Law Project (http://www.dmlp.org/legal-guide) that provide up-to-date information related to appropriate, responsible use of technology.

6. **Be Authentic. Be Professional. Be You.** There is a balancing act that you, as a new professional, have to engage in as you transition from being a student to a career employee at a college or university. You don't have to create separate accounts for your personal life and work, but use privacy settings wisely. Develop an online persona that best represents you and your brand.

Student affairs professionals need to be experts in knowing how students are engaged, involved, and best served on college campuses today. This chapter provides a foundation for new professionals to understand social media and technology use, but it is far from a comprehensive guide to all platforms you might encounter in this work. New professionals can take advantage of webinars, online chats and resources, and in-person professional development events to continue developing their competencies and enhancing their skills as student affairs professionals. Colleagues with expertise using social media and technology can also be approached for tips. Consider this advice from Stoller (2011), a student affairs technology expert: "Whenever/wherever you notice a new technology solution, thought piece, or tech-based recommendation, always ask a question: Is this relevant to the work that I do in student affairs?" (para. 1). If you find yourself saying yes to this question and you have implemented the use of a new technology, share your best practice through any social media platform or in person at a professional development event.

References

Barnard, C. A. (2003). The impact of cell phone use on building community. *Student Affairs Online*, *4*(4). Retrieved from http://www.studentaffairs.com/ejournal/Fall_2003/CellPhones.html

Barrett, W. (2003). Information technology in student affairs. In S. R. Komives & D. B. Woodard, Jr. (Eds.), *Student services: A handbook for the profession* (4th ed., pp. 379–396). San Francisco, CA: Jossey-Bass.

Burkard, A., Cole, D. C., Ott, M., & Stoflet, T. (2005). Entry-level competencies of new student affairs professionals: A Delphi study. *NASPA Journal*, *42*(3), 283–309. doi: 10.2202/1949-6605.1509

Cabellon, E. (2010, June 8). A student affairs social media plan. [Blog post]. Retrieved from http://edcabellon.com/tech/socialmediaplan

Conway, J., & Hubbard, B. (2003). From bricks to bytes: Building an online activities environment. *Student Affairs Online, 4*(3). Retrieved from http://studentaffairs.com/ejournal/Summer_2003/Bricks-to-Bytes.html

DeAndréa, D. C., Ellison, N. B., LaRose, R., Steinfield, C., & Fiore, A. (2012). Serious social media: On the use of social media for improving students' adjustment to college. *Internet and Higher Education, 15*(1), 15–23. doi: doi:10.1016/j.iheduc.2011.05.009

Dodson, L. F., & Dean, M. (2003). Career services 24/7: The online career center. *Student Affairs Online, 4*(3). Retrieved from http://studentaffairs.com/ejournal/Summer_2003/CareerServices24 – 7.html

Duderstadt, J. J., Atkins, D. E., & Van Houweling, D. (2002). *Higher education in the digital age: Technology issues and strategies for American colleges and universities.* Westport, CT: Praeger.

EDUCAUSE. (2010). *7 things you should know about backchannel communication.* Retrieved from https://net.educause.edu/ir/library/pdf/ELI7057.pdf

Fishman, S. (2012). Higher education administration with social media: Including applications in student affairs, enrollment management, alumni relations, and career centers. *Journal of Student Affairs Research & Practice, 49*(4), 471–474. doi:10.1515/jsarp-2012-6625.

Gemmill, E., & Peterson, M. (2006). Technology use among college students: Implications for student affairs professionals. *NASPA Journal, 43*(2), 280–300. doi: 10.2202/1949-6605.1640

Gruzd, A., Takheyev, Y., & Wellman, B. (2011). Imagining Twitter as an imagined community. *American Behavioral Scientist, 55*(10), 1294–1318. doi: 10.1177/0002764211409378

Hagler, S. (2011). Moving beyond just because: A theoretical approach to the use of social media as a relationship management tool for student affairs. *Campus Activities Programming, 44*(4), 24–26.

Heiberger, G., & Harper, R. (2008). Have you Facebooked Astin lately? In R. Junco & D. M. Timm (Eds.), *Using Technology to Increase Student Involvement* (New Directions for Student Services, No. 124, pp. 19–35). San Francisco, CA: Jossey-Bass.

Jenness, S. (2011). Rethinking Facebook: A tool to promote student engagement. *Journal of the Australian & New Zealand Student Services Association, 38*, 53–62.

Johnson, L. (2011). Build rapport with students by embracing social media. *Student Affairs Today, 13*(10), 12.

Joosten, T., Pasquini, L., & Harness, L. (2013). Guiding social media at our institutions. *Planning for Higher Education, 41*(2), 125–135.

Junco, R. (2012). The relationship between frequency of Facebook use, participation in Facebook activities, and student engagement. *Computers & Education, 58*(1), 162–171. doi:10.1016/j.compedu.2011.08.004

Junco, R., Dahms, A. R., Bower, M. L., Craddock, S., Davila, D. S., Hamilton, M., Kane, C., Koval, B. C., Kriegelstein, T., Mitchell, G. B., & Sanborn, D. (2010). Media review: #sachat on Twitter. *Journal of Student Affairs Research and Practice, 47*(2), 251–254. doi:10.2202/1949-6605.6178

Kleinglass, N. (2005). Who is driving the changing landscape in student affairs? In K. Kruger (Ed.), *Special issue: Technology in student affairs: Supporting student learning and services* (New Directions for Student Services, No. 112, pp. 25–38). San Francisco, CA: Jossey-Bass.

LeDuc, B., & Samaha, A. (2011). Using social media to hit a home run! *Campus Activities Programming, 44*(4), 15–17.

Leece, R. (2011). The use of social media by student affairs practitioners. *Journal of the Australian & New Zealand Student Services Association, 38*, 50–52.

Love, P. G., & Estanek, S. M. (2004). *Rethinking student affairs practice*. San Francisco, CA: Jossey-Bass.

Lovell, C., & Kosten, L. (2000). Skills, knowledge, and personal traits necessary for success as a student affairs administrator: A meta-analysis of thirty years of research. *NASPA Journal, 37*(4), 553–572. doi: 10.2202/1949-6605.1118

Lowery, J. (2004). Student affairs for a new generation. In M. D. Coomes & R. DeBard (Eds.), *Special issue: Serving the millennial generation* (New Directions for Student Services, No. 106, pp. 87–99). San Francisco, CA: Jossey-Bass.

Marklein, M. B. (2009, November 16). Social networks could help community college students. *USA Today*. Retrieved from http://www.usatoday.com/news/education/2009-11-16-ccsse16_ST_N.htm

Moneta, L. (2005). Technology and student affairs: Redux. In K. Kruger (Ed.), *Special issue: Technology in student affairs: Supporting student learning and services* (New Directions for Student Services, No. 112, pp. 3–14). San Francisco, CA: Jossey-Bass.

Reich, S. M. (2010). Adolescent's sense of community on MySpace and Facebook: A mixed-methods approach. *Journal of Community Psychology, 38*(6), 688–705. doi: 10.1002/jcop.20389

Renn, K. A., & Zeligman, D. M. (2005). Learning about technology and student affairs: Outcomes of an online immersion. *Journal of College Student Development, 46*(5), 547–555. doi: 10.1353/csd.2005.0055

Schawbel, D. (2013). *Promote yourself: The new rules for career success.* New York, NY: St. Martin's Press.

Stoller, E. (2011, January 18). *Social media, student affairs, and influence.* [Blog post]. Retrieved from http://www.insidehighered.com/blogs/student_affairs_and_technology/social_media_student_affairs_and_influence

Torres, M. (2012). Hi! I'm the new program advisor. *Campus Activities Programming, 44*(6), 33–35.

Twitter. (2014). What is a tweet? Retrieved from https://about.twitter.com/what-is-twitter/story-of-a-tweet

Wortham, F. B. (2013). Social networking: Engaging prospective and admitted African American and other minority students before they arrive on campus. *About Campus, 18*(1), 21–24. doi: 10.1002/abc.21108

MAKING PROFESSIONAL CONNECTIONS

CHAPTER NINE

Lori M. Reesor, Grace A. Bagunu, and Luke Gregory

The key to personal and professional success is having a strong support base of people who believe in you, challenge you, and help you grow—a recurring concept in many leadership books in the popular literature. In addition, it is a common belief that having positive and motivated people around you will have a positive impact on your destiny. As student affairs professionals, we try to create these kinds of conditions for our students. Sometimes we can be the positive change agents who make a difference in students' lives. Likewise, new professionals should establish a support system of connections, mentors, and professional involvement to enhance their professional growth and development. In this chapter we offer suggestions for networking with other higher education professionals, developing relationships with mentors, and recommendations for getting involved in professional organizations.

The Art of Networking

When I first became a professional, networking scared me to death. Going up to a stranger and striking up a conversation while pretending to be confident and smart seemed so tough. My taste of how easy it could be happened during a trip to NASPA IV-West. I decided to join the optional walk on one of the mornings to put myself out there. I enjoy walking, so I figured it was perfect. I ended up walking with another woman who was a professional in the field, and we talked about everything under the sun—personal, professional, etc. I found out after our walk that she was a very well-known and respected professional in the field. I laughed at myself, because I think if I had known who she was in the beginning, I probably would have shied away, but without the introductions and in the casual environment, I made a connection. Later on that morning, I realized I had networked and I didn't even know it! It wasn't as scary as I thought it was going to be. —Housing professional at a large public university

New professionals in student affairs establish their professional identity through professional involvement and connections with colleagues. In the scenario just recounted, the new professional had an "a-ha" moment: In this profession the opportunity to engage in casual conversations with colleagues abounds. For example, if you're in line to get popcorn at your university's basketball game—we all know how long concession lines can be—take advantage of these few minutes to meet those around you. If you exercise on campus, as many administrators and faculty members do, participating in group exercise classes is a great way to meet people from across campus. Networking can be intimidating, but it's also very basic and easy.

As colleges and universities change, the response of student affairs professionals must change as well, but change can be stressful. Having a network can be a stress reliever; it's comforting to realize that colleagues face similar issues. Having someone to bounce ideas off of can be a huge asset. Networks can help you stay knowledgeable about current events and opportunities in the field, recruitment processes, information technology trends, campus security issues, and opportunities for advancement.

For some people, the word *networking* has a negative connotation. They envision the old boys' network—meeting others to gain favors, loyalties, or personal influence (Pancrazio & Gray, 1982). Networking might sound artificial and manipulative, but it's simply a means of meeting new colleagues, and it can be a collaborative, collegial process. Networking can be beneficial for the individual as well as a collective group, particularly for White women and people of color, who can find support with others outside the dominant group of White

> **Networks enhance a profession by encouraging competence, communication, and support.**

males. Networks enhance a profession by encouraging competence, communication, and support. According to de Janasz and Forret (2008):

> Relationships built through networking make it easier to contact people who can share information about potential opportunities or introduce individuals to others who have this information. Whether through face-to-face, phone, written, or electronic means, individual attempts to "connect" with others who can provide needed information and opportunities. (pp. 630–631)

Networking is a valuable tool that can be used throughout your career. Networking skills can help you "increase your level of confidence; acquire mentors; tap into the 'hidden' job market; exchange valuable information, knowledge, resources, and contacts; give and receive advice and moral support; [and] form long-term personal and professional relationships" (Helfgott, 1995, p. 60).

> *To me, networking is all about shared learning—whether that's sharing what you know or tapping into the collective knowledge base of all the professionals around you. It is the vital process of building connections with others; learning while being reminded of how much more one can learn; grounding oneself in both how far one has come and how much more one can be.* —Housing professional at a large private university

Building a professional network is an important aspect of anyone's career, but it can be a puzzling experience. Here are some basic suggestions to help the new practitioner develop a professional network:

☞ **Network at all levels in the organization.** Networking is not just an up or down process. Although there can be value to networking with people at higher levels, there are also benefits to developing collegial relationships with peers and colleagues in other areas of the institution. For example, if you work in admissions, having contacts in the housing department can help you be more successful in your position.

I find networking easiest when I attend professional functions with another person who already knows many people and is able to introduce me. I find this less intimidating and easier to do.
—Admissions professional at a midsize public university

I now see networking as building relationships to have a network of professional support. It helps keep me relevant on hot topics and allows me to see things in a different lens. I think the length of many of the relationships I have with colleagues has allowed me to see networking differently. I may not see a colleague for a year or two and then get an e-mail asking to connect about a student or a practice my current institution is doing. That has nothing to do with moving up the ladder but rather about serving our students.
—Housing professional at a large private university

☞ **Make it a top priority to seek out colleagues.** If there's an administrator on your campus you especially respect and would like to get to know, take the initiative. Ask him or her to join you for a cup of coffee or lunch. Set up a meeting. Although most administrators welcome the opportunity to get to know new professionals, they have very busy schedules; therefore, make the meeting purposeful. Maybe the person is creating a new program you would like to learn more about, or maybe you're thinking about a doctorate one day and want to get his or her opinion. Most administrators and faculty members (even the very busy ones) will be flattered by your interest and will take the time to meet with you.

I've grown to learn that networking can happen at any and all times and you don't need an event to prompt it. I've learned the importance of following up with connections I make on my campus or across the country both within my functional area and outside of it. I've learned most of these skills from mentors and [conference] sessions on developing networking skills. This advice has helped to demystify networking for me. —Multicultural affairs professional at a large public university

☞ **Be sincere and genuine in your relationships.** If you're making artificial contacts with people you might be able to use, you're not networking. You can tell when someone is a fake and just schmoozing; others can tell, too. "People are quick to recognize and avoid those who are only interested in 'what's in it for me'" (Helfgott, 1995, p. 63). If you're sincerely interested in someone's background, values, thoughts, and opinions, this is a different type of relationship. Be yourself. In student affairs, most of us are connected in one way or another, or we share mutual colleagues. Impressions can be long lasting, so make sure they're positive.

It's not about how many people you have in your network but more about the quality of those relationships. The better quality relationships you have the more you'll get out of it in terms of assistance and growth as a professional. If you have such a large network with superficial relationships you'll never get any real feedback or growth. —Student activities professional at a large public university

☞ **Follow up.** Sincere follow-up efforts are the key to turning your network contacts into opportunities (Helfgott, 1995). Send a thank-you note to anyone who has given you a referral or provided support. Be prepared to engage in different ways to keep the relationship going. A one-time encounter is not networking. With some people, it takes a number of interactions before they remember you, get to know you, and consider you part of their network. Don't be discouraged if you meet someone a dozen times and they still don't remember your name. This happens to all of us; don't take it personally. It just means that you might not develop a significant relationship with that person.

Use online networks to follow up with contacts. Find an online networking site to share program ideas, discuss views on policy matters, and stay connected and up-to-date with colleagues across the country and even throughout the world. One thing to keep in mind about online networking: Always be professional, especially with postings and pictures—you never know when a potential employer might see what you've posted. Online social networking is great for follow-up and maintaining networks, but don't let the cyber world be your first interaction with other professionals; face-to-face is always the best place to make a good first impression. See Chapter Eight on social media and technology for additional advice in this area.

Forret and Dougherty (2001) identified five dimensions of networking behavior: maintaining contacts, socializing, engaging in professional activities, participating in church and community, and increasing internal visibility. Put yourself in networking opportunities that naturally fit into your daily routine. Attend a brown-bag lunch training session, which is an excellent way to meet other members of the campus community. Exchange business cards with a colleague and plan to have coffee together one day. Plan collaborative programs as a way to build a network across campus departments. You can showcase your strengths and learn from others as you build a useful network. Networks can also grow by the "spider web effect": Someone you know introduces you to someone else, and so on. A simple inquiry can help grow your network. Although networking can seem difficult and intimidating, it can be fun and very rewarding. The best way to begin is with the basics.

> *I've found that networking is the key to finding a job, and the resources you develop can prove invaluable later in life.* —Housing professional at a small private university

Mentoring

"The evidence is overwhelming in the literature that significant sources of social support, as well as 'learning,' are professional networks and mentoring" (VanDerLinden, 2005, p. 740). VanDerLinden (2005) said that although finding funding for professional development might be challenging, especially at smaller institutions such as community colleges, taking advantage of human capital can be very cost effective and often easily implemented. "Mentoring can be a life-altering relationship that inspires mutual growth, learning, and development. Its effects can be remarkable, profound, and enduring; mentoring relationships have the capacity to transform individuals, groups, organizations, and communities" (Ragins & Kram, 2007, p. 3).

Finding a Mentor

Various definitions exist for the word *mentor*. As adapted from Moore and Salimbene (1981), a mentor is a more experienced professional who guides, advises, and assists in numerous ways a less experienced, often younger, upwardly mobile protégé in the context of a close, professionally centered relationship, usually lasting a year or more. Kalbfleisch (2002) defined a mentor as someone who has "achieved personal or professional success and is willing and able to share covert and overt practices that have assisted him or her in becoming successful" (p. 63). Many research studies (Bell, 1996; Bolton, 2005; Caruso, 1992; Kelly, 1984; Kogler Hill, Bahniuk, Dobos, & Rouner, 1989; Kram, 1985; Rueywei, Shih-Ying, & Min-Lang, 2014) have shown that a mentor can have a positive effect on a person's career. In fact, some studies have shown that

> **Mentoring is an important part of our career development.**

those who experience supportive relationships such as mentoring have more opportunities for success, advancement, and achievement in their careers (Day & Allen, 2004; Kogler Hill et al., 1989; Wunsch, 1994). The profession of student affairs is no different. As new professionals, many of us learn that mentoring is an important part of our career development (Roberts, 2007). The question is how to develop mentoring relationships.

Networking can be an important factor in meeting a mentor (Bloomberg, 2014; Helfgott, 1995; Kelly, 1984; Scandura & Williams, 2001). In one research study, student affairs professionals suggested that new professionals take a proactive approach in initiating relationships with a mentor (Kelly, 1984). Many new professionals believe that the vice president for student affairs taps his or her magic wand and picks one new professional to be the protégé. Rarely does it happen this way; often, it is the new professional who initiates the relationship.

Zachary and Fischler (2009) recommended that to begin the mentoring process, you first assess your needs. What do you want from a mentor, what kind of help do you need, and who can provide it? Typically, you can expect a mentor to provide emotional support and direct assistance with professional and career development, and to act as a role model (Tentoni, 1995). It is also appropriate to look for different things from different mentors. Once you define your needs, ask colleagues to identify potential mentors. Create and take advantage of opportunities to interact. Put yourself in situations that allow you to be highly visible, and always do a good job at whatever you're doing (Zachary & Fischler, 2009).

> *I met my mentor at a training she did for us on campus. We had a natural connection as two women of color. We continued to stay in touch and she returned to campus several times. We also attended a few of the same conferences. I trust her because she listens well, advises based on what is best, not what I want to hear, and our relationship is a two-way street.* —Housing professional at a large private university

> *I find someone whose management or professional work style I agree with, and I try to build a relationship with this person in order to learn more about how he or she became successful.* —Admissions professional at a small private college

> *I found a mentor by attending a conference and hearing a speaker. I really understood and liked her ideas, and thought I could learn from her. So I approached her and introduced myself a couple times and then asked to work for her for free as an intern—anything to work for someone who could teach me something new.* —Orientation professional at a large public university

Zachary and Fischler (2009) have provided an excellent list of characteristics to look for in a potential mentor: a similar or shared value system, available time, professional competence in the area you want expertise, active contributions to the field, and a genuine interest in your professional development (a nurturing personality). The mentor should be someone you like and trust and be an open communicator. Fortunately, many people have these characteristics, so you'll have plenty of opportunities to select different mentors. "Effective mentors are like friends in that their goal is to create a safe context for growth. They are also like family in that their focus is to offer an unconditional, faithful acceptance of the protégé" (Bell, 1996, p. 7).

Selecting a mentor takes time, effort, and commitment, so be patient if a relationship takes a while to develop. Ideally, you'll have a number of mentors with different expectations to challenge and support you. As

Batchelor (1993) said, "Mentoring relationships often develop into rich and helpful lifelong friendships" (p. 381).

> *The benefit [of having a mentor] is having advice and concern from an individual who has already traveled down the career road you are traveling.* —Financial aid professional at a midsize public university

> *I talk to them about my identities and how I see them play out in relationships with others on campus. I talk with them about politics and creating change. I talk to them about balancing my personal life and how that impacts my career. I also talk to them about my dogs, my partner, and good beer.* —Housing professional at a large private university

Challenges with Mentors

Successful mentorships are beneficial not only for the individuals involved but also for the organization (Rosenbach, 1993; Sandler, 1993). As with any relationship, it takes two people to make it work; both have to cultivate the relationship.

> *The challenges of having a mentor are the challenges of any relationship—the investment of time and resources. It takes incredible intentionality in an era that intentionality is rare and time is a hot commodity. It also takes incredible trust to be authentic and vulnerable.* —Housing professional at a large public university

Here are a few recommendations, adapted from Trimble's (1994) suggestions for protégés, to make the most of the relationship with your mentor.

☞ **Clarify needs and expectations.** Acknowledge that each mentor won't be able to meet every one of your needs. By matching your needs with each mentor's particular strengths, you should both feel more successful in the relationship.

☞ **Be time conscious.** Most mentors are busy people, and although they might value the relationship, it's up to you to respect their schedules. Make an appointment in advance and have a specific purpose when you meet. Don't become a burden to your mentor.

☞ **Create a dialogue.** In any relationship, it's important to know when to stop talking and listen. Ask for clarification if necessary. Try to understand the values at work and the reasons for decisions. Ask your mentor to share experiences that might help you understand your own situation. Creating give-and-take communication challenges both of you and helps you gain new insights and make new discoveries.

☞ **Foster respect and appreciation for a valued professional.** As a protégé, you're seeking someone to support and care for you and your career. Show the same interest and care for your mentor. A caring attitude is important in the mentoring relationship. Provide the mentor with positive feedback, whether it's by writing a personal note, nominating him or her for an award, or just saying *thank you*.

Cross-race and Cross-gender Mentors

The most common mentoring relationships tend to be between members of the same gender and race (Blake-Beard, Murrell, & Thomas, 2007). Because many high-level administrators are White males, however, cross-racial and cross-gender mentoring might be the only choice for the professional development of underrepresented groups. Indeed, many have written about the importance and challenges of mentoring for women and people of color (Batchelor, 1993; Blake-Beard et al., 2007; Evans, 2000; Frankel, 2004; Hawks & Muha, 1991; Kelly, 1984; Luebkemann & Clemens, 1994; Murrell, Crosby, & Ely, 1999; Ragins, 2002; Smith & Davidson, 1992). Stanley and Lincoln (2005) asserted that "it is especially important that faculty of color be mentored effectively; majority administrators and senior faculty are likely to be perplexed by the task, because they may have no previous experience with minority colleagues to draw upon" (p. 46). Open and honest conversations can avoid the pitfall of miscommunication and the eventual dissolution of the mentoring relationship.

The literature relating to cross-racial mentoring shows mixed and sometimes conflicting results (Blake-Beard et al., 2007). Some research has shown that cross-racial mentoring relationships have not been as successful because of organizational and personal barriers (Luna & Cullen, 1995; Rosenbach, 1993). For example, protégés might feel pressured to participate only with individuals from a similar background when socializing and engaging in informal activities during mentoring.

According to Blake-Beard et al. (2007), cross-race mentoring can present a number of opportunities as well as challenges. Cross-racial mentoring relationships can even be extremely beneficial. Although the cultural adjustment can be challenging for new professionals of color, just as it can be for students of color, having a respectful mentoring relationship with a professional from a different race or ethnicity can be a great asset. In fact, some believe that sharing an affinity—whether it is race, gender, or position level—can have a negative impact on mentoring relationships (Murrel et al., 1999).

On the other hand, new professionals of color working in predominantly White institutions might want to connect with people from similar backgrounds or cultures. Same-race mentoring allows you to share cultural sensitivity and discover similarities rather than emphasize differences (Luna & Cullen, 1995). Ideally, you'll find this support within student affairs, but some institutions still do not have many professionals of color. You might find support groups or networks in larger institutions. Many campuses have affinity groups such as an Hispanic network or a Black faculty and staff council. These organizations can help you meet other staff members on campus who share common experiences. If the group you're looking for doesn't exist, this might be your opportunity to create it. You might also need to look outside your institution to community or civic organizations, or even colleagues at other institutions. Look for statewide networks or groups that you can join. Having multiple mentors, some you identify with based on race and others you do not, can help you to get the most out of your mentoring relationships. Regardless of the avenue you choose, it's important to develop relationships.

> *When I first came to campus, I made contact with the office of multicultural affairs. Through that office, I learned of the African American network. This group of faculty, professional staff, and support staff met monthly at a local restaurant. We also had a listserv so we could communicate through e-mail. It was a way for me to feel connected with others and learn about special cultural opportunities.* —Multicultural affairs professional at a large private university

Cultural differences might lead to misunderstandings, but Rosenbach (1993) said that "racism and sexism in the workplace will disappear as leaders learn to work in diverse teams and begin to view all members as friends and colleagues" (p. 148). Therefore, mentoring relationships that cross gender and ethnic lines can enhance learning opportunities and improve overall organizational climate (Luna & Cullen, 1995; Rosenbach, 1993; Sandler, 1993).

> *I have had a wonderful experience being mentored by a former professor. The fact that we are not the same race, I think, has made the experience more enjoyable and rewarding. It's fun to chat about our respective careers, and I know that I can call on her to receive good advice about my next career move. Plus, she gets the whole diversity thing and the challenges that I face. Talking with her about those struggles is pretty easy, and I definitely feel supported. The cultural differences we have also benefit me, being that I am a new professional of color working on a predominantly White campus. I feel that our relationship provides me insight into her culture, thus helping me navigate my own institution. I think the insight I provide benefits her in a similar manner. Although I do have a mentor who shares my ethnicity, I wouldn't give the relationship up with my White mentor for anything!* —Student activities professional at a small private college

> *When I started my first position out of graduate school, I soon realized that being the only person of color in my department would be quite an adjustment. I called my mentor to vent a little and ask for guidance. Even though she is not a person of color, she coached me on how to talk about my adjustment issues. We also discussed possible projects or appointments I could gain in multicultural affairs or other diverse areas. I found this a great relief! To see that she understood where I was coming from and that she even offered to coach me on how to talk about it with my supervisors was awesome.* —Multicultural affairs professional at a midsize public university

Much literature exists on the potential problems of cross-gender mentoring relationships. There are benefits and challenges with cross-gender mentoring (Ragin, 2002). At times, men and women might assume stereotypical roles in relating to each other (Rosenbach, 1993). One new professional said, "I greatly respect my mentor, but at times he acts like my father as opposed to my professional advisor." In issues related to gender or sexual orientation, as significant relationships develop, increasing intimacy and sexual tensions can result. "A more frequent disadvantage for women being mentored by men are the innuendoes about the relationship from people who find it hard to believe that any relationship between a man and woman is not sexual" (Sandler, 1993, p. B3). Develop appropriate boundaries so the intentions of the relationship are clear. As with any potential sexual harassment situation, "the dangers in the traditional mentoring model are not necessarily gender-related, but rather are a function of the imbalance of power within the relationship" (Johnsrud, 1991, p. 9). Sandberg (2013) encouraged senior men to champion and sponsor promising women in their companies. Although she wrote from a corporate view, Sandberg encouraged cross-gender mentoring, although she acknowledged some of the challenges and biases that can occur between both individuals.

Stages of Mentoring

Zachary and Fischler (2009) described a developmental process common to the relationship between mentors and protégés. In the early stages, the relationship tends to be more dependent. The protégé might rely more on guidance from the mentor and have a strong desire to please the mentor. Protégés might need more confirmation. As protégés move on to the independent stage, they are more likely to establish their purpose as distinct from the mentor. They might ask questions such as, Am I competent and independent if I am still being helped? Will I always be a protégé? At the interdependent stage, "Persons have the ability to fulfill for one another the yearning for connectedness and the yearning for identity" (Johnsrud, 1991, p. 15).

> **Mentoring relationships take time and effort. The result can be long-lasting, meaningful relationships that allow you to grow and develop as a person and a professional.**

Working through developmental stages with a mentor is a normal process. Just as our parents will always see us as children, mentors might always see us as their protégés. It's not uncommon to outgrow mentors or to disagree or have ethical conflicts with them. Mentors are not perfect; they are human beings and make mistakes. They might disappoint you. They might give you bad advice. At these times, reassess your needs and their strengths, and try to have realistic expectations for the relationship.

Although the mentoring relationship might include challenges, it's usually mutually beneficial and caring. If you have numerous mentors, you will be able to hear many perspectives on complex issues.

> *I have multiple people I identify as mentors. They all have very different personalities and ideas from one another, but their purpose as my mentor tends to provide me the same type of support.*
> —Academic advising professional at a large public university

Mentoring relationships take time and effort. The result can be long-lasting, meaningful relationships that allow you to grow and develop as a person and a professional. "With a supportive environment and the right attitude, mentoring can be a powerful force to empower followers to be leaders" (Rosenbach, 1993, p. 149). Fisher (2012) suggested that once you find a mentor or mentors, start looking for a sponsor—someone who is invested in helping you move through the career pipeline by providing opportunities for you to gain more experience. Sponsors can emerge from your pool of mentors, especially those mentors with whom you have a deeply rooted and mutually beneficial relationship. Bloomberg (2014) suggested professional associations as the best venue for finding a suitable career mentor.

Professional Associations

A common question asked by new professionals is, Should I get involved in professional organizations? The answer is a resounding, Yes! The reasons are many (Nuss, 1993). Networking and finding mentors are two ways of developing connections, but professional organizations provide different learning experiences from those obtained on your own campus. They allow new professionals to observe leadership styles in a different venue. They're outlets for socializing and identifying colleagues who share the same values and interests or hold positions you might aspire to in the future (Gardner & Barnes, 2007). For many, being involved in professional organizations involves a "sense of obligation to help advance the status of the profession and fund programs that assist it" (Nuss, 1993, p. 368). Professional organizations can also be a way to develop new friendships, networks, and mentors.

> *I have become involved in professional organizations by meeting others within my field, developing friendships, and then volunteering to serve on committees with these other professionals. This has*

been a great way to learn more about my field and other organizations and to grow professionally. —Career services professional at a small private college

My involvement in NASPA as a new professional in student affairs has definitely eased my transition from graduate student to full-time professional. As a graduate student, the student affairs world seemed so big, full of seasoned professionals, opportunities, and lots to learn. The resources and networking opportunities that NASPA provides have made things a lot less scary! I am now able to navigate the student affairs world with ease, and I know that it is really a tight-knit community of individuals who are passionate about student development, just like I am. My involvement in NASPA has also introduced me to members of the "NASPA family," new professionals like myself and experienced professionals across the nation whom I can turn to as a resource. —Orientation professional at a large public university

Preparing on the Home Front

There are various ways to get involved in professional organizations. Read through the list of the best known student affairs associations found in Appendix A and check out their websites. Before you rush out and join a number of professional organizations, make sure you have consulted appropriate individuals, discussed expectations, and evaluated the campus culture related to your potential involvement. For example, a hall director might be interested in getting involved in the American College Personnel Association (ACPA). The housing director might think ACPA involvement is inappropriate for the hall director and suggest that he or she get involved in the Association of College and University Housing Officers–International instead.

Talk to your colleagues, faculty, mentors, and other network members about the history, structure, culture, and purpose of the organizations in which you're interested. Consult with your supervisors about their thoughts on and support for professional involvement. Support might include financial assistance to attend conferences or meetings, time off from work (rather than using vacation time), and the use of office supplies (postage, phone calls, etc.). New professionals commonly receive some funding for a regional conference, but you might have to pay to attend a national conference with your own money. Sometimes this policy differs if you're presenting a program. Clarify all these matters in advance to ensure your supervisor supports your involvement and you're aware of the parameters. When you're performing to your fullest ability the duties and responsibilities of the job you were hired to do and meeting the expectations of your supervisor, you're ready to get involved in professional associations.

> *Many professional connections I made were a result of my supervisor pushing me to get involved in the National Association for Campus Activities (NACA), an organization that's very supportive and welcoming of new professionals. My experience with NACA paved the way to new volunteer opportunities in NASPA.* —Student activities professional at a large public university

Making the Most of Professional Conferences

Attending conferences is an effective way to get involved in and learn more about what a professional organization has to offer, who its members are, and what future opportunities it provides. For new professionals, it might be advantageous to start by attending state and regional conferences, drive-in workshops, or webinars. These events are usually smaller, allowing for more personal connections and easier navigation, than a national conference.

No matter what your position (whether you're a new professional or a mid-level manager), being a newcomer to a conference can be intimidating. You might feel as though everyone already knows one another and you're the outsider. Be careful before you make hasty judgments about the friendliness or openness of an organization on the basis of your initial observations. Student affairs professionals are rarely exclusionary. What might seem like a clique is really a group of friends and colleagues who have known one another for years and are getting together for their annual event.

> *I had just arrived at the hotel, tired because the plane was late and it took longer than I thought to arrange for transportation. I immediately felt like a new freshman on campus trying to find the registration area. After asking for directions several times, I found the area, only to notice several small groups of people talking. I wondered if anyone would ever talk to me. Then someone shouted my name—it was a good friend from graduate school. I realized*

that I, too, knew people here, and it would be okay. —Multicultural affairs professional at a large public university

Here are some important tips for making the most of your first (or second or third) professional conference (Swanson, 1996):

☞ **Attend the session for newcomers or first-time attendees.** This session will provide helpful information regarding the conference and the organization. Often, you'll have an opportunity to meet some of the leaders of the organization. You'll also meet other newcomers, so you can start building your own network at the conference.

☞ **Attend as many keynote speeches and interest sessions as possible.** Review the conference program guide carefully and mark the sessions you would like to attend. Select two or three options for each time block, as some sessions might be full by the time you get there. If you're with other staff members from your institution, split up and get to as many different sessions as you can. Arrive early at sessions, because some fill up quickly. Go to the opening session and the reception. This will help you get a sense of the conference, the association, and the leadership.

☞ **Meet new people.** Introduce yourself to people around you. Contacts are one of the greatest benefits of the conference. You'll be amazed at how small the world of student affairs is. If you meet someone you'd like to stay connected with, exchange business cards. Visit as many college- or university-sponsored receptions as you can. You'll meet a lot of people and learn how to get more involved. You could even end up with a full meal, which is important given the low budgets of new professionals. Attend task force or commission meetings.

☞ **Attend business meetings.** This is an opportunity to learn more about network, commission, or regional activities. Business meetings might sound formal and only for those who have formal positions in the organization, but most business meetings are open to all members. Again, these activities are a great time to volunteer and get involved.

Also, by attending your state or regional business meetings, you'll learn more about professional development activities closer to home.

☞ **Enjoy the time away.** Treat yourself to some fun and excitement. Use your free time and meals to get to know others and share ideas. If special tours or events are offered, try to take advantage of them. If you have a limited budget, look for low-cost activities that are often provided. If you're in a new area, visit some of the local highlights. Seeing new places is a perk of attending conferences—take advantage of the opportunity. Not all learning occurs in the interest sessions.

☞ **Reflect on the experience.** When the conference is over and you return to campus, it's natural to feel exhausted and exhilarated. Focus on what you learned. Share the information and handouts with your colleagues. Follow up on the contacts you made at the conference by sending a short note. Thank your supervisor for the opportunity to attend.

Whether you can afford to attend a professional conference or not, you can still gain a lot of useful information by following the backchannel: Search for the Twitter hashtag connected to the conference. Conferences are a rich source of professional development and networking, especially for new professionals. See Chapter Eight on technology and social media for other opportunities to network and engage with colleagues using online platforms.

Levels of Organizational Involvement

Over the course of your career, your interest in certain organizations might vary. Some new professionals maintain constant membership in a more general association such as NASPA or ACPA and, depending on their job responsibilities, also join a more specialized interest organization (Nuss, 1993). Once you determine which organization is most interesting to you, you can become involved at various levels (Nuss, 1993).

☞ **Passive member or consumer.** At this stage, you're an official member who receives the mailings to stay current in the profession. You can take advantage of some of the technological services provided by the organization—by join-ing a listserv, for example. At some point you might start attending the state, regional, or national conferences, but you still feel more like an observer or spectator. Consider joining one of the committees or special interest groups. For example, NASPA has a New Professionals and Gradu-ate Students Knowledge Community; other organizations might have a Black caucus. Some professional organizations also have electronic learning communities, which allow you to develop connections and gain new knowledge online. These organizations are effective ways to connect with oth-er professionals with similar interests. Once you're ready to increase your involvement in the association, the first step you can take is to volunteer at the conference. Volunteering is an excellent way to meet people and start learning about how the operation works. Find an area you're interested in and look for others who share that interest. Knowledge and interest groups form on almost every topic in student af-fairs. When you attend the conferences, be sure to go to the business meetings and socials. These events enable you to meet the leaders of the organization and hear about current activities and events. At almost every business meeting, of-ficers will ask for volunteers to help with future programs. This is your chance to get involved.

☞ **Contributor.** Another way to be involved in the profes-sional association is as a contributor (Nuss, 1993). You can write a proposal to present a program, write an article for the newsletter, participate in online discussions, or submit research results for publication. If you're interested in pre-senting a program, talk with people who have done it. Ask to see a copy of their proposal to get an idea of how to complete one. Ask a mentor or active member in the or-ganization to review your proposal and give you feedback. Ask one of your mentors or a colleague at another institu-tion to help you present. Volunteer to read proposals dur-ing the selection process to get an idea of what the reviewer might be looking for in proposals. Presenting is a great way to continue a networking relationship and become more involved at the same time.

☞ **Coordinator.** This means you're responsible for planning, coordinating, or directing the efforts of other volunteers (Nuss, 1993). Typically, this responsibility is on a state, regional, or national level; it might require a time commitment of 6 months to 2 years. You'll likely be working with volunteers all over the country (or world), which could involve interaction by phone, e-mail, or regular mail. You'll need good skills in coordinating, budgeting, and supervising, as well as strong interpersonal and communication skills (Nuss, 1993). The expectations for volunteers in professional associations are no different than those for employees. Be thorough, dependable, responsible, and effective. Although you're working for a volunteer association, the accountability and expectations of high quality are no less than those for your paid position.

☞ **Officer.** The highest level of involvement is governance (Nuss, 1993), being elected or appointed to a regional or national board. At this level, individuals affect policy and long-term planning for the organization. The time commitment can be significant. Although this is not typically the level at which new professionals participate, it's appropriate to set goals and plans to reach this stage at some point in your career.

Getting involved is not limited to professional organizations at the regional or national level; you can get involved in committees and associations within your campus community. There are a variety of opportunities to network and develop as a professional at your current institution. Search committees, steering committees, staff associations, and campus meetings are just a few venues to engage and network in your local community.

When I first started working at the university, I felt like an outsider. I walked the campus and didn't know any faces. I would have lunch with office coworkers who had worked at the university for multiple years, and they would know a number of other colleagues from other departments eating lunch around us. Working on a campus that was so large, I thought I would never be able to connect with colleagues.

Then I was asked to sit on a campuswide committee and a steering committee, and through both experiences I have networked with more colleagues around the campus. Now, when I eat lunch on campus, I run into colleagues I have networked with while serving on committees, and I feel like a connected member of the university. —Student activities professional at a small private college

So where do you start in this area of professional involvement? As always, it starts with self-assessment. What do you hope to accomplish? What talents do you have? How can you contribute? What are some areas you wish to develop? Once you have decided on your goals, let your mentors know of your plans. Have them introduce you to the leaders of the association. When you meet the leaders, instead of simply saying, "I want to get involved," tell them some of the specific things you'd like to do. If it seems appropriate, follow up in writing and include a résumé so the leader or decision maker can know how best to use your talents and skills. Following up with an e-mail is also useful. Finally, if it doesn't happen the first time, try again. Many leaders receive a lot of communication from their professional associations (and about their own work), so be patient and contact them again if you don't hear from them right away.

Professional associations play an important role in your career. The benefits include meeting valued colleagues and making friendships, learning about campus issues from new perspectives, and having access to cutting-edge research and vital federal, state, and local

> **Professional associations play an important role in your career.**

updates related to students and higher education. Research shows that involvement in professional associations influences the ability to network for future career opportunities and expands networks to foster future collaborations among colleagues (Gardner & Barnes, 2007). Once you become involved, you have an opportunity to establish a professional reputation beyond your campus, and you can influence the future of the profession. You are expected to be professionally involved, and the rewards are great.

Conclusion

Just as with the students on our campuses, it is important to ensure new professionals are retained in the profession, are successful, and are constantly learning and growing. One factor that helps new professionals remain in the profession is to develop connections. Making professional connections starts with building relationships with colleagues and mentors who can continue to help you develop in the field. Getting involved in a professional organization and attending conferences can help you build these support networks. Finding support on and off campus can help new professionals prosper in the student affairs profession. The suggestions and stories contributed by new professionals in this chapter illustrate the importance of developing and maintaining professional connections. With patience and perseverance, a new professional can network at any level, find a diverse group of mentors, and join professional organizations that will build a network of challenges and supports. These relationships foster growth and development throughout your professional and personal life. All it takes is a little courage, a bit of hope, and some know-how. It's up to you to begin the process. Although it takes time and effort, the personal and professional benefits make it worthwhile.

References

Batchelor, S. W. (1993). Mentoring and self-directed learning. In M. Barr (Ed.), *The handbook of student affairs administration* (pp. 378–389). San Francisco, CA: Jossey-Bass.

Bell, C. R. (1996). *Managers as mentors: Building partners for learning.* San Francisco, CA: Berrett-Koehler.

Blake-Beard, S. D., Murrell, A., & Thomas, D. (2007). The impact of race on understanding mentoring relationships. In B. R. Ragins & K. E. Kram (Eds.), *The handbook of mentoring at work: Theory, research, and practice* (pp. 223–247). Thousand Oaks, CA: Sage.

Bloomberg, M. (2014). The role of mentoring. *Physician Executive, 40*(2), 88–90.

Bolton, C. (2005). The role of mentors in our personal and professional lives. *College Student Affairs Journal, 24*(2), 180–188.

Caruso, R. E. (1992). *Mentoring and the business environment: Asset or liability?* Brookfield, VT: Dartmouth.

Day, R., & Allen, T. D. (2004). The relationship between career motivation and self-efficacy with protégé career success. *Journal of Vocational Behavior, 64*(1), 72–91. doi:10.1016/S0001-8791(03)00036-8 de Janasz, S. C., & Forret, M. L. (2008). Learning the art of networking: A critical skill for enhancing social capital and career success. *Journal of Management Education, 32*(5), 629–650. doi: 10.1177/1052562907307637

Evans, G. (2000). *Play like a man, win like a woman*. New York, NY: Broadway Books.

Fisher, A. (2012, September 21). Got a mentor? Good. Now find a sponsor. *Fortune*. Retrieved from http://fortune.com/2012/09/21/got-a-mentor-good-now-find-a-sponsor

Forret, M. L., & Dougherty, T. W. (2001). Correlates of networking behavior for managerial and professional employees. *Group & Organization Management, 26*(3), 283–311. doi: 10.1177/1059601101263004

Frankel, L. (2004). *Nice girls don't get the corner office*. New York, NY: Warner Business Books.

Gardner, S. K., & Barnes, B. J. (2007). Graduate student involvement: Socialization for the professional role. *Journal of College Student Development, 48*(4), 369–387. doi: 10.1353/csd.2007.0036

Hawks, B. K., & Muha, D. (1991). Facilitating the career development of minorities: Doing it differently this time. *Career Development Quarterly, 39*(3), 251–260. doi: 10.1002/j.2161-0045.1991.tb00397.x

Helfgott, D. (1995). Take 6 steps to networking success. *Planning Job Choices: 1995*. Bethlehem, PA: College Placement Council.

Johnsrud, L. K. (1991). Mentoring between academic women: The capacity for interdependence. *Initiatives, 54*(3), 7–17.

Kalbfleisch, P. J. (2002). Communicating in mentoring relationships: A theory for enactment. *Communication Theory, 12*(1), 63–69. doi:10.1111/j.1468-2885.2002.tb00259.x

Kelly, K. E. (1984). Initiating a relationship with a mentor in student affairs: A research study. *NASPA Journal, 21*, 49–54. doi: 10.1080/00220973.1984.11071881

Kogler Hill, S. E., Bahniuk, M. H., Dobos, J., & Rouner, D. (1989). Mentoring and other communication support in the academic setting. *Group & Organization Studies, 14,* 355–368.

Kram, K. E. (1985). *Mentoring at work*. Glenview, IL: Scott, Foresman.

Luebkemann, H., & Clemens, J. (1994). Mentors for women entering administration: A program that works. *National Association of Secondary School Principals Bulletin, 78,* 42–45.

Luna, G., & Cullen, D. L. (1995). *Empowering the faculty: Mentoring redirected and renewed* (ASHE-ERIC Higher Education Report, No. 3). Washington, DC: Association for the Study of Higher Education.

Moore, K. M., & Salimbene, A. M. (1981). The dynamics of the mentor–protégé relationship in developing women as academic leaders. *Journal for Educational Equity and Leadership, 2*(1), 51–64.

Murrell, A., Crosby, F., & Ely, R. (1999). *Mentoring dilemmas: Developmental relationships within multicultural organizations*. Mahwah, NJ: Erlbaum.

Nuss, E. M. (1993). The role of professional associations. In M. Barr (Ed.), *The handbook of student affairs administration* (pp. 364–377). San Francisco, CA: Jossey-Bass.

Pancrazio, S. B., & Gray, R. G. (1982). Networking for professional women: A collegial model. *Journal of NAWDAC, 45,* 16–19.

Ragins, B. R. (2002). Understanding diversified mentoring relationships: Definitions, challenges and strategies. In D. Clutterbuck & B. R. Ragins (Eds.), *Mentoring and diversity: An international perspective* (pp. 25–53). Oxford, United Kingdom: Butterworth-Heinemann.

Ragins, B. R., & Kram, K. E. (2007). *The handbook of mentoring at work: Theory, research, and practice*. Thousand Oaks, CA: Sage.

Roberts, D. M. (2007). Preferred methods of professional development in student affairs. *NASPA Journal, 44*(3), 561–577. doi: 10.2202/1949-6605.1836

Rosenbach, W. E. (1993). Mentoring: Empowering followers to be leaders. In W. E. Rosenbach & R. L. Taylor (Eds.), *Contemporary issues in leadership* (pp. 141–151). Boulder, CO: Westview.

Rueywei, G., Shih-Ying, C., & Min-Lang, Y. (2014). Career outcome of employees: The mediating effect of mentoring. *Social Behavior and Personality, 42*(3), 487–501. doi:10.2224/sbp.2014.42.3.487

Sandberg, C. (2013). *Lean in*. New York, NY: Knopf.

Sandler, B. R. (1993, March 10). Women as mentors: Myths and commandments. *The Chronicle of Higher Education*, p. B3.

Scandura, T. A., & Williams, E. A. (2001). An investigation of the moderating effects of gender on the relationships between mentorship initiation and protégé perceptions of mentoring functions. *Journal of Vocational Behavior, 59*(3), 342–363. doi:10.1006/jvbe.2001.1809

Smith, E. P., & Davidson, W. S. (1992). Mentoring and the development of African American graduate students. *Journal of College Student Development, 33,* 531–539.

Stanley, C., & Lincoln, Y. (2005). Cross-race faculty mentoring. *Change, 37*(2), 44–50. doi: 10.3200/CHNG.37.2.44-50

Swanson, R. M. (1996). *How to do a conference* [Brochure]. Washington, DC: American Association of Collegiate Registrars and Admissions Officers.

Tentoni, S. C. (1995). The mentoring of counseling students: A concept in search of a paradigm. *Counselor Education and Supervision, 35*(1), 32–42. doi: 10.1002/j.1556-6978.1995.tb00207.x

Trimble, S. (1994). A protégé's guide to mentoring. *National Association of Secondary School Principals Bulletin, 78,* 46–48.

VanDerLinden, K. (2005). Learning to play the game: Professional development and mentoring. *Community College Journal of Research and Practice, 29*(9–10), 729–743. doi: 10.1080/10668920591006575

Wunsch, M. A. (1994). Giving structure to experience: Mentoring strategies for women faculty. *Initiatives, 56*(1), 1–10.

Zachary, L. J., & Fischler, L.A. (2009). *The mentee's guide*. San Francisco, CA: Jossey-Bass.

RECONCILING LIFE AND WORK FOR THE NEW STUDENT AFFAIRS PROFESSIONAL

CHAPTER TEN

Joy Blanchard and Charlie Andrews

The answer to finding better work/life balance is to find the right blend between all our life activities—regardless of where and when they occur. (Sunnarborg, 2013, p. 7)

The notion of achieving a sense of balance between work and other aspects of life continues to elude many professionals and can be particularly difficult to achieve for those beginning a career in student affairs. For both new and seasoned professionals alike, the ability to find that balance has been linked to both short- and long-term professional success. According to many experts, the inability to demonstrate balance not only invites criticism from peers but can also jeopardize your health. As Sunnarborg's quote suggests, the key to balance involves understanding the integrated and overlapping nature of all life has to offer.

Within student affairs, this interconnectedness is often heightened by the fact that many professionals live with their students or spend long hours (outside the traditional work schedule) devoting themselves to ensuring that students grow, develop, and succeed. New professionals, in particular, often bear the brunt of this reality. So how do you achieve a work–life balance while also striving to establish a student-centered professional reputation? This chapter examines that topic by exploring the nature of the student affairs profession and offering suggestions for the new professional to keep in mind. Insights and suggestions from several higher education professionals with varying amounts of experience are included to help frame the discussion of a professional journey that strives toward establishing a balanced life.

Establishing Balance to Achieve Career Longevity

> *Balance is a constant dance that is different for every individual.*
> —Senior vice president at a privatized higher education company

Indeed, balance is an individualized concept; it is not simply time management (Roberts, 2008). Greenhaus, Collins, and Shaw (2003) defined balance as an *inter-role phenomenon* that recognizes an individual's priorities and dispositions across multiple life dimensions. Balance involves many factors: requirements of the job, internal motivations to succeed or achieve, home environment, priorities, and any other personal issues or interests that compete for your time and attention. The self-help literature suggests that we can achieve balance if we simply become more efficient, establish boundaries, and make choices that generate happiness. But if it's so simple, why is it so elusive?

Among student affairs professionals—and the global workforce at large—striking a balance invariably gets more challenging with time. As the marketplace becomes more sophisticated with increasingly more choices and increasingly more demanding consumers, the producers (i.e., employees) have borne the brunt to make everything better, cheaper, and faster (Guest, 2002; Reich, 2002). In student affairs, this translates into "being there" for the students. But is our philosophy and practice of being ever-present engendering burnout among our colleagues?

> *I've had supervisors who expected me (as a manager) to be the one to unlock the door and turn on the office lights in the morning, even if I was at an event until 10 p.m. or later the prior night.* —Director of student activities at a 4-year private college

According to some studies, more than half of student affairs professionals drop out of the field within the first 5 years of employment (Renn & Hodges, 2007). We have to wonder if that's directly linked to expectations that are sometimes placed on new professionals, especially those required to work longer or later hours (which is quite common for new professionals) and those with responsibilities related to living on campus. In essence, new professionals often focus on supporting their students without seeking the support they themselves need to live a balanced, happy life. Along those lines, more than half of American workers report that their jobs interfere with their personal lives and that they experience moderate to high amounts of stress (Christiansen & Matuska, 2006). Those who report having low levels of balance also have lower levels of job satisfaction and commitment to the organization (Beauregard & Henry, 2009). With those staggering statistics in mind, balance becomes even more vital in fostering the long-term careers of new professionals.

> **Balance becomes even more vital in fostering the long-term careers of new professionals.**

One major challenge for new professionals is securing friends and a social network outside the university (Renn & Hodges, 2007). When personal relationships outside work are underdeveloped, a void is created that causes you to invest even more energy in work, thus creating a dangerous cycle (Friedman & Greenhaus, 2000).

> *For the first 4 years of my professional career, I did not take a single vacation day except to see my parents at a holiday. I also ate lunch with my coworkers, socialized with them, went out for drinks with them, and I even exercised with them. My life became consumed by my institution and job. It wasn't until I made an active decision to meet other people and distance myself from my colleagues that I actually developed a work–life balance and came to enjoy my job.*
> —Director of student conduct at a 4-year religious college

New professionals should have open and honest conversations with their supervisors to outline work expectations and learn how to navigate the demands of the job while maintaining a sense of balance (Kernel, Kerenge, & Jauneaud, 2008). In addition to supervisors, seasoned colleagues and mentors can provide advice on how to achieve that sense of balance while maintaining an engaging, successful, and fulfilling connection to the profession. Recognizing that peak times and mandatory events are inherent to most student affairs jobs but that other times of the year might be less stressful will assist new professionals in developing their own system of time management. Scheduling time to get away and focus on personal interests is a crucial element in transitioning to life as a full-time professional. As such, new professionals should get connected in the community (e.g., through young professionals associations, community service organizations, adult recreation leagues) and find other opportunities that allow them to enrich their lives outside the job.

Socialization of New Professionals and Challenges for the Next Generation

Even more so than graduate preparation programs, the first job is key to the socialization of new professionals (Magolda & Carnaghi, 2014). Unfortunately, new professionals often internalize the message that they must work long hours in order to appear competent and fit within the office culture (Renn & Hodges, 2007). This message seems consistent among those at all levels in their student affairs career.

> *I believe most of us went into higher education for a specific reason— we wanted to support, grow, and develop students. We, in higher education, have a tendency to be martyrs and believe we're the only ones that can fix it. So there's great internal pressure to be that champion of students no matter how long it takes.* —Director of student activities at a 4-year private college

> *I believe that the lack of balance starts very early in a higher educa- tion career. Supervisors and more long-term staff don't always model positive life-balance behaviors. The message is often sent that in order to be considered successful you must put in long days and nights all the time.* —Vice president of student affairs at a 4-year public university

Senior professionals and supervisors play a key role in modeling posi- tive life balance skills. When newly minted graduates enter the field and observe their peers working too long in the office, it sends the message that they too must adopt this approach in order to be successful. However, the pressure and internal drive to work hard and strive for career advancement is not unique to student affairs and higher education. The phenomenon of the workaholic was first used to describe baby boomers' orientation to "paying your dues," the idea that to be successful you had to put in much more than the average 40-hour work week (Myers & Sadaghiani, 2010).

The generation of professionals currently entering the workforce—Millennials—do not espouse the same views about work as baby boomers or other generations did. In fact, neither Generation X nor Millennials construct their identities around their careers but instead use work as a means to support the lifestyle they desire (Myers & Sadaghiani, 2010). With growing demands in today's workplace and "the decline of work as a central life interest" (Guest, 2002, p. 258), achieving work–life balance can seem increasingly difficult to young professionals. It also can be more difficult for the later generations to socialize into work environments (Magolda & Carnaghi, 2014; Myers & Sadaghiani, 2010). In addition to the desire for more work–life balance, Millennials want close connections and relationships in the workplace; they seek regular feedback and want to be involved in decision making, regardless of where they are in the organizational chart. As a result, job satisfaction is higher when communication is open between them and their supervisors. This generation requires a great deal of praise in order to feel valued in the workplace, while at the same time they internalize a lot of pressure to succeed (Myers & Sadaghiani, 2010). As mentioned, it is paramount that new profes-

> **New professionals should offer practical solutions that enable them to feel a better sense of balance while negotiating the demands of the new job.**

sionals have open and candid conversations with their supervisors in order to gain a better understanding of their particular workplace culture and the expectations of that office.

Likewise, new professionals should offer practical solutions that enable them to feel a better sense of balance while negotiating the demands of the new job. These conversations are not always easy, but they're essential to the process of establishing this sense of balance. One approach new professionals should consider involves asking supervisors about the strategies they used in the past and what they have done to support the concept of balance among staff. Opening a dialogue early on, before the expectation of working long hours to cover programs and events has taken root, establishes boundaries. If done shortly after starting a new position, and with the reassurance (to the supervisor) that you're committed to getting the job done effectively, these conversations also serve to remind supervisors that it's in everyone's best interest to support a culture of balance in the workplace. New professionals need that balance to achieve greater job satisfaction which can, in turn, benefit supervisors through less turnover in entry-level positions.

Any cross-generational differences should not discount invaluable skill sets that the new generation of professionals brings to the workplace. Most notably, they're able to embrace and navigate the numerous and varied technologies that shape not only how we do business but how we interact with each other (Myers & Sadaghiani, 2010). These technologies, however, can also affect the work–life balance. Along those lines, conversations regarding supervisor expectations should also include a discussion regarding the use of technology for answering e-mails and completing tasks outside traditional working hours. Remote access to work-related tasks can be beneficial but can also contribute to burnout by making it difficult to disconnect. It stands to reason that the pervasive presence of technology has the potential to make it more challenging for student affairs professionals to achieve a true sense of balance. Although the constant connectivity provides a challenge to establishing boundaries, it can also afford the opportunity to be more flexible in your efforts to juggle both professional and personal demands.

> *For me, personally, social media and technology has helped me attain greater balance. I do believe there is a need to disconnect and, yes, there is such a thing as checking your e-mail too much, but I also think that having work at my fingertips helps me to negotiate freedom with myself and my job. I am not tied to one place and one desk and one computer. Additionally, social media has allowed me to connect with colleagues across the country who are doing similar work as I am and can help me with current problems or projects I am working on. I feel more connected, I feel more supported, and I feel as if the answers to many of my questions can be answered within seconds.* —Live-in academic advisor at a 4-year public university

> *Technology has assisted in helping me have a work–life balance as I can "check in" and handle issues from off-site. Technology has also assisted people who have many things going on in their life and cannot make it to campus for extra visits.* —Program coordinator at a 2-year public college

Personal and Familial Roles and Obligations

When discussing work–life balance, familial roles instinctively come to mind. Although the notion of family means different things to different people, student affairs practitioners often have to consciously carve out time to spend with those individuals who constitute their families. That time includes date nights or quiet time with partners, fulfilling childcare needs, socializing with friends who have become family, making time to adopt and care for pets, or perhaps caring for aging parents and grandparents. Cultivating and maintaining relationships in general requires a great deal of effort, even more so for those who exert the majority of their time and energy on work. Because new professionals in student affairs often feel added pressure to work long hours, they're susceptible to the stress and conflict that can strain and threaten their relationships.

For those professionals who are also parents, familial roles and obligations take on an added dimension. More and more couples with children have both partners working outside the home. Single parents experience added challenges and are increasingly faced with juggling the demands of work and family (U.S. Department of Labor, 2014). Working mothers continue to comprise a large segment of the workforce, and student affairs offices should adapt and provide accommodations when possible so as to not lose the strong human capital they provide. Still, women report having to become more efficient to juggle familial and work demands (Nobbe & Manning, 1997).

> *I can remember missing my son's first T-ball game because I was at a student retreat. I needed and wanted to be at the retreat and knew my son had many other games and plenty of people in attendance to support him. I made the choice to not go to the game, but it was on my mind while I was away.* —Director of orientation at a 4-year public university

The stereotype that women traditionally are caregivers gives rise to workplace theories that working mothers need more accommodation (Smithson & Stokoe, 2005), are less dedicated to their jobs, and are less competent than their counterparts (Fuegen, Biernat, Haines, & Deaux, 2004). As a result, working mothers tend to be held to a higher standard and scrutinized more than their non-mother counterparts (Fuegen et al., 2004; Nobbe & Manning, 1997). This perception of being less committed, according to some studies, might explain women's scarcity in top senior management positions (Doherty, 2004). Additionally, working mothers often shift priorities and delay pursuing doctorates, seeking promotions, or relocating (Nobbe & Manning, 1997) or, in some fields, opt to work part-time (Carr, Gareis, & Barnett, 2003).

> *Women are more likely to be questioned than men about particular situations. I notice in my current role men are more likely to "take time" while women "take time to take the children to the doctor, accompany a sick parent, etc." Women are more likely than men to give a reason why they are taking time. . . . I felt guilty and unsupported about opting out of certain events.* —Assistant director of career services at a 4-year public university

Although the standards regarding what is acceptable in the workplace are "gendered" in many ways, new professionals should avoid making their own assumptions about colleagues and perceived gender roles. The fact remains that inequities still exist. For instance, mothers might receive more pushback and scrutiny in the workplace when asking for accommodations than fathers do because they're more likely to ask for assistance and because of the persisting stigmas associated with caregiving roles. Pressures associated with caregiving stigmas and stereotypes make it that much more important for professionals to support one another in order to create inclusive environments that support the needs and life circumstances of all professionals and their diverse family units. Thoughts to consider: How do the demands of parenting affect single fathers or parents in same-sex relationships? How do demands of professionals who are maintaining or pursuing relationships outside work influence job performance? How do single professionals support colleagues while still maintaining their own sense of balance? The growing diversity of family units and our efforts to avoid double standards have broadened the discourse concerning how family obligations can complicate the elusive work–life balance. New professionals are encouraged to request necessary accommodations regardless of their family or personal circumstances and supervisors should be open to granting leave requests more equitably.

> *In a previous job, I was told it was okay for me to go on weekend-long retreats because I don't have a family at home to take care of. That statement, of course, is not okay. I no longer make excuses to take time off. I take time off because I need it or want it.* —Director of student activities at a 4-year private college

> *There's an assumption that those staff who are single and without children can more easily work weekends and or late nights. Although this might be that case, those staff should not be expected to take on those responsibilities, and the workload of that nature should be distributed equally among staff, allowing everyone to make arrangements in advance to fulfill those responsibilities. When these assumptions are expressed, someone in addition to those that are single, or perceived as single, and without children could challenge that assumption and provide support to their colleagues.*
> —Research administrator at a 4-year public university

As these two professionals noted, not everyone's familial roles include being a parent or caring for children; not everyone has a partner or aging family member to care for or even a dog at home who needs to be fed and walked. What new professionals need to keep in mind is that everyone has unique circumstances and obligations that are affected by a lack of work–life balance. Although it's certainly compassionate, or at the very least collegial, for you to offer to cover for a coworker because he or she has a family to get home to and you don't, it's also important to not be taken advantage of because your obligations are perceived to be less important. A single person should have the freedom to pursue outside interests and attend to personal concerns. A man should not feel nervous or ashamed about requesting time off for caretaking, even if he has a wife or partner. No one should expect the only nonparent in a work team to always work the less desirable hours. In essence, a new professional can expect that the pursuit of balance will intersect with the complexity of these familial roles and obligations and be prepared to request time off and support in order to address personal affairs.

Recommendations and Best Practices

There are many things that you can do to promote a healthier work–life balance. Your supervisor plays a vital role and can be an ally in establishing supportive work environments. Although there is no consensus theory or measure on how to achieve balance (Christiansen & Matuska, 2006), supervisors must recognize that employees value involvement in dimensions outside their life

> **Supervisors play an important role not just in modeling positive work–life balance but also in enabling their employees to strive for such balance as well.**

at work (Doherty, 2004). Organizational culture is important in establishing and recognizing efforts to establish work–life balance (Guest, 2002), and supervisors play an important role not just in modeling positive work–life balance but also in enabling their employees to strive for such balance as well.

> *I think it's important for student affairs professionals in managerial positions to understand that burnout is real. Accommodating a small request to avoid employee burnout and retain good employees is minor in the grand scheme of things.* —Assistant director of career services at a 4-year public university

> *I feel fortunate that from graduate school on I had supervisors that would help me be realistic about the number of hours worked and encouraged me to build a life with work as part of it, but not work as all of it.* —Associate dean of students at a 4-year private liberal arts college

Flextime, or "flexible working" (Smithson & Stokoe, 2005), can be a valuable perk to assist you in carving out time to seek balance and leads to greater employee satisfaction (Clark, 2001). Consider how to adjust your schedule and be sure to discuss those ideas with your supervisor.

> *I do give my staff comp time, especially because I cannot pay them more and they do work really hard. It helps with the morale!* —Director of student activities at a 4-year private college

> *My job requires late hours to attend events and meetings. When I have to be at work late I try to balance by coming in a little later the next day. I also try to balance by not attending more than three night or weekend events a week. Although this might not be possible during, say, orientation, I balance that with having a whole week of night or weekend free events when this busy time comes to a close.* —Associate dean of students at a 4-year private women's college

Additionally, childcare assistance can increase productivity up to 10% (Beauregard & Henry, 2009), and policies that allow employees to work from home, which are increasingly more possible given the advances in technology, increase performance and persistence (Casey & Grzywacz, 2008; Nobbe & Manning, 1997). Likewise, professionals who are able to involve their families in the fun of their work express increased satisfaction (Smith, 2001).

My son participates in the lifestyle by attending athletic events, programs, and being supportive in a college environment. —Director of student conduct at a 4-year private college

Consider these tips for increasing work–life balance:

☞ **Evaluate balance on a macro level.** Instead of looking to see if each day or each week was balanced—"crunch time" is inherent in the field—step back and analyze whether month to month or semester to semester your work allowed you to take time for yourself, your family, and your hobbies.

☞ **Find the right fit.** Choose an institution that meets your goals and personal expectations for a positive work environment (Magolda & Carnaghi, 2014). Such an environment might include available child care, benefits for domestic partners, wellness programs, flexible schedules, or mentoring programs.

☞ **Set boundaries.** Establish boundaries with your students so they know what's an appropriate use of your time and talents. Try to keep after-hours communication to a minimum and be cautious in sharing your personal contact information.

☞ **Make self-care a priority.** Recognize and accept that in order to be effective, sometimes you have to take time off to relax and rejuvenate.

I personally remember something that my graduate school supervisor told me when it comes to my philosophy to work–life balance, and that is "I am no good to others if I am no good to myself." On the days when I absolutely need a break, or need to be there for my family, or even just cannot fit one more thing into my schedule, I've learned to be good to me in those situations and say no. —Coordinator of student union event services at a 4-year public university

☞ **Know when to ask for help.** Learn early on in your career that you can't do it all. Even more so, learn that you're not in this alone. A successful professional, especially one who has aspirations to move up, must learn the art of delegation.

"The program or meeting or event won't occur without me there until 2 in the morning." Yes, it will. And if you were a good leader you'd empower others who could be there instead of you. —Director of academics for a not-for-profit study-abroad provider

☞ **Understand your new role.** Though you might be close in age to some of the students you work with, you must real-ize that your work–life balance relies on understanding that you are now a professional who just so happens to work on a college campus.

It's Not Just a Job, It's My Passion!

A discussion on work–life balance within student affairs would be incom-plete without reflecting on both the nature of the profession and the type of individuals it attracts. Much of the literature on this topic has been written through a corporate lens. Companies that exist in the fast-paced financial sector or high-stakes political realm require long hours from workers who must produce to maintain their job security. How does that translate to a helping profession like student affairs, where results are measured in human capital?

Higher education is a human services industry, and there are no 9-to-5s when dealing with human emotions, habits, attitudes, and behaviors. —Program coordinator at a 2-year public college

For years, the profession has attracted individuals motivated by their own positive collegiate experience to the extent that they feel the need to give back and devote their lives to helping other students. Although the motivation to help others is indeed noble, it can also become problematic if it evolves into a "need to be needed" situation. That's not to say that you shouldn't feel passionate about your work, but true balance is exhibited by those who don't allow their passions to consume them or detract from the other aspects of their lives.

Student affairs is what I call a caring profession. Practitioners display a heightened sense of care and responsibility for our stu-dents, our offices, and our campuses. —Director of student activi-ties at a 4-year private college

Working with students can be your passion and you can gain a lot from interactions and experiences with them, but your life should be

defined in whole, not only in connection to your work. —Associate dean of students at a 4-year private college

As mentioned earlier, student affairs professionals enter the field for altruistic reasons (Rhoades, Kiyama, McCormick, & Quiroz, 2008; Tull & Medrano, 2008). The pay often is not high, and the hours can be long. Still, many refer to it as a calling. As you progress through your career in student affairs, remember to not only take time for yourself but also keep in mind what attracted you to this profession.

Working in a field you're passionate about carries a higher risk of blurring the lines between personal and work than a standard 9-to-5 job you don't truly care about. This being said, I would much rather live passionately and work harder with greater rewards then punch a clock to do something that does not make a difference. Working some long days and late nights doing something I care about is more balanced than spending 40 hours of my week doing something I am not passionate about. —Senior vice president at a private higher education company

Although there is no exact formula for achieving proper balance and no universal instrument for measuring it, we encourage you to spend some time considering what balance looks like for you. Finding time for you, your outside interests, and those you love will not only help you avoid burnout but also enable you to be more present for your students when you *are* at work. Finding a rhythm that incorporates the multifaceted layers that help define who you are as both a professional and a person will put you in good stead for long-term success and enjoyment in the profession.

References

Beauregard, T. A., & Henry, L. C. (2009). Making the link between work–life balance practices and organizational performance. *Human Resource Management Review, 19,* 9–22. doi:10.1016/j. hrmr.2008.09.001

Carr, P. L., Gareis, K. C., & Barnett, R. C. (2003). Characteristics and outcomes for women physicians who work reduced hours. *Journal of Women's Health, 12*(4), 399–405. doi: 10.1089/154099903765448916

Casey, P., & Grzywacz, J. (2008). Employee health and well-being: The role of flexibility and work–family balance. *Psychologist-Manager Journal, 11*(1), 31–47. doi:10.1080/10887150801963885

Christiansen, C. H., & Matuska, K. M. (2006). Lifestyle balance: A review of concepts and research. *Journal of Occupational Science, 13,* 49–61. doi:10.1080/14427591.2006.9686570

Clark, S. C. (2001). Work cultures and work/family balance. *Journal of Vocational Behavior, 58,* 348–365. doi:10.1006/jvbe.2000.1759

Doherty, L. (2004). Work–life balance initiatives: Implications for women. *Employee Relations, 26,* 433–452. doi:10.1108/01425450410544524

Friedman, S. D., & Greenhaus, J. H. (2000). *Work and family: Allies or enemies? What happens when business professionals confront life choices.* New York, NY: Oxford University Press.

Fuegen, K., Biernat, M., Haines, E., & Deaux, K. (2004). Mothers and fathers in the workplace: How gender and parental status influence judgments of job-related competence. *Journal of Social Issues, 60,* 737–754. doi:10.1111/j.0022-4537.2004.00383.x

Greenhaus, J. H., Collins, K. M., & Shaw, J. D. (2003). The relation between work–family balance and quality of life. *Journal of Vocational Behavior, 63,* 510–531. doi:10.1016/S0001-8791(02)00042-8

Guest, D. E. (2002). Perspectives on the study of work–life balance. *Social Science Information, 41,* 255–279. doi:10.1177/0539018402041002005

Kernel, V., Kerenge, K., & Jauneaud, S. (2008). What are your tips for an effective work–life balance? *Communication World, 25*(1), 13.

Magolda, P. M., & Carnaghi, J. E., (Eds.). (2014). *Job one 2.0: Understanding the next generation of student affairs professionals.* Lanham, MD: University Press of America.

Myers, K. K., & Sadaghiani, K. (2010). Millennials in the workplace: A communication perspective on millennials' organizational relationships and performance. *Journal of Business and Psychology, 25,* 225–238. doi:10.1007/s10869-010-9172-7

Nobbe, J., & Manning, S. (1997). Issues for women in student affairs with children. *NASPA Journal, 34,* 101–111. doi: 10.2202/1949-6605.1014

Reich, R. B. (2002). *The future of success.* New York, NY: Vintage Books.

Renn, K. A., & Hodges, J. P. (2007). The first year on the job: Experiences of new professionals in student affairs. *NASPA Journal, 44*(2), 367–391. doi: 10.2202/1949-6605.1800

Rhoades, G., Kiyama, J. M., McCormick, R., & Quiroz, M. (2008). Local cosmopolitans and cosmopolitan locals: New models of professionals in the academy. *Review of Higher Education, 31,* 209–235. doi:10.1353/rhe.2007.0079

Roberts, E. (2008). Time and work–life balance: The roles of 'temporal customization' and 'life temporality.' *Gender, Work & Organization, 15,* 430–453. doi:10.1111/j.1468-0432.2008.00412.x

Smith, P. R. (2001). Parental-status employment discrimination: A wrong in need of a right? *University of Michigan Journal of Law Reform, 35,* 569–611.

Smithson, J., & Stokoe, E. H. (2005). Discourses of work–life balance: Negotiating 'genderblind' terms in organizations. *Gender, Work & Organization, 12,* 147–168. doi:10.1111/j.1468-0432.2005.00267.x

Sunnarborg, M. T. (2013). *21 keys to work/life balance: Unlock your full potential.* Minneapolis, MN: Author.

Tull, A., & Medrano, C. I. (2008). Character values congruence and person–organization fit in student affairs: Compatibility between administrators and the institutions that employ them. *Journal of College and Character, 9*(3), 1–16. doi: 10.2202/1940-1639.1118

U.S. Department of Labor, Bureau of Labor Statistics. (2014). *Employment characteristics of families summary.* Retrieved from http://www.bls.gov/news.release/famee.nr0.htm

PATHWAYS TO SUCCESS IN STUDENT AFFAIRS

CHAPTER ELEVEN

Jody Donovan and Maria R. Marinucci

Although the title of this chapter suggests there is a clear definition of success in student affairs, *success* is continually defined and redefined both personally and professionally based on context, culture, character, timing, and values. Deep soul searching, strategic planning, utilizing political savviness, and embracing ambiguity are necessary skills for long-term happiness and fulfillment in the student affairs profession.

Few children grow up dreaming of a career in student affairs (Blimling, 2002), except perhaps the children of happy student affairs professionals. Nonetheless, you began building your career a number of years ago by actively choosing your undergraduate major, seizing opportunities for campus involvement, engaging in leadership experiences, learning valuable job skills in part-time employment, and connecting with influential mentors. Perhaps you accepted a professional position after your undergraduate years and gained practical experience to draw on during your graduate school years. Earning your master's degree continued this career building process, as you applied newfound knowledge in assistantships, internships, and practicum experiences to broaden your portfolio of skills, knowledge, and curiosities. Career development is a series of beginnings, forward surges, regressions, steep climbs, lateral moves, and stop-outs with periods of rest, skill building, and reflection along the way.

This chapter focuses on how to maximize your graduate school experience to set yourself up for your first professional position, the realities of "climbing the ladder" versus utilizing "lattice-like" or nontraditional career paths, strategic considerations regarding enhanced academic credentials, professional development opportunities, and a holistic and satisfying student affairs career. The chapter concludes with recommendations for your pathway(s) to "success."

Starting with Self-awareness

Building and maintaining a successful student affairs career begins with self-awareness—a personal foundational competency identified for student affairs professionals by the American College Personnel Association (ACPA) and National Association of Student Personnel Administrators (NASPA) (2010) and described as:

> the knowledge, skills, and attitudes to maintain emotional, physical, social, environmental, relational, spiritual, and intellectual wellness; be self-directed and self-reflective; maintain excellence and integrity in work; be comfortable with ambiguity; be aware of one's own areas of strength and growth; have a passion for work; and remain curious. (p. 24)

> *Being able to take a step back and reflect on a frequent basis has been a lifesaver to find and maintain clarity and focus in the midst of chaos and complexity. It has allowed me to continue to grow and learn while staying fresh, passionate, engaged, and motivated in the midst of continuous change and ambiguity that oftentimes dominate the experiences of new professionals in our field. —*Assistant director of cultural programs at a large 4-year public university

As you imagine yourself fulfilled and satisfied as a student affairs professional, let your soul searching begin with a question posed by Sinofsky (2013), "Do you view your career as a journey or a destination?" (para. 1). If your career is a destination, you might have your eyes set on the prize—an ultimate title or position that brings status and responsibility. The vice president for student affairs position might be your career goal, and every decision and choice is made with that destination in mind. It's critical, however, to be aware of the opportunity pyramid with numerous entry-level positions and relatively few senior-level positions on most college campuses (Hamrick & Hemphill, 2009). Alternatively, you might be more interested in having varied experiences and soaking up extensive information to build a broad career, seeking joy in the journey. Holding a variety of positions in a number of functional areas and working at diverse institutional types might better fit your vision of a fulfilling career during a lifetime. Certainly, destination and journey are not mutually exclusive, but self-awareness is an important component to building a career (Sinofsky, 2013).

> *You don't need to hustle for success if you know that by being who you are, you can accomplish anything. Live life courageously but most important in a way that makes you happy and fulfilled not just as a professional but as a human being.* —Assistant director of cultural programs at a large 4-year public university

Pathways Begin in Graduate School

Pathways into and through student affairs vary widely, depending on the needs and goals of each individual. However, there are some common experiences shared by many in the field, particularly new professionals. For example, one study found a majority of student affairs professionals surveyed reported their perceptions of the field and student affairs work and the subsequent desire to pursue such a career began during their own undergraduate years (Silver & Jakeman, 2014). Some develop an aspiration to affect college students' lives as a result of the

> **Pathways into and through student affairs vary widely, depending on the needs and goals of each individual.**

support by student affairs staff they once received as well as contact with professionals who positively impacted their own collegiate experience.

Although your interest in the field of student affairs might have been sparked by your undergraduate involvement, your formal introduction to the profession likely occurred in graduate school. A master's degree is increasingly a minimum requirement for entry-level student affairs positions. More specifically, employers tend to prefer a degree in higher education administration, student affairs, or a field closely related (McClellan, 2010). As a result, pathways into the field frequently begin with a graduate education, and entry-level professionals often report they developed professional knowledge and abilities through their graduate preparation programs (Dickerson et al., 2011). Graduate school is your time to truly invest in learning opportunities within and beyond the classroom to adequately prepare for professional work.

At the same time, the stress of a graduate program can trigger feelings of inadequacy and lack of confidence in your ability to succeed, an experience known as "imposter phenomenon" (IP). According to Craddock, Birnbaum, Rodriguez, Cobb, and Zeeh (2011), IP is defined as "the feelings students experience when they compare themselves to peers and believe they have significantly less preparation or intellectual ability" (p. 430). If you experience IP, it's easy to feel as though you're not smart enough to be in graduate school and worry about whether you made the right choice. This is a common feeling and is normal, particularly in a setting where you are unfamiliar with expectations (Craddock et al., 2011).

Understanding expectations for new professionals potentially offsets feelings of IP or simply helps all students make the most of their time in graduate preparation programs. The skills and competencies needed to succeed as a professional, frequently developed through graduate programs and other ongoing professional development opportunities, are somewhat universal. As you engage in your graduate education, you'll probably explore the field and choose to participate in a variety of opportunities to maximize your experience. Some individuals enroll in graduate school full-time and are offered student affairs positions prior to completing their master's degree. Taking advantage of these opportunities, as well as reflecting on your values and learning how to align them with higher education institutions, allows you to best prepare for your work as a new professional. If you have prior professional experience, use this to your advantage in graduate school as well. It can be beneficial, particularly when learning about student development theory, to reflect on previous interactions with students and how to respond with knowledge about where students are in their developmental journeys.

Understanding Skills Necessary for Success

Preparing yourself for a career in student affairs begins with an understanding of the skills and competencies required for such work. Knowing what is expected of you in your first position and beyond helps you examine areas where you already excel and those requiring more work. This anticipation can facilitate your ability to tailor your preparatory experience to develop in a purposeful way.

Mid- and senior-level administrators are well situated to articulate those skills essential to entry-level positions. By surveying 104 of these experts on the responsibilities, skills, and theories important for new student affairs professionals, Burkard, Cole, Ott, and Stoflet (2005) identified 32 different skills as "essential to entry-level positions in student affairs" (p. 293). When divided into themed competency areas, two arose as especially important: personal qualities and human relations skills. Personal qualities included such characteristics as flexibility, time management, critical thinking, strong communication (both written and oral), and assertiveness. Human relation skills included counseling, working with and developing a team, multicultural competency, supervising and advising, and conflict management (Burkard et al., 2005). This list is intuitive, because much of the work of student affairs involves engaging with others and responding to them in a positive and appropriate manner. Also important to mid- and senior-level administrators were the ability to plan and develop programs, set goals, engage in research, manage a budget, and successfully perform administrative or management tasks (Burkard et al., 2005).

In another study, entry-level professionals were asked to report the skills they used to a great extent in their first professional positions and compare them to skills developed during their master's program (Waple, 2006). The skills most utilized on the job, yet for which they felt underprepared, were supervision, strategic planning, budget management, and the use of technology. Many of these skills aligned with what seasoned professionals reported they expect of new professionals (Burkard et al., 2005). In addition, both administrators and faculty reported a need for, yet deficiency in, knowledge and skills related to fiscal management, assessment, and legal issues (Dickerson et al., 2011), a finding that mirrors the expectations of mid- and senior-level professionals (Burkard et al., 2005) and reflects the skills new professionals report using in their first positions (Waple, 2006).

The skills required and used by new professionals are seemingly limitless. Nevertheless, understanding at least a portion of the wide-ranging competencies expected of new student affairs professionals helps graduate students modify their experiences to get what they need to be effective student affairs professionals. This effort can be accomplished through classroom education, professional experiences such as practica or internships, or informal interaction with classmates, faculty, and mentors.

I held practicums and internships related to assessment. This led to volunteer and assigned committee participation, as well as hired consultant work for grant-funded assessment projects. All of these opportunities provided experience that impacted my career path.
—Assistant director of assessment at a proprietary college

I used internships, practicum, and assistantships to help me support my own learning, regardless of the professional positions to come later. Sharing community with people whose backgrounds and experiences were unlike mine helped me develop additional ideas on how I could support students from underrepresented and under-resourced communities. I don't know that I thought very strategically about those decisions, except to say that I knew I had a lot to learn because of my relatively privileged background. —Assistant dean of students at a large public university

A new professional had a similar experience and considers an interaction outside of the classroom with a member of her cohort to be one of the most lasting and important learning experiences from graduate school. During this conversation, she reflected on her privilege and how it affected her ability to be an inclusive professional. These learning moments are crucial to identify and then reflect on as you grow. We seek these moments for our students and must do the same for ourselves, particularly once we're out of graduate school.

Both awareness and skills in diversity and assessment were identified by mid- and senior-level administrators as critical to entry-level positions (Burkard et al., 2005). Although faculty sometimes report that graduate students are underprepared in multicultural competence and senior administrators perceive a gap in preparedness for assessment (Dickerson et al., 2011), there is ample opportunity to explore such areas, and many others, beyond the classroom.

Realistically, it is unlikely your formal education includes discussions of all of the aforementioned competencies; there are more skills to develop than can be covered in the limited time available for classroom experience within a master's program. Therefore, enhancing these skills falls largely on your shoulders as an emerging professional. Take initiative to understand where you lack

> **Take initiative to understand where you lack skills and work to find opportunities to develop them.**

skills and work to find opportunities to develop them. Knowing that your professional development is primarily your responsibility is vital; many graduate students expect faculty and other mentors to cater to their needs without taking ownership of their experience (Renn & Hodges, 2007). Personal development is also important in terms of self-awareness with regard to identity and privilege; developing personal multicultural competence will assist you in your professional career. Spend time thinking about your goals and areas for growth.

> *In graduate school I spent a lot of time reflecting on my personal and professional goals. Through this reflection I was able to determine what experiences I wanted to gain as a graduate student that would positively impact my career in student affairs.* —Coordinator for student activities at a large public university

Engaging in such reflective experiences is crucial, because only you can determine what you want and need for your career. Once you make such decisions, which can be broadly or narrowly defined, you can seek out opportunities to prepare you for that path.

Choosing to Specialize or Be a Generalist

One significant decision to consider is whether you want to pursue experiences in a wide range of functional areas or take time to specialize in a specific area. One senior-level student affairs professional advised the former. "[T]he pool of candidates for entry-level positions is likelier than ever to include people with previous professional experience, and it might help your chances to have a varied background rather than a narrow one" (McClellan, 2010, para. 8). McClellan (2010) advised practica and assistantships across areas, both to make yourself more marketable and to "try out a variety of specialties and find your niche" (para. 4).

While I knew I wanted to work in housing, I intentionally chose my assistantship, practicums, and became involved with experiences that would provide different skills. This worked well for my career choice as housing professionals typically utilize a wide variety of skills. This made me very marketable for entry level positions. —Interim associate director of residence life at a midsize public university

Another new professional pursued opportunities beyond where she thought her career path might lead. She began her career in residence life and housing and knew she loved this functional area. When she enrolled in graduate school, her goal was to explore other areas to determine whether they fit with her long-term professional vision. She used assistantships and practicum experiences to explore parent and family programs, retention initiatives, access programs, Greek life, and support and safety assessment. Doing so allowed her to more specifically identify which aspects of student affairs ignited her passion, and—equally as important—which did not. In addition, she was able to connect her work with her ultimate priority of serving students, regardless of functional area.

As you explore the field, note what you do and do not love and use this to determine why you want to engage in this work.

I took on additional practicums and volunteer experiences to expand my assistantship outside of residence life—I didn't want to be pigeonholed into only being seen as someone who could work in residence life. I also completed a graduate certificate in women's studies to help inform the work I wanted to do on women's issues and interpersonal violence. I also took the opportunity to focus as many of my papers and projects on the area of women's issues and sexual assault to give me additional preparation and experience for a career path in women and gender support services. —Mid-level professional in a women's center at a public university

By focusing papers and projects on various subject and functional areas or student populations, you can supplement, enhance, or even expand on practical work experiences outside the classroom, providing additional means to learn and apply theory to practice. Whether you explore many functional areas or refine your abilities in a single area, reflect on your goals, experience the possibilities within student affairs, and continuously expand on your skill sets.

Although graduate school is the point of entry into the field of student affairs for many, and perhaps the majority of, new professionals, it "is not the only launching pad" (McClellan, 2010, para. 9). New professionals may also enter the field directly from a bachelor's degree or find their way from another career, both of which provide valuable experience and support graduate study.

Another growing phenomenon within student affairs is post-baccalaureate certificate programs (McClellan, 2010, para. 10). These programs provide formal education in critical areas such as budget, finance, and law, but they're not as time consuming as a master's degree program. Certificates also enhance the skills of those who hold a master's, making candidates even more attractive to potential employers (McClellan, 2010). Such credentials might become necessary in the future. NASPA and ACPA created professional certification programs so even those who have completed formal degree programs can explore various certificates to stay abreast of changes in the field and expand on the work they're qualified to do (Stoller, 2012).

> *I have only pursued certifications and specific training programs post-master's. I have not pursued any degree-seeking or degree-related education post-master's. The reason I have pursued certifications and trainings (i.e., MBTI, StrengthsQuest, Self Defense, Ropes Course Facilitation, etc.) is because I find these certifications and qualifications extremely applicable and helpful in the positions I have held both in and out of the higher education field.* —Associate director of a career center at a midsize state college

Although there are countless ways to gain experience prior to or while working professionally in student affairs, what is perhaps most important is reflecting on your identity and values. Silver and Jakeman (2014) found that an inability to connect your work to the institutional mission and to your identity and values can lead to exiting the field. Similarly, Renn and Hodges (2007) advised, "Particular attention should be paid to the impact of incongruence between the individual's characteristics and the institution's characteristics" (p. 385). As you navigate your graduate school experience, explore your values and identity as a critical piece of your professional development. Developing skills, exploring functional areas, building multicultural competence, and seeking opportunities to grow also pave your way into a more fulfilling and meaningful career within student affairs.

Exploring your values extends beyond institutions and positions to how you live your life outside of work as well. When thinking about balance, the picture of the scale—with work on one side and everything else on the other side—often comes to mind. Instead, find a rhythm for your life, which assumes timing, choreography, flexibility, and passion. At any given time in life, different roles take precedence; if you are not intentional, the student affairs profession can be all encompassing. Consider all aspects of your life and how they affect one another, both at the beginning of and throughout your career. See Chapter Ten for strategies and suggestions for work–life balance.

Finding Institutional and Positional Fit

The diversity of postsecondary institutions and functional areas within student affairs can be overwhelming; however, such diversity means nearly unlimited choice and flexibility to fit your strengths, talents, skills, and interests. As silos fall between student affairs, academic affairs, athletics, alumni, and advancement divisions, student-affairs-like positions are found across campuses (Kuk, Banning, & Amey, 2010).

> *Graduate students need to know that there is not one correct way to get your foot in the door.* —Entry-level student affairs professional in Greek life at a large public university

Conduct a thorough self-assessment of your negotiable and non-negotiable factors, particularly institutional considerations, geographic influences, positional components, and personal elements, when planning your career. An academic advising position can be very different when working at an online, for-profit institution as opposed to an urban, 4-year research intensive institution. Supervising and advising a student-alumni programming and fundraising council within a pressure-filled institutional advancement division at a midsize teaching institution provides a unique experience compared to working within a traditional campus activities unit at a rural, private, religiously affiliated campus. Completing informational interviews, shadowing, networking, and learning about specific institutions, departments, staff philosophies and roles are valuable methods to get an inside view and perspective on culture, climate, and fit (Henning, Cilente, Kennedy & Sloane, 2011; Magolda & Carnaghi, 2004; Renn & Hodges, 2007).

> *I truly believe the one informational meeting I had is the sole reason I obtained an interview for the part-time position which eventually led to my full-time job.* —Mid-level professional in a women's center at a large public university

Your early professional experiences provide the foundation on which future decisions and strategic planning is based, but they shouldn't be viewed as defining or restricting opportunities over the length of your career. Worrying about being pigeonholed or labeled a "job hopper" is not uncommon for new professionals (Hamrick & Hemphill, 2009); however, these first student affairs positions are useful for identifying your passions as well as eliminating options based on poor fit or lack of interest. Unexamined assumptions made about functional areas, institution types, or geographic regions can result in closed doors that could have offered significant opportunities and fulfillment.

Institutional crossover, or moving from one institutional type to another, requires strategic preparation to understand the unique mission, vision, and values of the new institution. You need to adapt your language to fit the culture and demonstrate transferrable skills (Hamrick & Hemphill, 2009). As enrollment at 2-year, 4-year, public, private, for-profit, and online institutions continues to increase (National Center for Education Statistics, 2013; National Student Clearinghouse Research Center, 2013), it's even more critical to explore student affairs career opportunities at all institutional types. Focusing on person–organization fit throughout your career acknowledges the need for a good match between your values and the institution's values, feeling comfortable in the environment, having job satisfaction, and embracing the institutional culture while being authentically you (Tull & Medrano, 2008).

The search for professional and personal fulfillment is highly valued among today's young new professionals. Emerging adults—those between 18 and 29 years old (Arnett, 2004), might be best suited for careers in student affairs with the breadth of opportunity and value for flexibility inherent in the profession. The ability to explore your identity in work and play, the relative lack of permanency in entry-level positions, the opportunity to take advantage of all the educational and growth experiences on a university campus, and the unbridled hope and optimism within higher education are qualities that appeal to many student affairs professionals, young and old.

> *New professionals must realize that the decision to work in a public or private institution does not have to be permanent. Select the best setting for yourself, but realize that the career decision-making process does not end with your first job. Research and evaluate the different settings and make a professional decision about your future.* —Dean of students at a large public university

For one senior-level administrator, being open to the possibilities and saying yes to opportunities early on provided a fulfilling career in housing, career counseling, Greek life, student conduct, and ultimately a generalist position as dean of students. Residence life can be a key starting place, because new professionals quickly gain valuable experience in supervision, advising, student development, facility management, budget management, student conduct, programming, and crisis management (Blimling, 2002; Hamrick & Hemphill, 2009; Henning et al., 2011).

Within a 10 to 20 year period, you might work as a coordinator for 3 to 5 years at a large institution, move to a similar-sized institution for an assistant director position, make a lateral move to a larger institution, be promoted to associate director, and eventually become director at a different university. This progression can exist in one functional area for an entire career, fostering a professional reputation based on a specific expertise. Conversely, student affairs professionals at small institutions are often expected to become generalists, holding several collateral assignments and fulfilling numerous job responsibilities. Career movement within small institutions can be more fluid, with upward progression occurring more quickly because of flat hierarchical structures (Hirt, 2006).

> *My initial advancement to director was simple. My director left and we were a two-person office—they offered me the position.*
> —Director of student activities at a small liberal arts college

Another student affairs professional at a small private liberal arts institution was quickly promoted to director of residence life in 3 years and assistant vice president for student affairs after being in the profession a short 8 years.

> *On a smaller campus, professionals at all levels wear many hats! This was a great opportunity for me to experience a vibrant student life experience. When you work hard to establish credibility, you're often rewarded with more responsibilities.* —Associate dean of students at a large public university

Embedded in the image of a career as a path or a ladder is forward or upward movement, but not all student affairs professionals move in a straight direction (McClellan, 2010). Think of your career as a lattice with "both vertical and lateral movement" between jobs that "frequently span multiple organizations because movement within one organization may not be possible" (CareerOneStop, n.d., para. 3).

Everyone wants to be a dean; it's okay to not be that. The path is more like climbing a tree, you have some branches that help you up, some are too frail, so you have to climb over or down until you find one that can hold you. —Residence director at a private liberal arts institution

Having positions end expectedly (and unexpectedly) have all influenced my career path. I have not intentionally left the field, but have had two periods of brief unemployment while job searching. —Associate dean of students at a large public institution

McClellan (2010) suggested being flexible and expanding the scope of your search from a position and geographic perspective, stating, "You might find that a part-time position—or more than one—becomes the path of entry into student affairs" (para. 7). Other factors might influence your job search as well.

After graduate school, I only did a local search so I could be close to my partner and family. I was unemployed for 4 months and then had to work two part-time jobs in higher education before I was able to secure a full-time position 11 months after graduation. —Mid-level professional in a women's center at a public university

I did not restrict myself geographically, because I wanted to learn and explore. As long as my job was in an institution where I could connect with the people and do the work I was passionate about, I was happy. —Assistant director of cultural programs at a large 4-year public university

After spending 10 years at the same institution, an assistant vice president for student affairs left her position to support her partner's career move to a new geographic region. She was fortunate to obtain a mid-level position in residence life at a significantly larger institution within commuting distance. Over a period of 16 years, she actively sought opportunities to improve her skills and abilities, enhance her academic credentials with a doctoral degree, increase her multicultural competence, build relationships, and earn trust to eventually regain her title with a deeper and broader set of responsibilities as assistant vice president for student affairs at a 4-year, research intensive university. Rather than a ladder, her career path resembles a carefully crafted lattice with strategic decisions woven throughout. Similarly, Larry Roper, former vice president for student affairs at Oregon State University, emphasized the need to manage your career: "Nobody should ever take your goals and aspirations more seriously than you" (Blimling, 2002, p. 29).

> *Consider taking on lateral moves to get different experiences rather than insisting on moving up every time you change jobs. A lateral move gave me the experience and network I needed to get a job I am so passionate about—if I'd held out for a promotion I might still be unemployed.* —Academic advisor for international and English language programs at a large public university

There is not one standard career pathway within student affairs; instead, multiple ways exist to navigate your journey into and through the profession, depending on interests, identities, values, strengths, and personal circumstances, not to mention institutional types and functional areas. Spending time reflecting on your assets, negotiable requirements, goals, and opportunities together with strategic future thinking will serve you well as a new, mid-, and senior-level student affairs professional.

> **Rather than a ladder, her career path resembles a carefully crafted lattice with strategic decisions woven throughout.**

Developing as a Professional

Dickerson et al. (2011) noted that "practitioners who work with entry-level professionals should anticipate a greater need for on-the-job training and development for new professionals, especially in competency gap areas such as collaboration, reflection, and the application of theory to practice" (p. 476). Though these competencies are not necessarily different from those used in graduate school, they need to be refined and adapted for professional work. Graduate school and other formal and informal education surely provide a solid foundation upon which to build your student affairs career, yet it's the on-the-job training and opportunities within your professional positions that allow you to apply that knowledge. In addition, these experiences—including committee involvement, professional association membership, and finding a mentor—orient you to your institution; they deepen and broaden your development within and across functional areas.

As new professionals begin to settle into their first positions, they often realize they can take charge of their experience and be proactive about closing gaps in professional and personal competencies (Renn & Hodges, 2007). In a longitudinal study of new professionals' first year on the job, Renn and Hodges (2007) found that to take responsibility for their professional development, individuals volunteered to serve on various committees and projects. Doing so helped them "see how decision making works" at their institution, a lesson not easily taught in the classroom (Renn & Hodges, 2007, p. 387). Serving on committees can help you understand institutional culture and general procedures.

> *The experience I gained by serving on campuswide committees and search committees, volunteering for campus leadership retreats or conferences, and even taking shift-work with student center operations and maintenance staff crews informed much of my depth of knowledge about our campus operations. Seeking ways to serve the campus beyond my required responsibilities has also informed much of my administrative knowledge and connections across campus.*
> —Assistant dean of students at a midsize public university

Another student affairs professional had a similar experience. Though only in her first professional position at a small public college prior to enrolling in graduate school, she developed a solid understanding of Title IX responsibilities as they pertain to sexual misconduct by attending a conference sponsored by the U.S. Department of Education's Office for Civil Rights. The knowledge she gained helped her discover new areas to explore more deeply. She would have missed this opportunity had she not volunteered to represent her office on various campuswide initiatives. Curiosity and a willingness to go above and beyond opened doors to further opportunities to broaden her skill set and knowledge. Developing knowledge of institutional practices through committee and other volunteer work helps you as a new professional "[find] your voice" and realize you "have valuable insights and perspectives to share" (Hamrick & Hemphill, 2009, p. 155). This is important, particularly early in your career, and we highly encourage you to be proactive in seeking out such opportunities.

Mentoring is another way to engage with the profession. As student affairs professionals, we tend to reach out and help those with whom we work; we must be willing as well to seek assistance when we need it. Mentors are valuable resources, and you must be willing to accept their support and guidance. Though both types of growth opportunities are discussed in other chapters, we felt it important to briefly note their significance here as well. We advise reviewing Chapter Nine for a detailed discussion of the importance of networks and mentoring relationships.

Supervision is perhaps one of the most significant areas for continued professional development (Harned & Murphy, 1998; Henning et al, 2011; Renn & Hodges, 2007; Tull, 2006; Winston & Creamer, 1997), a topic covered extensively in Chapter Four. We encourage you to continuously reflect from two perspectives—as supervisor and as supervisee—as you develop supervision skills throughout your career. Doing so not only helps you become a more effective and responsive supervisor to those you manage, but it also allows you to better communicate your needs to those who supervise you. Learning and growth continue well beyond your graduate years. To develop throughout your career, look for opportunities beyond your job responsibilities at your institution, join and fully engage in professional associations, and find good mentors. These are invaluable ways of continuing your education and exploring all the field has to offer.

> *Through my graduate assistantship, I took advantage of opportunities to work with faculty on conference presentations, give presentations on writing in APA Style, volunteer at local conferences, and network with higher education professionals on other campuses. I am grateful for having had excellent mentors who taught me how to maximize my graduate school experience!* —Mid-level professional in international student services at a large public university

This can—and in fact *should*—extend well beyond your graduate school years. Don't be afraid to acknowledge areas of needed growth and interest; seize opportunities to move forward in your career. Continue reflecting on your identities and engaging with others from different backgrounds to enhance your cultural competence as well.

Continued Academic Advancement and Enrichment

At some point in your career, you might think about getting a terminal degree or other academic credentials. Professional credibility and legitimacy becomes increasingly important as you engage with faculty, university leaders, and external constituents as a mid- and senior-level professional (Komives & Taub, 2000).

> *A terminal degree will be a necessary step for me in the next few years to build my political, economic, and social capital, which can only be built when I am seen as a credible leader.* —Assistant director of cultural programs at a large 4-year public university

Contributing to students' academic experiences as well as adding to the knowledge base within student affairs are additional considerations as you progress in the field. The exposure to current research and intellectually challenging discussions and the opportunity to create new knowledge provide a platform for influencing institutional or systemic change. Pursuing a doctorate requires discipline, clarity of purpose, and persistence; therefore, it must be a personal decision not taken lightly. Hamrick and Hemphill (2009) wrote that enrolling in a doctoral program,

> signifies the pursuit of knowledge that contributes to a field that promotes personal growth and development. New professionals who understand the complexities of higher education should see the doctorate as an opportunity to continue discovering themselves as learners, while promoting both professional and intellectual skill building. (p. 157)

Although a doctorate is not required for success in student affairs, certain doors might be closed for future promotion and advancement without it. Most senior-level job postings on higher education websites, in publications, and in various search firms' announcements identify the terminal degree as preferred, if not required. Certainly, salaries are also influenced by educational rank, with a doctorate earning more than a master's (Engstrom, McIntosh, Ridzi, & Kruger, 2006; Reason, Walker, & Robinson, 2002).

You may also consider earning a Juris Doctor or a Master of Business Administration, based on your interest, availability of educational programs, and institutional preferences or requirements. If your long-term plans include moving into a faculty role, you might need a doctorate in an academic discipline rather than an administrative discipline. If you've completed a master's degree, the thought of returning to school might send you running straight for the door and for good reason. Matching your educational credentials with your professional work experience makes you a more effective professional. Prior to enrolling in a doctoral program, it's beneficial to work professionally at least 3 to 5 years. Bringing valuable work experience to doctoral coursework enriches your learning, adds perspective, and contributes to your scholarly growth. Hamrick and Hemphill (2009) cautioned, "Combinations of work experience and graduate education, rather than only one or the other, now constitute superior preparation for career advancement" (p. 158).

It makes sense after a few years for me to pursue doctoral studies. Unfortunately, though, educational status and credibility are correlated, and it's often hard to be credible if your educational status doesn't match your position. —A new professional in multicultural affairs at a large public university, returning to school for a doctorate

Earning an advanced degree includes personal considerations, such as whether to keep working full-time and studying part-time or to enroll in a full-time doctoral program. You can choose an online program to accommodate your geographic restrictions and need for flexibility or move across the country to be immersed in school. Again, self-awareness and reflection are helpful as you determine whether, how, and when to pursue your advanced degree. It's not an easy decision.

Over the years, many people encouraged me to return for my PhD. When the time was right, it was an easy decision. Trust your own experiences about if, how, and when to pursue it! —Associate dean of students at a large public university

Whether you choose to continue your education beyond the master's degree, we encourage you to strive to become a scholar–practitioner through lifelong learning, reading, and writing (Bloom & Lowenstein, 2013). Regardless of degree status, you can stay current through professional development, engaging in challenging philosophical and practical discussions related to higher education and student development, and giving back to the field through presentations and publications.

> **We encourage you to strive to become a scholar–practitioner through lifelong learning, reading, and writing.**

Recommendations and Conclusion

This chapter began with a caution related to the definition of success in student affairs. Your definition of success will likely change as you mature in this profession. Initially, you might jump in with both feet, focusing on understanding the philosophical, historical, and theoretical foundations of the field while in graduate school and then shifting to applying this knowledge to practice as a new professional.

Throughout this chapter, we have provided several suggestions for maximizing your graduate school experience and navigating your pathway to and through student affairs. We acknowledge this is just the beginning; professional development is a continuous process that involves assessing your skills, competencies, goals, and satisfaction. After contacting a number of colleagues in the field and asking their advice for current graduate students and new professionals, several themes emerged. These recommendations come from individuals who were in a similar position as you not long ago and reflect what they wish they had known. Take time to reflect on this advice, and note how it might affect how you approach your job search and performance.

☞ **Determine your work–life balance expectations.** Think about whether you want to work within the confines of a 9-to-5 job, whether you're open to night and weekend responsibilities, whether you want to work at a large institution, or whether other institutional variables are significant. Only you can determine what the right path is for you, and this will almost certainly evolve over the course of your career. Ask yourself these questions and seek positions aligned with your values.

Spend time thinking about what kind of life you want to live when you are working as a professional. —Resident director at a private religiously affiliated university

☞ **Be open to experiences outside your plan.** Maintain curiosity about the field, and be willing to expand skills and abilities with new positions.

Pursue opportunities that leave you with options. While you may have your heart set on working in one functional area for your career now, you might develop new interests or life circumstances that would be better accommodated in another functional area. —Residence life coordinator for education and engagement at a large public university

☞ **Engage in lifelong professional development.** Invest yourself in the opportunities available within and beyond your position at your institution and within the field to learn more about what a career in student affairs has to offer. Get involved to further your strengths and improve areas where you have limited experience.

Be proactive. Look for opportunities to try out new things, learn about current trends in higher education, network with other professionals, and take on leadership positions. Don't shy away from 'other duties as assigned,' they are all experiences that can help with your professional development and skill set. —International student services advisor at a large public university

Pursuing opportunities outside student affairs, and even outside higher education in general, might take you on a lattice pathway as opposed to the ladder. Follow your interests and be willing to try new things to explore potential future paths. If possible, do not rush the process; be patient and explore those positions that advance your career.

☞ **Do your best work.** When you arrive at your first, second, or third position, work hard. Every day is an interview. By that, we mean it's important to put forth strong effort each day. Your graduate and new professional years set up your career. This is the time you make a name for yourself. Be someone others want to hire.

Excelling in all aspects of the job you were hired to perform is the best professional development; nothing will help you develop trust and respect in a large organization more effectively than performing well in all aspects of your position. —Assistant director of residence life at a large public university

Clearly, "every day is an interview" transcends beyond graduate school. It's a mantra that will support your career at all levels.

☞ **Learn from your mistakes.** At the same time, don't be afraid to make an error or seek assistance when needed. Reflect on missteps and learn from them; they teach you lessons not possibly learned in any other way.

Ask for help when you need it—which is a sign of strength and professional maturity. I think as a new professional I believed I

had to be perfect and competent at everything, which is both impossible and unrealistic. Now I have confidence in my skills, and the perspective that seeking help from my colleagues and supervisor is a key strategy for success. —Associate dean of students at a large public university

> You are not expected to have all the answers as a new professional. Learn from those with practical experience and embrace the knowledge they have acquired over their careers.

Last, and perhaps most important:

☞ **Remember you are more than a student affairs professional.** Reflect on what you want personally and professionally. Working hard, being dedicated, and committing to your work is crucial, but you must also think of yourself as a whole person with personal needs as well.

Remember that you are not your job. Taking time to take care of ourselves and having an enriching, balanced, and purposeful life outside of the job actually makes us more effective and amazing in our professional roles and gives us the ability to be true role models to our students who we hope not only excel academically but are happy and whole and empowered within all aspects of their lives during and after college. Finally, don't ever feel that there's one way to succeed in this field or that there's one version of what success in this field looks like. This field requires people of different talents, abilities, backgrounds, skills, and knowledge. —Assistant director of cultural programs at a large 4-year public university

Your path is unique to you. Only you can define success for yourself, and this is what we must model for the students we serve.

References

American College Personnel Association & National Association of Student Personnel Administrators. (2010). *Professional competency areas for student affairs practitioners*. Washington, DC: Author.

Arnett, J. J. (2004). *Emerging adulthood: The winding road from the late teens through the twenties.* Oxford, UK: Oxford University Press.

Blimling, G. S. (2002). Reflections on career development among student affairs leaders. In J. C. Dalton & M. McClinton (Eds.), *Special issue: The art and practical wisdom of student affairs leadership* (New Directions for Student Services, No. 98, pp. 27–36). San Francisco, CA: Jossey-Bass.

Bloom, J. L., & Lowenstein, M. (2013). Embracing lifelong learning for ourselves. *About Campus, 17*(6), 2–10. doi:10.1002/abc.21099

Burkard, A., Cole, D., Ott, M., & Stoflet, T. (2005). Entry-level competencies of new student affairs professionals: A Delphi study. *NASPA Journal, 42*(3), 283–309. doi: 10.2202/1949-6605.1509

CareerOneStop. (n.d.). Develop a career ladder/lattice. Retrieved from http://www.careeronestop.org/CompetencyModel/userguide_cll.aspx

Craddock, S., Birnbaum, M., Rodriguez, K., Cobb, C., & Zeeh, S. (2011). Doctoral students and the imposter phenomenon: Am I smart enough to be here? *Journal of Student Affairs Research and Practice, 48*(4), 429–442. doi: 10.2202/1949-6605.6321

Dickerson, A. M., Hoffman, J. L., Anan, B. P., Brown, K. F., Vong, L. K., Bresciani, M. J., Monzon, R., & Oyler, J. (2011). A comparison of senior student affairs officer and student affairs preparatory program faculty expectations of entry-level professionals' competencies. *Journal of Student Affairs Research and Practice, 48*(4), 463–479. doi: 10.2202/1949-6605.1638

Engstrom, C. M., McIntosh, J. G., Ridzi, F. M., & Kruger, K. (2006). Salary determinants for senior student affairs officers: Revisiting gender and ethnicity in light of institutional characteristics. *NASPA Journal, 43*(2), 243–263.

Hamrick, F. A., & Hemphill, B. O. (2009). Pathways to success in student affairs. In M. J. Amey & L. M. Reesor (Eds.), *Beginning your journey: A guide for new professionals* (3rd ed., pp. 147–171). Washington DC: National Association of Student Personnel Administrators.

Harned, P. J., & Murphy, M. C. (1998). Creating a culture of development for the new professional. In W. A. Bryan & R. A. Schwartz (Eds.), *Strategies for staff development: Personal and professional education in the 21ˢᵗ century* (New Directions for Student Services, No. 84, pp. 43–53). San Francisco, CA: Jossey-Bass.

Henning, G. W., Cilente, K. M., Kennedy, D. F., & Sloane, T. M. (2011). Professional development needs for new residential life professionals. *Journal of College and University Student Housing, 37*(2), 26–37.

Hirt, J. B. (2006). *Where you work matters. Student affairs administration at different types of institutions.* Lanham, MD: University Press of America.

Komives, S. R., & Taub, D. J. (2000). Advancing professionally through doctoral education. In M. J. Barr & M. K. Desler (Eds.), *The handbook of student affairs administration* (pp. 508–534). San Francisco, CA: Jossey-Bass.

Kuk, L., Banning, J. H., & Amey, M. J. (2010). *Positioning student affairs for sustainable change: Achieving organizational effectiveness through multiple perspectives.* Sterling, VA: Stylus.

Magolda, P. M., & Carnaghi, J. E. (Eds.). (2004). *Job one: Experiences of new professionals in student affairs.* Lanham, MD: University Press of America.

McClellan, G. S. (2010, November 17). Getting a start in student affairs. *The Chronicle of Higher Education.* Retrieved from http://chronicle.com/article/Getting-a-Start-in-Student/125391

National Center for Education Statistics. (2013). Table 301.10: Enrollment, staff, and degrees/certificates conferred in degree-granting and non-degree-granting postsecondary institutions, by control and level of institution, sex of student, type of staff, and level of degree: Fall 2010, fall 2011, and 2011–12. *Digest of Education Statistics.* Retrieved from http://nces.ed.gov/programs/digest/d13/tables/dt13_301.10.asp

National Student Clearinghouse Research Center. (2013, December 11). *Report: Current term enrollment report—fall 2013.* Retrieved from http://nscresearchcenter.org/currenttermenrollmentestimate-fall2013

Reason, R. D., Walker, D. A., & Robinson, D. C. (2002). Gender, ethnicity, and highest degree earned as salary determinants for senior student affairs officers at public institutions. *NASPA Journal, 39*(3), 251–265. doi: 10.2202/1949-6605.1169

Renn, K. A., & Hodges, J. P. (2007). The first year on the job: Experiences of new professionals in student affairs. *NASPA Journal, 44*(2), 367–389. doi: 10.2202/1949-6605.1800

Silver, B. R., & Jakeman, R. C. (2014). Understanding intent to leave the field: A study of student affairs master's students' career plans. *Journal of Student Affairs Research and Practice, 51*(2), 170–182. doi: 10.1515/jsarp-2014-0017

Sinofsky, S. (2013, March 28). What's your career path: Journey or destination? [Blog post]. *Pulse*. Retrieved from https://www.linkedin.com/pulse/article/20130328160626-2293107-what-s-your-career-path-journey-or-destination

Stoller, E. (2012, January 12). Certification for student affairs professionals [Blog post]. *Inside Higher Ed*. Retrieved from http://www.insidehighered.com/blogs/certification-student-affairs-professionals#sthash.flQ9h7DS.dpbs

Tull, A. (2006). Synergistic supervision, job satisfaction, and intention to turnover of new professionals in student affairs. *Journal of College Student Development, 47*(4), 465–480. doi: 10.1353/csd.2006.0053

Tull, A., & Medrano, C. (2008). Character values congruence and person-organization fit in student affairs: Compatibility between administrators and the institutions that employ them. *Journal of College and Character, 9*(3), 1–16. doi: 10.2202/1940-1639.1118

Waple, J. N. (2006). An assessment of skills and competencies necessary for entry-level student affairs work. *NASPA Journal, 43*(1), 1–18. doi: 10.2202/1949-6605.1568

Winston, R. B., & Creamer, D. G. (1997). *Improving staffing practices in student affairs*. San Francisco, CA: Jossey-Bass.

MANAGING THE FIRST
JOB SEARCH PROCESS

CHAPTER TWELVE

Brent G. Paterson and Christa Coffey

The first major job search can be exhilarating, a climax to the successful completion of a graduate program and recognition that you have made it. It can also be scary, exhausting, and harmful to your finances. In this chapter, we offer our joint experiences with job searches: as candidates, as employers, as members and chairs of NASPA Career Services and The Placement Exchange, and as faculty in master's degree programs in student affairs. We focus on those conducting their first major job search. While there are many paths into the field that don't require a degree in student affairs, most people experience similar issues in conducting a job search, regardless of the path they take.

Competencies

The first stage of the job search involves knowing yourself—identifying your strengths, weaknesses, and values. Investing time and effort in this process helps you find a position that suits you.

As a starting point, we suggest that you review *Professional Competency Areas for Student Affairs Practitioners*, a 2010 joint publication of the American College Personnel Association (ACPA) and the National Association of Student Personnel Administrators (NASPA), to determine your current and desired ability level for a variety of important competencies in the field. This document lists competencies for student affairs professionals in the areas of advising and helping; assessment, evaluation, and research; equity, diversity, and inclusion; ethical professional practice; history, philosophy, and values; human and organizational resources; law, policy, and governance; leadership; personal foundations; and student learning and development. Within each area, the competencies are grouped by proficiency level: basic, intermediate, and advanced.

In addition, each functional area requires certain competencies or levels of competence. Many skills are transferable not only among functional areas in student affairs but also between positions inside and outside the field. To determine what competencies are essential for the areas in which you're interested, refer to the professional associations that specialize in those areas (e.g., Association of Fraternity/Sorority Advisors) and speak with colleagues who work in them.

Before the beginning of the second year of your graduate program, identify—perhaps with the help of a supervisor—your strengths and weaknesses in terms of skills and abilities. Understanding the areas where you need improvement lets you focus on them; analyzing your strengths allows you to search for positions that maximize those abilities and helps you sell yourself to potential employers. Matching the competencies you possess with the requirements of a position is one aspect of finding "fit," which leads to less job stress and greater job satisfaction.

Matching the competencies you possess with the requirements of a position is one aspect of finding "fit," which leads to less job stress and greater job satisfaction.

Once you understand the competencies essential for entry-level work, you must be creative in demonstrating how your competencies fit those required for the position. For example, if you have experience advising student organizations, you should be able to connect that competency to a position that provides financial aid counseling to students. If you need help making these connections, ask a supervisor or mentor to assist you.

Values

If you're in your final quarter or semester of graduate school, or looking for your first position, it can be nerve-racking to have no idea where you'll be living or what you'll be doing in 6 months. But even if you're in a desperate situation, don't accept a position just because it's offered. You will have a better experience, one in which you can grow professionally, if you accept a job in which your values match those of the institution, department, and supervisor. This is the other part of fit—the part that goes beyond ensuring a match between your competencies and the job responsibilities. This part of fit matches your personality and preferences with those of the organization, institution, and supervisor.

> *Don't waste time on institutions that will be a bad fit or in areas that you don't like. If you do the work right and have the patience to support it, you can find the place you really want to work.*
> —Graduate student at a midsize public university

Many soon-to-be professionals don't realize how different the environment can be from one institution to the next, and how important it is to think about professional values. Institutions and departments differ in what they value, perhaps because of who funds them or the influence of their leaders. For example, some institutions are organized to provide staff-driven programming for students, while others provide student-driven programming. Imagine your ideal institution and department. What values would it have (e.g., regarding student development and staff)? What is your advising style in working with students? What is the advising style of the department or institution you're interested in? What values and management style would your ideal supervisor have, and how do these line up with those of your potential supervisor?

> *Make sure you pay very close attention to the climate of the department or division you're interviewing with, and ask a lot of questions to try to figure out if the mission, vision, and goals of the department or division match your own.* —Coordinator of new student orientation at a midsize public university

Although your values and the values of the institution, department, and supervisor might not match perfectly, it's important that you don't feel as though you're compromising your personal student affairs values in the execution of your responsibilities.

Types of Positions

The field of student affairs offers a variety of ways to work with and for college students. They are typically grouped by functional areas, which can be found via the search categories of the two major placement conferences and websites (see "Finding Available Positions" in this chapter). The wording might differ slightly from one placement entity to another, but candidates can generally search for the following types of positions: adult, commuter, and off-campus student services; campus or student activities; career services; counseling services; enrollment management and admissions; gay, lesbian, bisexual, and transgender (GLBT) services; Greek affairs; health, wellness, and drug and alcohol services; housing and residence life; judicial affairs; leadership development; multicultural or diversity services; orientation and new-student programs; and service–learning and volunteerism. For additional information on the history, purpose, role, function, and even entry-level qualifications for most of these functional areas, review *Rentz's Student Affairs Practice in Higher Education* (MacKinnon, 2004).

Although these are the most common functional areas in student affairs, the distribution of positions is uneven. At least for the two major placement conferences, housing and residence life positions typically outnumber the combined total of all other positions, comprising slightly more than 50% of available positions. The next largest category has traditionally been campus or student activities, comprising 10% to 15% of total positions.

Types of Institutions

A common question from job seekers is: Does it matter at what type of institution I work? The simple answer is that it doesn't matter as long as you're comfortable at that institution. But be aware that institutions of the same type might not be similar.

Your graduate program should expose you to student affairs work at different types of institutions. Student affairs faculty members often encourage students to complete a practicum at a different type of college or university from their undergraduate or graduate school. For example, if you're attending a public university, you might be surprised to find that you like the student affairs work environment at a community college or a religiously affiliated liberal arts college. Adding experience at a different type of institution can only enhance your résumé and make you a more viable candidate.

In *Where You Work Matters*, Joan Hirt (2006) described student affairs work at different types of institutions: liberal arts colleges, religiously affiliated institutions, comprehensive institutions, research universities, historically Black colleges and universities (HBCUs), Hispanic-serving institutions (HSIs), and community colleges. Hirt's characterization of student affairs workers at different types of institutions provides helpful insights for anyone considering a position at one of these institutions. For each type of institution, Hirt describes the professional life of a student affairs staff member in terms of the nature of the work environment, the nature of relationships, and the nature of rewards.

Hirt (2006) called student affairs staff at liberal arts colleges *standard bearers*. She said they "believe in working closely with students to encourage development across a broad array of realms" (p. 19). They have a holistic approach to their work that closely follows the philosophy of student affairs. She called staff members at religiously affiliated institutions *interpreters*, because they spend their time and energy "interpreting their personal faith in light of their professional responsibilities and interpreting their professional responsibilities in light of their personal faith" (p. 40). Hirt viewed student affairs staff at comprehensive colleges as *generalists*, and those at research universities as *specialists*. At the latter type of institution, expertise in one functional area is common, and relationships tend to be intradepartmental. Hirt noted that student affairs staff at HBCUs view themselves as surrogate family for their students. At HSIs, change is a way of life. Staff members deal with changes in their institutions (academic, programmatic, cultural, and administrative); the changes with students' experience; and the change in how they view themselves as a result of working at an HSI. Hirt referred to these staff members as *guardians*. Finally, Hirt viewed student affairs staff members at community colleges as *producers*, who provide high-quality services for a diverse population of students, typically with fewer staff than other types of institutions. We encourage you to explore other institutional types and student affairs work environments in Hirt's book.

Size of Institution

Does institutional size really matter? The size of the institution does make a difference in the work environment, job duties, and how you'll interact with students. Size often correlates with type of institution. For example, small institutions (fewer than 2,500 students) tend to be private religiously affiliated liberal arts colleges, whereas institutions with enrollments greater than 20,000 are often public research universities.

Student affairs professionals at small institutions are frequently generalists with responsibilities in more than one area. For example, a staff member might be a hall director and director of student activities. Because there are fewer layers in the student affairs organization at a small institution, a new professional might hold the title of director or associate dean. In addition to titles, small colleges might offer other perks not found at larger universities, including the possibility of building closer relationships with faculty and senior administrators, because of the flattened hierarchy, or of teaching an undergraduate course from time to time.

By contrast, student affairs professionals at large universities are specialists. They have very specific duties and usually have a limited scope of interaction with students. The staff member responsible for student conduct might never encounter a particular student in another setting. The size and decentralized nature of the student affairs division at a large university also means that student affairs staff members might have limited interactions with each other and with other units on campus. At times, student affairs professionals at large universities may feel as though they deal with numbers rather than students.

Location of Institution

Geographic location is an important factor to some job seekers. Location is more than just climate; it includes the culture of an area. It's easier to adapt to a new culture in some communities than in others. Community values and beliefs about issues such as religion, race, politics, and the environment can affect whether you would be comfortable living and working in that community.

Some job seekers are geographically bound by their spouse's or partner's employment or schooling or by family responsibilities. Or they might simply like a certain area. If you fall into this category, you might limit your job opportunities and career advancement. Many people happily and successfully spend their entire career at the institution where they graduated; however, there is a hiring bias toward student affairs professionals who have experience at more than one institution. Innovation and creativity are valued traits in student affairs professionals; if you have worked at only one institution, the assumption is that you know only one approach to student affairs work.

I was geographically bound due to my spouse's job. As late June arrived, I began looking about two to three hours away. I additionally began applying for jobs at community colleges and for additional positions that I did not consider earlier in my search. I definitely began to consider positions I didn't have direct experience in, but knew my skills were transferrable because I knew time was of the essence. —Coordinator of retention services at a large public university

The size of the community also has implications for the job search. An urban community often offers endless social and entertainment opportunities, but the cost of living (i.e., housing, transportation, food, utilities) can be high. It might be cheaper to live in a rural setting, but shopping and social and entertainment opportunities are usually limited. Living in an urban setting allows a greater measure of anonymity for the student affairs professional; in a rural community, the interplay between the institution and the community can appear seamless, and it can be hard to get away from students. Suburban institutions sometimes have the best of both worlds.

Career Goals

Although high aspirations can be motivating, we suggest that you establish realistic career goals for the near future (the next 5 to 10 years) and reevaluate them periodically. The general rule of thumb is that a person should stay in his or her first professional position for approximately 3 years. After 3 years in an entry-level position, you should consider moving into a more responsible position or transitioning into another functional area of student affairs.

The general rule of thumb is that a person should stay in his or her first professional position for approximately 3 years.

New professionals are often concerned about being pigeonholed in one area of student affairs. If you seek opportunities to gain knowledge and skills in areas outside your primary responsibilities, you'll have little difficulty selling your transferable skills when you apply for a position in another area of student affairs. If you work in housing but want to move into programming, find opportunities to do programming for your hall or the campus residence hall community. Co-program with the campus programming board. Volunteer to help with a campus program. The number of ways to build your skills and gain experience is limited only by your imagination.

Finding Available Positions

You can search for positions in various ways. Most search methods are available exclusively online, which allows you to search at any time and from anywhere.

Professional Associations

NASPA and ACPA each offer two methods candidates can use to look for jobs. The first is the online job board, which allows candidates to search for positions and post résumés free of charge. The second method is used by many aspiring entry-level professionals: the placement conference connected to annual national conventions (The Placement Exchange, held prior to the NASPA Annual Conference; and Career Central, held prior to the ACPA Annual Convention). Both associations typically hold their conferences in March or April, so this avenue is very popular for candidates who want to start working in the summer or early fall. If you don't limit yourself to a specific geographic or functional area (e.g., admissions, enrollment), you'll probably benefit from attending a placement conference.

> *Placement was, without a doubt, my greatest ally in my search. While the entire process and system was daunting, I am so grateful for the experience. It allowed me to test the waters of a lot of different factors within my search criteria. I interviewed for positions in residence life, student activities, orientation, and leadership and at institutions in several states. Ultimately, I got a great feel for "fit" with four different positions.* —Conference coordinator at a large public university

The Placement Exchange serves as a collaboration of several student affairs professional entities, including NASPA; the Association of College and University Housing Officers–International; the National Association for Campus Activities; the National Orientation Directors Association; the Association for Student Conduct Administration; the Association of Fraternity/Sorority Advisors; and HigherEdJobs. Professional associations that specialize in other functional areas of student affairs—such as academic advising, admissions and enrollment, or career services—might have their own online job boards or conference placement services. These services can be especially helpful if you know you want to work in a certain area. We encourage you to review the positions listed with the specialized professional associations, even if the functional area you prefer (e.g., admissions) is one of the major search categories of the NASPA and ACPA processes.

Institutional Websites

If you're looking to work in a certain city or at a specific institution, the most effective approach is probably the institutional website; most institutions require that positions be posted through their human resources (HR) department. For a list of higher education institutions and links to their HR websites, go to http://www.academic360.com.

The challenge in searching for positions on some HR websites is that the descriptions are limited and you might not be able to distinguish among them, especially if the department or office is not listed. For example, you might see five "coordinator" positions listed on the HR website, but if the department or office is not listed, you'll have to figure out if it's a student affairs coordinator or a library coordinator. We suggest that you also check the websites of the student affairs division and the department or office related to your functional areas of interest. If these sites have job listings, they will generally be more descriptive than the ones posted by HR.

Networking

In the business world, many people find positions through networking; student affairs is no different. The profession is a small one—not in the numeric sense but in "degrees of separation"—so networking is a powerful means of searching. Networking is especially helpful if you're in graduate school. Your faculty members, assistantship and practicum supervisors, and mentors have professional colleagues at institutions around the world. Let them know when you begin your job search, and tell them what you're interested in, including geographic and functional areas. As you apply and interview for jobs, keep them informed of your progress. If you have developed strong relationships with these people during graduate school, they'll be more than willing to tell you about potential opportunities, introduce you to colleagues at other institutions, and put in a good word to potential employers. See Chapter Nine, Making Professional Connections, for more information about networking.

Other Sources

In addition to those sponsored by professional associations, online services exist for student affairs and higher education job searches (including faculty positions). These services generally offer more specific functional area search capabilities than the professional association services, and several include search functions for city, state, institution, and institutional type (including community colleges). You can find online job boards by searching for "student affairs" and "jobs" in your favorite Internet search engine.

Application

The great challenge in applying for a position at an institution of higher education is that there are almost as many processes as there are institutions. Although almost all institutions require that an application be submitted to the HR department at some point, the timing differs from institution to institution. For example, some institutional HR policies require that a potential candidate submit an application before the hiring unit can make any kind of contact with the candidate. Some policies allow the hiring unit to have a few informal conversations before the candidate submits an application. Still others allow the hiring unit to conduct a few interviews (such as at a placement conference) before requiring an application.

Many institutions use an online application process through their HR website. Even if you gave the interviewer at a placement conference a letter of interest, a résumé, and references, the institution will likely require you to complete the online application process. This may also be true if you sent information directly to the student affairs department.

Résumé

Student affairs allows for some creativity in how you present yourself through cover letters and résumés. There's nothing wrong with creating your own style, as long as it's professional, organized, easy to read, and consistent.

The purpose of a résumé is to secure an interview, not to describe every experience or skill you have. Employers who conduct a search—whether at a placement conference or through the institution's HR process—typically receive a large number of applications. In the early part of the process, as they weed out applicants, they typically don't read each résumé in depth. Therefore, especially for entry-level positions, it's best to limit your résumé to two or three pages plus a reference page.

Employers are always busy, so use formatting (e.g., boldface, different font sizes, and underlining) to draw their attention to specific words, sections, or phrases to ensure that they extract the most important information from your résumé as easily as possible. People read left to right and top to bottom, so place the most important information in the upper left quadrant of the page and in the upper left portion of each section of the résumé (e.g., education, student affairs experience, certifications).

You'll always need a generic résumé, but you should also tailor your résumé to each position of interest, or at the very least to each functional area. Many student affairs competencies are transferable, but, for example, some of the skills needed by a Greek advisor are different from those needed by a residence hall director or judicial officer. Organize your résumé to highlight the skills, knowledge, and experience needed in the specific position as explained in its job description. Quantify and use specifics whenever you can—numbers look great. For example, instead of saying that you have budgeting experience, say that you managed a $20,000 budget.

We cannot stress enough the importance of a grammatically correct and error-free résumé. Some employers see a mistake as a lack of attention to detail or even a lack of interest in the position and will not consider your résumé, despite your qualifications. Ask several people, including at least one professional who coordinates hiring in your functional area of interest, to review your résumé (including content and formatting) and give you feedback.

Finally, print your résumé on paper that copies well. Whether you're at a placement conference or an on-campus interview, the employer might make copies of your résumé for an interview team. You want to make sure the copies will be clear. Experiment on a copy machine before you decide what kind of paper to use.

Cover Letter

A typical cover letter is three to five paragraphs and not more than one page. It should be consistent (in font, formatting, header, and paper) with your résumé. It might include the following information: the position for which you're applying, how you learned of the position, why you're interested, why you think you're qualified, what you think you can bring to the position, experiences that are relevant to the position, your current position and significant job responsibilities, contact information, and a request to discuss the position and your qualifications. As you do with your résumé, tailor each letter, highlighting the competencies and experiences that will help get you an interview for the specific position. The cover letter is your first chance to explain your résumé in more detail, including, for example, time gaps between positions held and information related to the position requirements and your qualifications.

Try to avoid addressing a letter with "To whom it may concern" or "Dear Sir or Madam." If you don't know the name of the person you're addressing the letter to, call the corresponding department or office and get the name. If you can't get a name that way, address your letter to a specific person in an upper-level position.

References

An infrequent topic in the job search discussion is the selection of references. Your references could be the tipping point in your ability to secure an interview, which is why we suggest that you include a list of references as the last page of your résumé, rather than stating that references are "available upon request."

You need three to five references. If you're about to complete or have completed a student affairs graduate program, your list should include one or two student affairs supervisors (graduate assistant, practicum, or internship); ideally, one of these is your current supervisor. You also want to include one or two faculty members. Finally, consider using a student with whom you have worked in an advising or mentoring role. This combination of references showcases a variety of perspectives on your experience and talents.

How do you decide which individuals to select? Create a list of professional staff, faculty, students, and non-student-affairs contacts you have worked with. Then select three to five people who have observed your strengths and abilities (for at least one quarter or semester) and who can speak about them in depth. Including a "big name" professional on your reference list can help you secure an interview, but if the person doesn't have a close relationship with you, he or she might not be able to sell you over another candidate. In the long run, using someone who knows your skills and talents is a lot more helpful in securing a position.

If you're entering the field from outside the graduate school track or you don't have student affairs graduate program connections, we suggest selecting references who can talk about the skills and experiences you have that would be transferable to the position. Depending on the amount of time that has passed since your undergraduate career, you might also consider using a reference related to collegiate involvement (e.g., resident assistant or orientation leader).

After you have selected the people you want to serve as references, ask each person if he or she is willing to serve in that role. If they agree, provide them with information about yourself and your search, including a copy of your résumé, and keep them informed of your progress—including the positions for which you have applied, where you are in the process, and your level of interest in each.

Keep in mind that people who are not your "official" references can serve in an unofficial capacity, especially at professional conferences. Make sure your mentors, colleagues, program faculty, and peers know about your interests. These people can connect you to potential job opportunities.

Interview Types

Placement Conference

Interviewing at a placement conference is a unique experience, one that requires great patience, energy, and stress management skills. Placement conference interviewing can be overwhelming, but it's popular because of the potential to meet with a number of institutions in one location.

Placement conferences might differ in minor procedural matters, but most schedule interviews in a similar way. At the conference, the scheduling process begins when you receive written verification (if you requested the interview) or a written request to schedule an interview from an employer who identifies you from the placement registry you completed. Upon receipt of that note, contact the placement conference staff to set a time to meet with the employer.

Interviews are typically scheduled in 30-minute blocks; some employers might invite you back for a second, hour-long interview, which might occur on the same day or later in the placement conference. We strongly encourage you not to schedule back-to-back interviews, in case the first one runs long. Always leave at least a 30-minute block between interviews. This ensures that you're never late to an interview and gives you time to collect your thoughts after one interview and relax before the next one.

Although the setup varies somewhat from one location to another and from one association to another, the concept is similar: Several hundred tables are placed in the convention facility, very close to each other on all sides. During your interview for a position, other interviews will be going on simultaneously at tables all around you—the facility can get very noisy. Because of this setup, and because candidates and employers are constantly walking up and down the narrow aisles between the rows of tables, you have to work hard to maintain your concentration and eye contact during the interview.

You might have several interviews in one day. No matter how tired you are of talking and interviewing, you must stay enthusiastic. Even if you're asked the same question over and over again, you must act as if it's the first time. The employer perceives a lack of enthusiasm as a lack of interest in the position.

Telephone and Video Interview

The telephone interview is common in student affairs, and the video interview is growing in popularity. Typically, hiring entities use one of these methods to narrow the field of candidates and determine who will continue to the next step in the process, which might be a campus interview. These calls are also a great follow-up to interviews at placement conferences, because they allow the hiring entity to involve a number of interviewers, perhaps the entire hiring committee.

If you're invited to participate in a phone interview, find a quiet area where you won't be disturbed. Don't use a mobile phone, as reception is not generally as clear as on a landline. If you have nearby family or friends who still have a landline, ask if you can use theirs. Worst case scenario, request permission from your supervisor to conduct the interview at work. As long as you're not making a personal long-distance call, interfering with the work environment, or interviewing during your work hours, this scenario allows you to maintain a high level of ethics. Finding a landline might seem like an unnecessary challenge, but it can be worth it, because you don't want any distractions or obstacles to the interviewers hearing your responses clearly. During the introductions, it can be helpful to write down the name and position of each interviewer, so you can make personal connections with people during the conversation. Have notes and other references in front of you, as if you were taking an open-book test.

Many institutions have begun to use video conference interviews in place of phone interviews. If you're extended the opportunity for one of these, be sure you have sufficient bandwidth at the location you plan to use for the interview so that the connection is constant and the picture and sound are clear. These interviews can be awkward, because you might be looking at a room with people sitting around a conference table but be unable to clearly see faces and determine who is talking. Remember, they are looking at a monitor during the interview, so they see facial expressions on a big screen. They also see what's behind you, so wherever you are, make sure you have selected a place (e.g., in front of a wall) where there's no possibility of movement or activity going on behind you.

Campus Interview

Typically, when the hiring entity has narrowed the search to three to five candidates, it offers them on-campus interviews. This interview gives you the opportunity to experience the campus and department or office environment personally. Entry-level interviews are typically 5 to 8 hours long over the course of a day; you meet and interview with potential coworkers, student affairs division colleagues, students, and the supervisor. It's very strenuous to be interviewed all day, especially if you traveled far to get to campus, so do whatever you can to keep your energy level up (e.g., eat

> **Remember, no matter how many times you're asked the same question, act as though it's the first time you have heard it.**

little snacks, drink water, walk around on breaks). Remember, no matter how many times you're asked the same question, act as though it's the first time you have heard it.

> *At on-campus interviews, be incredibly observant. Watch how your on-campus hosts interact, not only in the formal parts of the interview, but the informal parts as well. This is going to be your LIFE, you need to ensure it's a good fit for you both professionally and personally.* —Coordinator of orientation, new student, and family programs at a metropolitan research university

Regardless of the type of interview, it's important to be prepared. Lack of preparation is obvious to the interviewer, who might think you're not really interested in the position and might, therefore, not want to continue the process with you.

Preparation for interviewing begins with knowing who you are (i.e., your strengths, weaknesses, values, and student affairs philosophy), as discussed earlier in this chapter. Think about your experiences, the skills required for the position, and specific situations you have encountered. Think about why you're interested in working at that type of institution and within that functional area. If you haven't thought about these things, you won't be able to answer the inevitable questions. Review the position description carefully and prepare responses about how you have the skills and experiences listed in the qualifications, as well as how you're the type of person they are seeking. Ask your professors and supervisors for a list of typical questions, and look for them on professional association placement websites. Practice your responses.

Not only do you need to prepare answers for questions you might be asked, you also need to make a list of questions to ask the potential employer. Employers expect and appreciate these questions; candidates who don't ask at least a few questions might appear not to be interested. What do you want to know about the position, department or office, and institution that will help you decide if it's the best fit for you? This part of the process is very important; after all, you're interviewing them as much as they're interviewing you. Typically, the interviewer will ask if you have any questions. In 30-minute placement conference interviews, you'll probably receive 5 to 10 minutes for questions. You won't be able to ask all your questions in this short amount of time, so group them into several sets, starting with the most important ones. If you progress to additional interviews with the same employer, you can proceed down your list of questions, each of which delves deeper into employment issues.

We're often asked when it's appropriate to talk about salary. Everyone has an opinion on this topic; generally, you should not ask about salary in your first interview with a prospective employer. The human resources or department website sometimes specifies the salary in the job posting or description. If it doesn't, try to hold out as long as you can before asking, because employers usually bring up salary issues on their own, typically after a few meetings with the candidate. If it still hasn't come up, ask before you accept an invitation to a campus interview.

In addition to general research, you should prepare specifically for the position by reviewing the institutional, divisional, and departmental or office websites. This task is difficult at placement conferences because of the quick turnaround and the number of interviews in a short time. When you attend a placement conference, set up some interviews before you get there. That way, you can do this research in advance, thus freeing up some onsite research time and building in some flexibility to add new interviews.

Preparation is not complete without practice. Mock interviews give you the experience of the interviewing environment, the opportunity to practice providing answers on the spot, a chance to determine how to sit comfortably yet professionally, and the opportunity to receive immediate feedback. Most mentors, supervisors, and professional staff in your functional areas of interest are happy to do mock interviews with you. The career center on your campus might also offer interview practice sessions.

Follow-up

Immediately after an interview, take a few moments to reflect on it. Write some notes or impressions of the interview, including the position and institution, the interviewers' names, and the discussion points. At a placement conference—where you'll meet many employers in a short time—these notes are crucial for helping you remember each interview later.

> *As you are applying to jobs and going through the interview process, keep some sort of record to track it all. I created a master excel document of every school I applied to, the position title, and then whether or not I received a phone interview, second phone interview, on-campus interview, and job offer. This was really helpful as I was searching for new jobs to keep everything straight.* —Assistant director of student success at a private liberal arts college

The next step is the thank you. The choice of e-mail or handwritten note is still highly debated in the profession. A general rule of thumb is to send a note using the method by which the employer has conducted most communication with you. You might think it's easier to send both an e-mail and handwritten letter to cover your bases, but consider this: If you complete the typical interviewing cycle (i.e., one or two at a placement conference, a phone or video conference, and a campus meeting) with an employer, that yields at least six notes, which is a bit excessive. As employers who have hired new professionals in the last few decades, during the time that e-mail became the most common delivery method of written work communication, we suggest that you write an e-mail (as recommended by at least one of the larger placement conferences) or handwritten note at a conference, because the employer will receive it soon after an interview. Send an e-mail after a phone or video conference interview so that the employer receives it immediately, in the event that there's a quick turnaround for the employer to select candidates for campus interviews. Finally, if you complete a campus interview, send an e-mail (for the reason just stated) as well as a handwritten note to show additional sincerity and effort by engaging in this lost art.

Regardless of the method, always be gracious, whether or not you're still interested in the position. Send a thank-you note within 24 hours to whoever interviewed you by telephone, video, or on campus; at a placement conference, the thank you note should be sent within hours of the interview. Be sure to spell the name of the institution and the interviewer correctly. If you decide that you're not interested in the position, a simple thank you and a statement that you're no longer interested is sufficient. If you're sincerely interested in the position after an interview, your note should express your appreciation for the interview; reiterate your interest in the institution and the position; and briefly note how your education, experience, and interest align with what the institution is seeking.

The interviewing process doesn't end with the formal interview at a placement conference or scheduled meetings during a campus interview. You're being observed and evaluated throughout the placement conference and throughout the time you're visiting the campus. The way you interact with interviewers before and after the formal interview and your behavior in general are always being evaluated.

Be patient. The search process takes time. Different institutions and even different departments within institutions operate at different paces. University calendars, commitments of search committee members, and availability of candidates all contribute to delays in hiring decisions. In addition, some institutions require departments to seek approval from the HR or affirmative action office before they can offer a position. Sometimes a department must wait for budget approval. It's appropriate to check with your contact at an institution about the status of your candidacy, but don't be a pest. As a general rule, contact the institution if you haven't heard anything in 3 weeks, unless you have been given a specific date or time frame by which you'll be informed. Don't panic. In the end, you're very likely to find a position that you like.

> **Be patient. The search process takes time.**

The hardest part of the job search for me was waiting after having an on-campus interview while still doing other interviews and having to weigh options beforehand in case an offer came and what to do in that situation. For this, I had to consider everything I wanted in a job that was non-negotiable and what options provided me the best professional opportunity. —Coordinator of Greek life at a large public university

Evaluating an Offer

You receive a job offer from the institution of your dreams in a progressive department with a caring supervisor. What could be better? Before you respond, consider some practical things from a financial perspective. Assuming that housing is not provided, look at salary comparison and cost of living sites on the Internet to determine the cost of living in the city or town where the institution is located. A salary might sound great until you discover the cost of living in the area. Also, consider the benefits package at the institution. What type of health insurance coverage is provided? Can you take free classes at the institution? What are your retirement benefits, and what is the vesting period? Typically, institutions have a 5- to 10-year vesting period. If you leave an institution before this period, you'll receive your personal contributions to retirement, but you won't receive the institution's contributions to retirement. What are the parking fees? Will you receive special rates on athletic tickets or tickets to entertainment on campus? Are funds available for traveling to professional conferences? Will your moving expenses be covered?

For entry-level positions, salaries often are not negotiable. Because an institution might be hiring several people for entry-level positions with similar requirements for education and experience, salaries must be consistent. Also, supervisors are leery of offering a new hire a higher salary than that of someone who is already employed in a similar position. However, there might be some flexibility with perks. The institution might help with moving expenses or put you on payroll earlier to provide additional income. It might arrange for housing at a reasonable price in property owned by the institution. It might provide temporary housing until you find permanent living arrangements. It might be willing to provide additional funds for travel to conferences. Be creative in asking for perks, and note that a private institution likely will have more flexibility in this area. However, do not make a final decision on accepting a position based solely on perks.

You receive an offer from an institution that is not your top choice, and the institution wants an answer in 48 hours. What do you do? It's reasonable to ask for an extension. Institutions know that you probably have interviewed with more than one institution and usually are willing to grant a few more days. Contact your first-choice institution and explain that you have an offer from another institution but you're still very interested and would appreciate knowing the expected time frame for them to make a hiring decision. Chances are, they will give you an honest answer concerning when you might hear about the position. If you aren't being seriously considered, they'll probably tell you.

What if your first-choice institution won't be making its decision for another 2 weeks? Do you accept the offer you have or turn it down and wait to hear from your first choice? The timing could make a difference. If it's April and you're still a serious candidate for several other positions, turning the offer down might be the right thing to do if you're not excited about the institution, the department, or the position. If it's July and you're not a candidate at other institutions, you should probably consider taking the offer, assuming the fit is strong enough.

Financial Issues

Searching for a job has financial implications. Save money for the semester you'll be interviewing. You'll need money for travel to placement conferences and interviews, moving expenses, and temporary housing. As a graduate student, you probably have a closet full of casual clothes, but you might not have suitable clothing for interviewing. Be prepared to buy some professional clothing.

Institutions handle travel arrangements for campus interviews differently. Some institutions make the arrangements and pay for your flight and hotel; some require you to pay for everything. Some institutions reimburse you for travel within institutional or state guidelines, possibly depending on whether you're offered a position and accept it. If you're interviewing at more than one institution over a 3- or 4-week period, your credit card might reach its limit while you're waiting for reimbursement. Even after you submit receipts, it often takes 3 or 4 weeks to receive a check from an institution. If finances are a concern, ask the potential employer how travel arrangements are paid.

The good news about being a poor graduate student is that you likely don't have a lot of furniture and belongings to move; the bad news is that it's still expensive to move. Unless you can fit everything you own into your vehicle, you'll probably have to rent a moving trailer or truck. Along the way, you'll have fuel, food, and lodging costs. You might also have the cost of temporary housing, either in your current location or in the new community. Remember that moving also means deposits for an apartment, utilities, cable, and so on. Rarely do you graduate and start your new job the next week. Many entry-level positions have start dates tied to the opening of residence halls, the start of the fall semester, or the beginning of a new fiscal year. You need funds to make it through this transition period.

Finding Balance

Searching for a job can be very stressful. You might be finishing graduate work, leaving the comfort of a familiar institution, leaving friends, perhaps moving a spouse or partner or family, and heading off into the unknown. The search process is like a marathon; you need to pace yourself. There is excitement one day and disappointment the next, and this pattern is repeated throughout the process. You can do many things to prepare yourself for each step of the process, but it takes commitment to focus on a job search and not neglect yourself; those around you; or your responsibilities to work, school, and family.

Remember that you're still a graduate student. If you're in a student-affairs-oriented master's program, your faculty understands that you'll be interviewing in the spring semester, but they still expect you to attend class and complete assignments on time. Missing one class for an interview might be acceptable, but missing several classes in March and April (typical interview season) is unacceptable. Your graduate assistant supervisor has similar expectations—you're still an employee with a job to do. All graduate assistants cannot be away from campus at the same time; someone has to be there to run the residence halls, implement programs, and provide services.

Pay attention to your family and friends. It's easy to become so wrapped up in your own situation that you forget about those who care about you. Find time to spend with family and friends. They're your support system, and you'll likely need them as you face some difficult decisions during the search process.

> *It is a stressful process, and it's okay to occupy your time with things other than the job search to relax. There is a job out there for you; just be patient.* —Coordinator of fraternity and sorority life at a metropolitan public university

Finally, take care of yourself—get enough sleep, eat right, and exercise regularly. This is easier said than done, but it has been proven over and over that regular exercise and a proper diet help reduce stress and lead to better sleep.

Other Search Considerations

Accommodations for Disabilities

If you require an accommodation (e.g., captioning, wheelchair accessibility) during the interview or search process, don't hesitate to request assistance. If you have a hearing impairment, placement conference interviewing might be a challenge because of the physical setup. Any reputable placement service will provide accommodation (e.g., a sign language interpreter, a different location for interviews) and should help you contact the employers with whom you're interviewing to communicate the details of the accommodation. If you're attending a placement conference or a campus interview, touch base with the staff or hiring entity in advance to explain your requests and ensure that your accommodation is in place.

Strategies for LGBTQ Candidates

For a candidate who identifies as lesbian, gay, bisexual, transgender, or queer (LGBTQ), environmental fit and a safe climate are especially important. To begin your exploration of the campus climate for LBGTQ individuals, you should examine the institution's nondiscrimination statements and policies, particularly as they relate to sexual orientation, gender identity, and gender expression. Next, check on the availability and type of domestic partner benefits. You need to decide if and when to come out (e.g., during the interview or after you're in the position). During a second phone interview or on-campus interview, you might want to ask about the climate for LGBTQ students, faculty, and staff. The answers to this question provide another basis for determining the campus climate. During the campus interview, you might ask to speak to an LGBTQ-identified professional staff member. You probably can have a more frank discussion about the campus climate for LGBTQ persons with this staff member than in a group setting or with the hiring supervisor. Ultimately, it's a personal decision that depends on your comfort level.

Strategies for Dual Career Couples

Dual career couples are not uncommon in student affairs and other professions, but it does complicate the job search. Dual career couples face all the challenges and pressures of individuals involved in a job search, plus some additional challenges, including:

> whether, when, and how to reveal to prospective employers that your spouse [or partner] is also looking for a job; deciding whether (and for how long) you and your spouse [or partner] are willing to live apart for the sake of one or both careers; and even choosing how you (as a couple) will make choices. (Science Education Resource Center, n.d.)

The first step in determining your job search strategy is to identify what you value most in your life (e.g., family time, income, location) and which aspects of your job (e.g., salary, title, responsibilities, career opportunities) are most important. You should complete this step individually and then as a couple (University of Michigan, n.d.). Next, discuss possible models for dual careers: one primary career with a "trailing spouse" or partner, taking turns at beneficial career moves, two careers of equal importance, or "linking career decisions to the timeline of the primary caretaker of children" (University of Michigan, n.d.).

> Not only did we talk openly about our frustrations and disappointments . . . we also had to develop a willingness to explain our parameters or limitations to each other. (Gardner & Woodsmall, 2004, p. 48)

Some online job boards, such as http://www.higheredjobs.com, provide a search function specifically designed to assist dual career couples. Many institutions can provide assistance with relocation of dual career couples, but you really need to take charge of your own search. It's highly unlikely that you'll find two dream jobs in the same geographic location. If you're conducting two job searches simultaneously, one person might receive an offer of a position while the other partner has no leads in that area.

Conclusion

Each year, hundreds of soon-to-be professionals enter the job market, eager for their first interviews and the prospect of finding the job of their dreams. The job search process requires dedication and patience, as well as a sense of humor. Remember that many people have followed a similar process as they began their student affairs career. If you have prepared properly, you'll be successful. And so your student affairs career begins.

> *Every person's search is different, but the best pieces of advice I yielded from my experience is to be patient, be open and honest (with yourself and any other key people involved in your search), and trust in your skills and abilities. The right job is out there.*
> —Conference coordinator at a large public university

References

American College Personnel Association & National Association of Student Personnel Administrators. (2010). *Professional competency areas for student affairs practitioners*. Retrieved from https://www.naspa.org/images/uploads/main/Professional_Competencies.pdf

Gardner, K., & Woodsmall, C. (2004). The art of compromise and other secrets of the dual career job search. In P. M. Magolda & J. E. Carnaghi (Eds.), *Job one*. Lanham, MD: University Press of America.

Hirt, J. B. (2006). *Where you work matters: Student affairs administration at different types of institutions*. Lanham, MD: University Press of America.

MacKinnon, F. (Ed.). (2004). *Rentz's student affairs practice in higher education* (3rd ed.). Springfield, IL: Charles C. Thomas.

Science Education Resource Center. (n.d.). The job search: Dual career couples: Preparing for academic careers in the geosciences. Retrieved from http://serc.carleton.edu/NAGTWorkshops/careerprep/jobsearch/dualcareer.htm

University of Michigan Human Resources. (n.d.). *Dual career couples and the job search*. Retrieved from http://www.provost.umich.edu/programs/dual_career/DualCareerTips.pdf

WORDS OF WISDOM

CHAPTER THIRTEEN

Shannon E. Ellis

Y ou have chosen well. It doesn't matter whether you fell into the student affairs profession by accident or have methodically studied and planned your career. The exemplary vice presidents for student affairs who contributed their perspectives to this chapter have shaped successful careers from both origins. They would all concur with Cheo Torres, vice president for student affairs at the University of New Mexico, who has pursued a career both in and out of higher education: "All the years I have worked in student services have been the best years of my life."

Each senior administrator would agree that you are destined for a life full of fascinating people, provocative problems, global exploration, critical change, deep sadness, and high elation—all because you have the daily capacity to create a better world. We are fortunate to have found a career that offers such challenges and satisfaction. As Gage Paine, vice president of student affairs at the University of Texas, Austin, describes it: "We are breathing rarified air on a college campus. We work in places where people care about ideas, equity, and justice. That doesn't happen everywhere." Our wisdom is intended to help you be the best you can be at the start of and throughout your career. We hope it will make your journey to becoming an exemplary student affairs professional all the more enjoyable and rewarding.

As you begin your career, we encourage you to start where you are. You don't know everything and should continue to explore new information and different ways of thinking. In the beginning, you're likely to focus on what you don't know, but you'll see progress as you read, observe, reflect, and practice. As we share advice, remember that we are practitioners who have been doing this and learning, most of us, for more than 30 years. We started with the same passion you have for helping students. Our objective is to help you coordinate your love of college students with strong organizational, administrative, and communication skills. As you practice the wisdom we share here, you'll work with greater skill, effectiveness, confidence, and enthusiasm.

Be Values Driven

This is a values-centered profession. Knowing your values is a significant tool in becoming the professional you aspire to be. Values are an important barometer for personal career paths as well as professional decisions. If you know what's important to you, you'll know your parameters and priorities. Paine advises, "The sooner you can be clear about your values and what's important to you, the sooner you spend your energy in those places." This can be hard work according to Patrick Day, vice president for student life at the University of the Pacific. "Do the hard work to challenge yourself and others about clarifying your values and beliefs. You will differ. You will disagree with others. But you *will* be clear," Day assures. What do you do when personal values and institutional values do not align? Larry Moneta, vice president of student affairs at Duke University, says, "Don't sacrifice your values, but don't stand on ceremony. Issues of institutional preference trump *your* preference. Try to fit."

Maintain Perspective

Often, as a new professional, the smallest issue can seem like the biggest thing. Perspective colors how people look at a situation and their ability to handle it in the best way. It's not uncommon for new professionals to take everything too seriously. Moneta says, "Stop taking yourself so seriously. If you haven't laughed during some part of each day, you've wasted the day. And make sure you go home for dinner."

As a new professional, "You want to develop a wider perspective on how things work," advises Deneece Huftalin, vice president of student services at Salt Lake Community College. Paine warns new professionals about being so overwhelmed and enamored with what they do that they forget there's a bigger university. "Develop an insatiable curiosity," Paine suggests. Huftalin and Paine tell new professionals to get involved in bigger campus initiatives, ask to be appointed to institutionwide committees, and volunteer for different opportunities. "Remember that you are a citizen and leader of the academy." Moneta urges new professionals to be conversant on what's happening in the world as well as in our field and in higher education. "I'm a firm believer that smart people do very well. One indicator of this is to be conversant in world events," he says.

Find Storytellers, Effectors, and Mentors

Campus storytellers provide the context and history to educate a new person quickly. Huftalin urges new professionals to identify the "effectors" at their institution: "Campus effectors are the people who get things done." Moneta warns against staying "nested." "A successful student affairs professional is multilingual. They listen to and talk with a cadre of folks, from the parking guard and mail carriers to parents and alumni." Paine warns that "just because you have a master's degree doesn't mean you know more than the person answering the phone."

> **Campus storytellers provide the context and history to educate a new person quickly.**

Mentors focus on your success and provide you with opportunities to learn and grow by doing and observing. Les Cook, vice president for student affairs and advancement at Michigan Technological University, always looks for the "trusted sage" on campus. "They have your best interests in mind," he says. Huftalin looks for mentors on and off campus, in and out of student affairs: "Try to work for amazing supervisors. I've worked for some passionate, smart, and engaging people. They were not only great mentors but became good friends." Remember to spend time with the vice president for student affairs on campus: They can be great role models, advisors, and teachers.

Commit Yourself and Work Hard

Loving what you do for a living is a great way to spend your life. Don't shrink from the joy you find in pursuing your craft just because other people don't feel the same way. There is no greater feeling than the flow of a productive workday, where aspirations are high and achievements are realized. The "good tired" that you feel at the end of such a day is the result of personal satisfaction in a job well done. Although it's always nice to be recognized by others for doing a good job, learn not to expect or need it. A sure sign of professional maturity is to be self-motivated and satisfied without needing praise from others. Loving your work is nothing to be ashamed of; in fact, having a passion for your career is to be envied and shared. Day advises new professionals to "develop professional resilience. Your career will not be handed to you just because you show up. Go get the experience. Commit to things and know that things won't go well all the time."

> Loving what you do for a living is a great way to spend your life.

Seek Out and Develop Relationships

Relationships are the way you build a career and get things done. New professionals should seek out and develop relationships with as many people as possible; do this with frequent conversations and shared experiences. From the moment you meet another person, you're working on the terms of your relationship and your expectations of one another. Even if you never discuss relationship building directly, you're always deciding whose interests deserve attention, whose opinion matters, and how cooperative you'll be.

Cynthia Cherrey, vice president for campus life at Princeton University, says, "The most important relationships new professionals have are with their students. In order to do this well, they need to think strategically about where their work intersects with the needs and priorities of the institution." The best way to build a lasting relationship is to link your own interests to the other person's needs. Enhance this sense of connection by engaging in genuine dialogue while you make time to build relationships during your busy day.

Understand Campus Politics

Politics is about relationships with people. Many vice presidents for student affairs express regret that as new professionals they didn't understand this key to navigating politics on their campus. Moneta says, "The nature of politics means there are vested interests, and the nature of humans is competitive. The secret to success is through relationships and information." Student affairs professionals have the strong interpersonal skills necessary to be effective campus politicians.

Early in her career, Huftalin was a young woman in a big power structure dominated by men. She says, "Don't be afraid to navigate the political landscape with your interpersonal skills. It can only strengthen your role so you can be effective." She recommends new professionals immerse themselves in the entire campus culture, not just student affairs. "I had a lot of conversations with my new colleagues throughout the institution, especially academics. It was a great way to build allies around issues to move things forward. I also served on collegewide committees that exposed me to curricular and personnel issues, not just student issues," Huftalin says.

"We can't do this work alone," Cherrey advises. "We must work with our academic colleagues." She encourages new professionals to develop relationships with a minimum of five faculty members. "Really understand their role," she says. "Your work and their work don't have to intersect, but try to understand their work and build a relationship."

Be a Great Supervisor

Huftalin admits that she was nervous about her first job, where she supervised 20 people. "I was comfortable with my programming skills, but when I became a supervisor, all I could think was, 'I don't know how to do this,'" Huftalin says. She advises calling colleagues. "I called people and asked them to tell me about the best boss they ever had *and* the worst," she says. "I learned that it's important to develop the ability to lead and to coach so you don't kill your employees' spirit." Learn how to do things, like supervising, by doing them.

Moneta stresses the need to "be clear about expectations and be okay about being wrong." You will make mistakes. Mike Segawa, vice president for student affairs and dean of students at the University of Puget Sound, adds an important piece of advice about turnover: "If you don't know what you are going to do if you lose a staff member, then you have a problem. No one should be irreplaceable."

As both a supervisor and an employee, recognize the multigenerational workplace. Day advises new professionals to take the time to understand the life experiences that have shaped their colleagues and to consider how that affects their professional values and work style.

Be a Great Employee

What about the other side of the job—being an employee? "It's just as important to make sure you understand your boss's expectations. If they don't tell you, go ask," advises Juanita Chrysanthou, vice chancellor for student success at Lone Star College. Honest performance reviews are not only helpful in clarifying what you're supposed to do and how you're doing; they give you goals for learning and contributing. Chrysanthou says, "Remember that your boss also reports to somebody, and you need to support him or her in achieving that boss's goals."

Surprise Your Mother

Do the things you think you cannot do. "Surprising your mother" means taking the opportunity to be someone your mother doesn't know. If she sees you as meek and mild, be assertive and powerful. If she can't imagine you getting people to do things for you, become a supervisor of 20 people. If she thinks you can't balance your checkbook, get a job managing a $12 million budget. If she believes you would never leave the area where you grew up, apply for a job 1,000 miles away. Do things others do not expect of you. It's the same advice we give our students, just framed a different way: Unshackle yourself from the expectations of others—a boss, a partner, a faculty member, a colleague. Don't hold yourself back.

Don't Be Afraid

Because you're a new professional, some people at the institution will make you feel small and unimportant. Day advises new professionals to "develop confidence," especially if you are female. "I see generations of educated, talented women who have deep confidence issues. Instill confidence in female colleagues and students." Moneta observes, "Sometimes new professionals try to position themselves as equals to faculty and then take umbrage when they're not. Student affairs is critical but not comparable." Everything we do augments classroom education. Moneta adds, "Be okay with the role of enlivening your students' learning in and out of class."

Looking back on his own career, Cook says, "Don't be afraid to move around. New professionals shouldn't be afraid to go someplace for 2 or 3 years and then move on to someplace new." Occasionally, you can do this within your own institution, but Cook says, "Don't be afraid to look at different types of institutions. Expose yourself to a lot of different experiences."

Have Broad Shoulders and Small Tear Ducts

There's no doubt about it: This can be a tough profession. Every day, the student affairs professional faces critics, controversy, public tensions, and endless problems to resolve. Perhaps that's exactly why we love this work—because of the opportunity to develop skills that allow us to lead the campus in creating a positive environment for student learning. Even the best student affairs professionals make mistakes, but they learn from their mistakes by reflecting, evaluating, and accepting constructive feedback and criticism from others. "Stop worrying about people liking you or your decisions," says Huftalin. Thick skin, a commitment to the bigger picture, and a self-assurance that allows for improvement will not only sustain a successful career in this field but ensure it. It's Segawa's experience that "most of the time someone's anger isn't about you. If I get a disproportionate response to a situation, I need to dig deeper to find the real issue."

Dick McKaig, retired vice provost for student affairs and dean of students at Indiana University Bloomington, was correct when he said, "Student affairs is not for the weak of heart or the insecure." He added that the one factor that makes all the difference for a fulfilling career in student affairs is "institutional fit."

Respect the Mission of the Institution

McKaig explains, "In student affairs, you can be a change agent, but you start in a context that is set by the history, tradition, and mission of the institution."

Select an institution that's a good fit for you and one that you can fully embrace. Chrysanthou loves the values of community colleges: "The mission fits with my character—opportunities for everyone." Huftalin has worked at 2- and 4-year colleges as well as private and public institutions. She says, "The advice about understanding institutional mission transcends institution type. An understanding of politics, organizational dynamics, people, and problem solving are needed by student affairs professionals at all institutions." Cook says, "Students are students are students. The foundations are the same." Paine remembers a speech by U.S. President Barack Obama on her campus. He said, "We are all members of a relay race. Someone before you did the work, hands it off to you, and you will hand it off to someone else." Remember the people who paved the way. Paine adds, "We stand on foundations built by others."

Don't try to make your institution be what it wasn't intended to be. Participate in and benefit from the best of what it is and accept the problems. Use language that is valued and understood by your on-campus audience and avoid student affairs jargon. Often this means learning the vocabulary of academicians. Paine advises new professionals to be a student of their organization. "Read the journals, the campus newspaper, understand which are the popular campus sports teams *and* exemplary academic programs. Know who the provost is so you don't ask him or her, 'What do you do on campus?'" Know more about your campus than just your program.

Stay Learner Centered

Staying learner centered is the vice president for student affairs' way of saying, be completely connected to the academic mission of your institution. Of her division's mission, Cherrey says, "We aspire to be student centered and learning focused in creating a distinctive experience. This means we are always thinking about how student affairs can help students map out a learning environment." Totally "embrace the student services mission" says Segawa, which is to help students learn. Beware, however, of the term *cocurriculum* for student affairs work. Segawa is clear, "We don't have a curriculum, especially not one that hangs together like a course of study in a major. What we are doing is purposeful, but we don't use a true curricular approach." Don't confuse the two when being learner centered. Moneta observes that the term *learner centered* can be cosmetic, a veneer, just words. "We are truly learner centered when we develop our programs through the lens of the learner rather than that of the administrator." Cherrey adds, "We must be very intentional in our work. There is structure to a learning environment, and it is the questions we ask that help a student process through a new program or policy." Chrysanthou urges focus: "Everything you do is about helping students have the best educational experience possible."

Respect the Historical Perspective of Campus Colleagues

The newcomer will be working with colleagues who remember events from the past and who have a long-term view of the college. It can be frustrating to be told that an idea will not work based on something that occurred 10 years ago; but to be successful, new staff members should convey a respect for the past and strive to understand the perspective of those who have a protracted view of time. If you're promoting an idea that has been tried before, you'll not only have to be sensitive to the past, you'll also need to be persuasive about why past conditions no longer apply.

Bend Rules and Get Rid of the Dumb Ones

It's a great joy to realize that because we make the policies and rules, we can change them. It's motivating to answer the question: If we were truly student centered, what would this campus be like? with acts of real change led by speedy and strategic thinking. We're inspired by staff, faculty, and students who not only raise the questions but bring answers, too.

Be a Student of Students

No one should know your students better than you. Your understanding of demographics, attitudes, trends, and pending changes, and your ability to make predictions for the campus will make you an invaluable asset to the institution. This is only true, however, if you share the results of your studies openly, regularly, and widely. Your ability to share knowledge about your students will greatly increase the impact of successful pedagogy, satisfaction with services, and student learning. Be sure to spend time with students, as opposed to merely assessing, developing, and analyzing. Paine reminds new professionals to "be inspired by your students."

> **No one should know your students better than you.**

Be a Problem Solver

Chrysanthou says that new professionals must never lose sight of the fact that their job is to resolve institutional issues and meet institutional needs, "not the other way around. Solve the problems we hope an organized community can solve on campus." Meaning is found in many parts of our work. The ability to bring people together to resolve issues is extremely satisfying. By sharing your knowledge about students, facilitating conversations among diverse campus constituencies, and listening to the wisdom of others, you can help the community become one that curbs substance abuse and violence, retains students, and makes them smarter as they learn more.

Advocate for Student Interests, Not Your Personal Agenda

Student advocacy requires careful representation of the concerns of individual students and groups of students: Make it clear whether you're trying to reflect what students are saying or whether you're talking about what you believe is in the best interest of students. Try not to project your beliefs or agenda onto students. Looking back on his long career, McKaig advises that "the needs of students will change over your student affairs career. It is more important to know how to assess student needs and facilitate change than it is to understand what you and your peers wanted as students."

When Paine became dean of students at Southern Methodist University, she didn't know how to answer when people asked, "What do you do?" "I decided it was to make sure the institution works for all students. I have since decided that is the job of everybody, not just the dean."

Join Professional Organizations

"NASPA taught me early on the value of getting to know other new professionals," says Segawa. Start your network now. Like all the vice presidents for student affairs who contributed their perspectives to this chapter, Huftalin's professional involvement led to a personal network of hundreds of colleagues across the country who are valuable resources for advice and ideas on professional issues.

Don't consider professional activities as something extra that helps you get ahead. The myth still exists that you can get ahead simply by doing your job and that things such as professional involvement are the cream. You want to be professionally active because that is *how* you can do your job well. Solutions to problems, development of new skills, forecasts of upcoming issues, job contacts, mentors, leadership opportunities, models of best practice, and much more await the student affairs professional who takes advantage of all that associations have to offer.

Review Professional Standards and Ethical Codes

Many vice presidents for student affairs expect new professionals to follow the standards set for our profession. Start now and continue throughout your career to review codes of ethics and statements regarding good practice. These publications include *Statement of Ethical Principles and Standards* (American College Personnel Association [ACPA], 2006), *Principles of Good Practice for Student Affairs* (ACPA & NASPA, 1998), *Professional Competency Areas for Student Affairs Practitioners* (ACPA & NASPA, 2010), and *Statement of Shared Ethical Principles* (Council for the Advancement of Standards in Higher Education, 2012). These publications reflect the judgment of experienced professionals and are helpful guidelines regarding best practices. The interplay of your personal ethics with professional standards and principles is an important key to happiness and effectiveness in the job. Be clear with yourself about your unshakeable values and core beliefs. As you advance into jobs with greater responsibilities, your personal ethics will be a useful guide in your role as an exemplary student affairs professional.

Develop Professionally Throughout Your Career

Moneta advises new professionals to "take all you learned in graduate school and contextualize it with your first experiences, because the world is far more complicated." For example, diversity is different today from 30 years ago. "Now it's about social justice and equity, which is where new professionals need to learn and lead," says Segawa. Day advises new professionals to "focus on right now *and* the future." Day also tells new professionals to prepare to do more than one thing. "Prepare to be an administrator, leader, teacher, financial planner and forecaster, and enrollment strategist."

Professional development encompasses clear values, broad capabilities, and valuable work experiences. Vice presidents for student affairs stress the need to:

☞ Follow through on commitments.

☞ Avoid self-promotion. It gets old!

☞ Become a good writer by rewriting until it's right.

☞ Always arrive prepared.

☞ Think hard before saying no to a request or an assignment.

☞ Seize opportunities to learn and demonstrate new qualities.

☞ Learn from new professionals when you're no longer one yourself.

☞ Teach if you're qualified.

☞ Develop trust.

☞ Learn to distinguish the urgent from the important, and the useful from the useless.

☞ Create a context for the work you're doing so you see its larger purpose.

All vice presidents for student affairs were new professionals once. Although it was a long time ago, we all remember it as a time of great fun, when we knew everything and nothing, tried to listen and learn from those more senior while forging our way with new ideas and fresh approaches, read everything in the field, and felt fortunate to attend student affairs institutes and conferences. We quickly learned that all the cutting-edge knowledge we had gained in our graduate programs (if we were in a college student development program) served us well for the next few years; after that, the learning cycle needed to be rejuvenated forever. Many of us recall thinking that when we achieved a certain position in the field, we would change things. And many of us have.

Integrate Your Personal and Professional Life

Striving for balance between your personal and professional life is a losing battle. "I've quit talking about work–life balance," says Paine. Now I talk about living an integrated life." Try integrating all facets of your life so that there is no division, only complementary actions and thought. Personal and professional values are the same, as are constantly shifting priorities of family and staff, activity and reflection, managing and socializing. It doesn't have to be "either–or" but rather "this, then that." Integrating still allows for boundaries and limits when it comes to personal relationships with students, and for modeling the responsible use of alcohol and the ethical use of money. When living "life as career," you're always on the job, because your personal behavior affects your professional reputation. Fair or not, it's a fact that how you're perceived on campus and in the town will enhance or diminish your ability to be an effective advocate for a student-centered campus.

Day advises new professionals that emotional intelligence at work is critical to effectiveness and success. "We've convinced ourselves that authenticity means you tell everything about your life to everybody. It's not okay, especially in the workplace. Demonstrate emotional intelligence." New professionals fresh from graduate programs should recognize the differences and relish the complexity of the workplace.

Develop a Vision of the Possible

People enjoy being around those who are optimistic and positive in the face of realistic challenges and adversity. Become known as a person who acknowledges the problem but overcomes the negatives with creative thinking and new alternatives. Develop a vision of the possible. Make this vision congruent with the vision of senior campus administrators. Infuse your vision with current and future thinking.

Your vision should take a long look into the future—the future of college students, of higher education, of the student affairs profession, and, most of all, of you. Create and promote this vision so that at first it becomes a possibility and eventually, a reality. Think of yourself and everyone else as a resource in developing competencies and personal influence. Adopt the right mindset, participate willingly, build success for others, and model personal and professional development by leading with integrity.

Paddle Faster Than the Current

Good student affairs professionals are not victims, swept away by powerful currents over which we exercise little influence. At first it seems as though we must either paddle upstream, battling all the way, or just go with the flow, hoping we can float along undisturbed. But skilled student affairs professionals, like skilled whitewater rafters, discover that neither paddling against the current nor going with the flow is a productive tactic. The best way to get where you want to go when negotiating rapids is to paddle faster than the current. The best of us anticipate the trends and look far ahead for the issues. This allows us to capture energy and create initiatives, strategies, new rules, and philosophies.

Conclusion

What kind of student affairs professional will you become? What values will you hold and act on in this profession as you compose yourself? This concluding chapter is meant to inspire you rather than intimidate you. Developing into a great student affairs professional takes patience and practice. We promise you'll get better as you acquire skills over time. Many of us wish we could relive our first years in the profession. It's a time of discovery, when you're aware of your commitment to students and seek to become more effective at your work as an administrator, educator, programmer, and counselor.

Don't forget your excitement and passion for the job. Chrysanthou observes, "As time goes by, you will have colleagues who are jaded. When *you* cross the line to that place, pull back and remember the time you received the offer of your first job and how excited you were to come onto campus and do great things." Don't abandon ship psychologically while remaining physically.

We offer the following tips and challenges as you embark on a life in service to students, learning, and higher education:

☞ Look into a student's eyes when you're listening.

☞ Walk up and introduce yourself to the scariest faculty member on campus.

☞ Have the courage to challenge authority.

☞ Stop in the middle of the craziest part of the day and admire a piece of art.

☞ Find a handful of colleagues along the way you can turn to with your problems and worries for honest advice, sympathy, and friendship.

☞ Take risks, push the envelope a little more, make some mistakes.

☞ Change lives, lots of lives, every single day.

☞ Cry when a student is a heroin addict, a survivor of incest, or has an abusive partner.

☞ Celebrate when a student is 6 months into recovery, gets a "B" in statistics, or has moved into a shelter.

☞ Change yourself because of their tragedies and achievements.

☞ Craft a vision for your own personal and professional journey just as you do for your organization.

☞ Be funny. Make people laugh, put them at ease.

☞ Read what your students are reading; listen to their music on the latest technology; and ask them about their hopes, dreams, and fears.

☞ Struggle with a real-life ethical dilemma at least once a day.

☞ View criticism and negative feedback as a gift.

☞ Be the one who always asks, "How is this best for our students?"

☞ Reflect once in a while.

☞ Travel to a foreign land every year to remember what it's like to be a new student on a strange campus.

☞ Remember birthdays.

☞ Go to funerals.

☞ Communicate in person more than in text.

☞ Help realize dreams

☞ . . . especially your own.

The inspiration and advice shared by successful vice presidents for student affairs from a variety of institutions, backgrounds, and beliefs are given to you, the new professional, as a gift. Learn from our mistakes, be motivated by our insights, and fully embrace the wonderful life you have chosen as a student affairs professional. You will occasionally have your doubts, and you will most certainly know failure, conflict, and sadness. Be assured that these will be far outweighed by the triumphs, easy comfort of career fit, your personal commitment, and the realization of dreams—both yours and those of your students.

Welcome to the finest profession in the world. Welcome to our world.

References

American College Personnel Association. (2006). *Statement of ethical principles and standards.* Retrieved from http://www.acpa.nche.edu/sites/default/files/Ethical_Principles_Standards.pdf

American College Personnel Association & National Association of Student Personnel Administrators. (1998). *Principles of good practice for student affairs.* Retrieved from https://www.naspa.org/images/uploads/main/Principles_of_Good_Practice_in_Student_Affairs.pdf

American College Personnel Association & National Association of Student Personnel Administrators. (2010). *Professional competency areas for student affairs practitioners.* Retrieved from https://www.naspa.org/images/uploads/main/Professional_Competencies.pdf

Council for the Advancement of Standards in Higher Education. (2012). CAS statement of shared ethical principles. In Council for the Advancement of Standards in Higher Education (Ed.), *Professional standards for higher education* (8th ed., pp. 21–22). Washington, DC: Author.

Professional Organizations in Students Affairs and Higher Education

American Association of Community Colleges (AACC)

Category: General Higher Education for Community Colleges
E-mail: None
Website: www.aacc.nche.edu

American Association of Collegiate Registrars and Admissions Officers (AACRAO)

Category: Admissions and Student Records/Registrars
E-mail: info@aacrao.org
Website: www.aacrao.org

American Association of State Colleges and Universities (AASCU)

Category:	General Higher Education for Regional Institutions
E-mail:	None
Website:	www.aascu.org

American College Health Association (ACHA)

Category:	Student Health
E-mail:	contact@acha.org
Website:	www.acha.org

American College Personnel Association (ACPA)

Category:	General Student Affairs
E-mail:	info@acpa.nche.edu
Website:	www.acpa.nche.edu

American Council on Education (ACE)

Category:	General Higher Education for Senior-level Administrators
E-mail:	None
Website:	www.acenet.edu

Association of College Unions International (ACUI)

Category:	Student Unions
E-mail:	acui@acui.org
Website:	www.acui.org

Association of College and University Housing Officers–International (ACUHO–I)

Category:	Student Housing
E-mail:	office@acuho-i.org
Website:	www.acuho-i.org

Association of International Educators (NAFSA)

Category: International Students
E-mail: inbox@nafsa.org
Website: www.nafsa.org

Association of Fraternal Advisors (AFA)

Category: Fraternities and Sororities
E-mail: ryan@afa1976.org
Website: www.afa1976.org

Association of Public and Land-Grant Universities (APLU)

Category: General Higher Education for Senior-level Administrators at Research Institutions
E-mail: none
Website: www.aplu.org

American Association for Employment in Education (AAEE)

Category: Career Services for Education Majors
E-mail: office@aaee.org
Website: www.aaee.org

Association for the Study of Higher Education (ASHE)

Category: Higher Education Faculty and Administrators
E-mail: ashemsu@msu.edu
Website: www.ashe.ws

Association for Student Conduct Administration (ASCA)

Category: Student Judicial Affairs
E-mail: asca@tamu.edu
Website: www.theasca.org

National Academic Advising Association (NACADA)

Category: Academic Advising
E-mail: nacada@ksu.edu
Website: www.nacada.ksu.edu

National Association for Campus Activities (NACA)

Category: Student Activities
E-mail: info@naca.org
Website: www.naca.org

National Association of College Admissions Counseling (NACAC)

Category: Admissions
E-mail: info@nacacnet.org
Website: www.nacacnet.org

National Association of Colleges and Employers (NACE)

Category: Career Services
E-mail: mmackes@naceweb.org
Website: www.naceweb.org

National Association of College and University Residence Halls (NACURH)

Category: Housing for Student Leaders
E-mail: nic@nacurh.org
Website: www.nacurh.org

National Association of College Auxiliary Services (NACAS)

Category: Auxiliary Services
E-mail: info@nacas.org
Website: www.nacas.org

National Association of Student Financial Aid Administrators (NASFAA)

    Category: Financial Aid

    E-mail: web@nasfaa.org

    Website: www.nasfaa.org

National Association of Student Personnel Administrators (NASPA)

    Category: General Student Affairs

    E-mail: office@naspa.org

    Website: www.naspa.org

National Conference on Race and Ethnicity in American Higher Education (NCORE)

    Category: Multiculturalism and Diversity

    E-mail: pnabavi@ou.edu

    Website: www.ncore.ou.edu

National Intramural-Recreational Sports Association (NIRSA)

    Category: Recreation Services

    E-mail: nirsa@nirsa.org

    Website: www.nirsa.org

National Orientation Directors Association (NODA)

    Category: New Student Orientation

    E-mail: noda@umn.edu

    Website: www.nodaweb.org

THE AUTHORS

MARILYN J. AMEY is professor of higher education and chair of the Department of Educational Administration at Michigan State University. She received her bachelor's degree in elementary and special education from Wittenberg University, master's degree in college student personnel from The Ohio State University, and doctorate in higher education from The Pennsylvania State University. Previously, she was a faculty member at The University of Kansas, and she has student affairs experience in residence life and student activities. She served two terms as a NASPA Faculty Fellow, has been a member and chair of NASPA's Dissertation of the Year committee, and received the 2014 Robert H. Shaffer Award for Excellence as a Graduate Faculty Member.

CHARLIE ANDREWS is director of academic advising and first-year programs at Florida International University. He received his bachelor's degree in mathematics education from Florida International University, master's degree in college student personnel from Bowling Green State University, and doctorate in higher education from Florida International University. He has worked primarily in academic advising, new-student orientation, and student activities during the past 20 years. He also served as the president of the National Orientation Directors Association from 2004 to 2007.

WILLIAM H. ARNOLD is assistant professor and coordinator of the master's in higher, adult, and lifelong education program in the Department of Educational Administration at Michigan State University. He received his bachelor's degree in exercise and health science from Alma College, master's degree in student affairs administration from Michigan State University, and doctorate in higher education administration from Bowling Green State University. Prior to assuming a faculty position, he held several student affairs administrative positions involving work in residence life, Greek life, student orientation, enrollment, and campus programming.

GRACE A. BAGUNU is currently studying full time toward a doctoral degree in leadership studies and working as a graduate teaching assistant at the University of San Diego's School of Education and Leadership Sciences. She received her bachelor's degree in psychology and master's degree in higher education administration from the University of Missouri–Kansas City. She has worked in the areas of student activities, student organizations, communication, leadership development, social justice, and orientation, and she is actively involved in NASPA at the regional and national levels.

KEVIN W. BAILEY is vice president for student affairs at the University of West Florida. He received his doctorate in higher education administration from Bowling Green State University, and his bachelor's and master's degrees from Indiana University of Pennsylvania. He previously worked at Tulane University, Millersville University, Bowling Green State University, and the University of North Carolina at Charlotte.

JOY BLANCHARD is assistant professor of higher education at Florida International University. She earned an honors baccalaureate in French education from the University of Louisiana at Lafayette, master's degree in higher education from Florida State University, and doctorate from the Institute of Higher Education at the University of Georgia. She previously was assistant dean of students at the University of Louisiana at Lafayette and has worked in several areas of student affairs, including residence life, student conduct, service–learning, and student activities. She currently serves on the board of directors of the Education Law Association.

ASHLEIGH BROCK is an assistant director of career services in the Office of Alumni and Career Services at the University of Richmond. She has a bachelor's degree in rhetoric and communication studies and journalism from the University of Richmond, and a master's degree in student affairs administration from Michigan State University. She is the technical editor for the *Journal of Student Affairs Research and Practice* and vice chair of professional development for ACPA's Commission for Career Services. She has administrative experience in career services, first-year programs, and admissions.

CHRISTA COFFEY is the director of student activities at the University of North Texas. She has a bachelor's degree in mathematics and a master's degree in educational administration from Texas A&M University, as well as a doctorate in educational leadership from the University of Central Florida. She previously worked in student activities at Missouri State University and the University of Central Florida. She served on the NASPA Career Services committee for 6 years and as the inaugural NASPA cochair for The Placement Exchange in 2008.

CAMILLE CONSOLVO is chief student affairs officer at Great Falls College Montana State University, a 2-year campus in the Montana State University system. She received her bachelor's and master's degrees from Missouri State University, and her doctorate in counseling psychology from Florida State University. Camille worked previously at Eastern Oregon University, Bowling Green State University, Washburn University, Kansas State University, and Missouri University of Science and Technology. She has worked in counseling, career services, residence life, orientation, student conduct, disability services, and enrollment management, having held administrative positions in both student affairs and academic affairs.

JODY DONOVAN serves as the assistant vice president for student affairs and dean of students at Colorado State University. She is also an assistant professor in the School of Education, teaching in the student affairs in higher education graduate program. She earned a bachelor's degree in psychology from Nebraska Wesleyan University, a master's in counseling and college student development, and a doctorate in higher education student affairs leadership at the University of Northern Colorado. She also serves as a NASPA Faculty Fellow.

KARI ELLINGSON is the associate vice president for student development at the University of Utah, where she has also served as director of the counseling center. She has faculty appointments in the departments of educational psychology and educational leadership and policy. She earned a bachelor's degree in English from the University of Virginia, and a master's in counseling and a doctorate in counseling psychology from the The University of North Carolina at Chapel Hill. She has served in several regional and national positions with NASPA, including Region V vice president.

SHANNON E. ELLIS is vice president of student services at the University of Nevada, Reno. She received her bachelor's degree in journalism from the University of Illinois at Urbana-Champaign, master's in public administration from the University of Massachusetts Amherst, and doctorate in higher education from the University of Southern California. She is a past president of NASPA.

LUKE GREGORY is an assistant director of residential life at Washington University in St. Louis. He received his bachelor's degree in business administration and sociology from the University of St. Thomas and his master's degree in higher education administration from the University of Kansas. He previously worked as a residential college director at Washington University in St. Louis and a residence hall director at Iona College.

JENNY HAMILTON serves as the student government operations coordinator at the University of West Florida. She received her bachelor's degree in communication with an emphasis in public relations from Mississippi State University and her master's degree in college student personnel administration from the University of West Florida, where she served as the leadership graduate assistant. She previously served as a residential learning coordinator at Virginia Polytechnic Institute and State University.

ERIC R. JESSUP-ANGER serves as director of student involvement at the University of Wisconsin–Milwaukee and teaches at Marquette University and Michigan State University. He received his bachelor's degree in English and education from the University of Wisconsin–Madison; master's degree in college student personnel from Bowling Green State University; graduate certificate in women's studies from Colorado State University; and doctorate in higher, adult, and lifelong education from Michigan State University. He previously worked in residence life, student life, judicial affairs, and academic affairs.

MARIA R. MARINUCCI is assistant director for residence education at the University of Scranton. She received her bachelor's degree in psychology from Colgate University and her master's degree in student affairs in higher education from Colorado State University, where she worked with parent and family programs and retention initiatives. She previously worked in residence life at Castleton State College and served as a NASPA graduate associate.

CARLA R. MARTINEZ is dean of student life at Golden West College, a community college in Orange County, California. She earned her bachelor's degree in business administration with a concentration in marketing from California Polytechnic State University, San Luis Obispo, and her master's degree in counseling with a specialization in student development in higher education from California State University, Long Beach. She has worked in the areas of leadership development, student life, international education, and judicial affairs.

JONATHAN O'BRIEN is assistant professor of educational leadership and coordinator of the student development in higher education master's program at California State University, Long Beach. He earned a bachelor's degree in English and a master's in college student personnel administration from the University of Central Missouri, and a doctorate in education from the University of California, Irvine. His research interests include applied ethics and professional dispositions in student affairs practice. His professional experience includes leadership development, student media, career services, student conduct, and academic advising.

ANNA M. ORTIZ is professor and department chair of educational leadership at California State University, Long Beach. She earned a bachelor's degree in human development from the University of California, Davis; a master's in higher education and student affairs from The Ohio State University; and a doctorate in higher education and organizational change from the University of California, Los Angeles. Her student affairs administrative experience was in residence life and career services. Her research interests include ethnic identity, Latino students in higher education, multicultural education, and professional issues for student affairs administrators and faculty. She has been involved in several student affairs and higher education associations, most recently serving as the inaugural director of NASPA's Faculty Division.

BRENT G. PATERSON is vice president for student affairs at Illinois State University. He earned a bachelor's degree in elementary education from Lambuth College, master's degree in counseling and personnel services from Memphis State University, and doctorate in higher education administration from the University of Denver. Brent formerly served as senior associate vice president for student affairs at Illinois State University and dean of student life at Texas A&M University. In 2001, he served as chair of NASPA Career Services.

DANIELLE N. QUIÑONES-ORTEGA is assistant director for first-year programs and leadership development at the University of California, Santa Barbara. She is four parts Gaucho and two parts Aztec. She received her bachelor's degree from the University of California, Santa Barbara, and her master's degree in postsecondary educational leadership with a specialization in student affairs from San Diego State University. She has been involved with NASPA since she began her student affairs journey as a NASPA Undergraduate Fellow at the University of California, Santa Barbara. Her involvement has extended to the Graduate Associate Program and Latino/a Knowledge Community (LKC) leadership team.

LORI M. REESOR is vice president for student affairs at the University of North Dakota. She received her bachelor's degree from the University of Wisconsin–Whitewater, master's in higher education from Iowa State University, and doctorate in educational policy and leadership from the University of Kansas. Previously, she was an associate vice provost for student success at the University of Kansas, was the dean of students at Wichita State University, and worked at the University of Missouri–Kansas City. She currently serves on the NASPA Foundation Board of Directors.

BARBARA SNYDER is vice president for student affairs at The University of Utah. She received a bachelor's degree in home economics and speech communication from The Ohio State University, master's in counseling from St. Cloud State University, and doctorate in higher education from Iowa State University. Previously, she was vice chancellor for student affairs at the University of Nebraska at Kearney. She has held several positions within NASPA, including chair of the NASPA Annual Conference, regional vice president, and president of the NASPA Foundation.

AUSTIN SWEENEY is a residential college director at Washington University in St. Louis where he chairs the residential life assessment committee. He earned his bachelor's degree from Miami University and his master's degree in student affairs administration from Michigan State University. While at Michigan State, he worked as a graduate assistant with the sexual assault and relationship violence prevention program. He also has worked as a research team member for BACCHUS Network's National Peer Educator Study.

CONNIE TINGSON-GATUZ is vice president for student affairs and mission integration at Madonna University and adjunct assistant professor in the higher education and student affairs master's program, located in Metro-Detroit, Michigan. Honored with the 2013 OCA Pioneer Community Educator Award, she continues to develop students and professionals in higher education. For more than a decade, she has been a lead trainer for the Gates Millennium Scholars program and a consultant for a national college student leadership development program and other national college scholarship programs. She is a 2014 Asian Pacific American Women's Leadership Institute Fellow. She earned a bachelor's degree in political science and a master's degree in college and university administration from Michigan State University.

DAWN WATKINS is a partner and vice president of Plaid, an organizational management firm that focuses on effectiveness in higher education and higher-education-related organizations. Prior to joining Plaid, she spent more than 20 years in higher education administration in roles ranging from academic advising to student involvement to serving as vice president for student affairs and dean of students. She has also published and presented extensively in such areas as crisis management, women and leadership, sexual misconduct and Title IX, strategic planning, and student mental health issues. She received her bachelor's degree in English and her master's degree in counseling and student personnel services from Virginia Polytechnic Institute and State University, and her doctorate in higher education administration and organizational management from The University of North Carolina at Greensboro with a research focus on strategic planning and its effect on recruitment and retention in colleges and universities.

MATTHEW R. WAWRZYNSKI is associate professor in the department of educational administration and coordinator of the higher, adult, and lifelong education programs at Michigan State University. He received his bachelor's degree in biology from Canisius College, master's in college student personnel from Indiana University, and doctorate in higher education from the

University of Maryland. Previously, he was an AERA Research Fellow and has student affairs experience in residence life, student activities, first-year programs, and orientation. He is executive editor for the *Journal of Student Affairs Research and Practice* and a NASPA Faculty Fellow.

EUGENE L. ZDZIARSKI II is vice president for student affairs at DePaul University. He holds a bachelor's degree in business administration from Oklahoma State University, a master's degree in student personnel and higher education from The University of Tennessee, Knoxville, and a doctorate in educational administration from Texas A&M University. He previously served as vice president for student affairs and dean of students at Roanoke College, and dean of students at the University of Florida. He has served as vice president for NASPA's Region III.

INDEX